NET INCOME

Other VNR titles of interest:

Thomas Anderson, *Java for Business*

Bill Bysinger and Ken Knight, *Investing in Information Technology*

Mary Cronin, *Doing More Business on the Internet*

Mary Cronin, *Global Advantage on the Internet*

Richard J. Gascoyne and Koray Ozcubucku, *Corporate Internet Planning Guide: Aligning Internet Strategy with Business Goals*

Daniel S. Janal, *101 Successful Businesses You Can Start on the Internet*

Daniel S. Janal, *Online Marketing Handbook, 1997 Edition*

Thomas Koulopoulos, *Corporate Instinct*

Thomas Koulopoulos, *Smart Companies, Smart Tools: Transforming Business Processes into Business Assets*

Amit K. Maitra, *Building a Corporate Internet Strategy*

Eugene Marlow, *Web Visions: An Inside Look at Successful Business Strategies on the Net*

Bob Schmidt, *The Geek's Guide to Internet Business Success*

NET INCOME

Cut Costs, Boost Profits, and Enhance Operations Online

WALLY BOCK   **JEFF SENNÉ**

VAN NOSTRAND REINHOLD
I(T)P™ A Division of International Thomson Publishing Inc.

New York • Albany • Bonn • Boston • Detroit • London • Madrid • Melbourne
Mexico City • Paris • San Francisco • Singapore • Tokyo • Toronto

Van Nostrand Reinhold is an International Thomson Publishing Company.
ITP logo is a trademark under license.

The ideas presented in this book are generic and strategic. Their specific application to a particular company must be the responsibility of the management of that company, based on management's understanding of their company's procedures, culture, resources, and competitive situation.

The term TACTICS used throughout this book is a protected trademark of Jeff Senné and Wally Bock.

Printed in the United States of America

Visit us on the Web   www.vnr.com

For more information contact:

Van Nostrand Reinhold
115 Fifth Avenue
New York, NY 10003

Chapman & Hall GmbH
Pappalallee 3
69469 Weinham
Germany

Chapman & Hall
2-6 Boundary Row
London SEI 8HN
United Kingdom

International Thomson Publishing Asia
60 Albert Street #15-01
Albert Complex
Singapore 189969

Thomas Nelson Australia
102 Dodds Street
South Melbourne 3205
Victoria, Australia

International Thomson Publishing Japan
Hirakawa-cho Kyowa Building, 3F
2-2-1 Hirakawa-cho, Chiyoda-ku
Tokyo 102 Japan

Nelson Canada
1120 Birchmount Road
Scarborough, Ontario
M1K 5G4, Canada

International Thomson Editores
Seneca, 53
Colonia Polanco
11560 Mexico D.F. Mexico

1 2 3 4 5 6 7 8 9 10 QEBFF 01 00 99 98 97

Library of Congress Cataloging-in-Publication Data available upon request.

ISBN: 0-442-02558-0

Production: Jo-Ann Campbell • mle design • 213 Cider Mill Road, Glastonbury, CT 06033

Jeff:

This book is dedicated to four wonderful people who have each made important contributions to the quality of my life: my mother and father, Margaret and Clifford Senné, who have always believed in me: my life partner, Michelle Murphy, who is my closest counsel, friend and the source of much joy for me; and to my co-author, Wally Bock, who provides both inspiration and a model of excellence in our strategic alliance.

Wally:

To Absent Friends

> *Tom Mandel*
> *Officer Mike Soto*

and all the others who would be in the midst of this excitement if they weren't names chiseled on walls of honor.

ACKNOWLEDGMENTS

This project really began on a hot summer afternoon a couple of years ago. We were having a telephone discussion about the Net and the Web and all the things it meant for business. Jeff had been connecting it up to his background in sales leadership and in facilitating sales culture change in banks and other financial institutions. Wally was bringing up the stuff that he'd learned from years of working on effective business and marketing with his clients, most of whom, as he puts it, usually make or carry physical product.

The discussion turned to what book we should recommend to our clients to tell then about this exciting new technology that we saw as transforming business. And the silence got pretty long.

The fact is, that even then, there were lots of good books out there. Most of them, though, fell into one of two broad categories. There were technical books about the specifics of TCP/IP and HTML and filled with screen shots. There were, and are, a lot of marketing books. What we were looking for, and couldn't find, was a book about business strategy and how to use this new technology to make it more effective while increasing productivity, cutting costs, and boosting profits. So we decided to write one.

The further we got into this material, the more excited we got. You'll probably catch our excitement from several pages in the book. It's not that we're not old-time business folk who see the obstacles that are out there. Instead, it's the fact that after a couple of decades in business, we've stumbled on something that we think makes business strategy work the way it should. That something is

Net and Web technology.

To make this book happen we looked at the experiences of over a hundred companies and made extensive use of the resources and tools available on the Internet and the Web. We conducted interviews with many people who took time from their busy schedules to speak with us at length, share their information, and sometimes share access to their private networks. This book and the quality examples would not exist with out the help of the following:

Bill Andiario, Lockheed Martin
Suzanne Anthony, Netscape Communications Corp.
Dr. Robert Atherton, Sun Microsystems
James Barksdale, Netscape Communications Corporation
Gary Base, Community Credit Union
Frank Berrish, Vision Federal Credit Union
William Buonnanni, Lockheed Martin
Ian Campbell, International Data Corporation
Jerry Cellucci, Johnson Controls
Bruce Chovnick, General Electric Information Services
Dave Copeland, Intuitive Technologies
Lorraine Darrell, Arkansas Federal Credit Union
Carolyn Drake, Fort Knox Federal Credit Union
Bob Edelman, Marshall Industries
Troy Eid, InfoTest International
Tod Fetherling, Columbia/HCA
Katie Finneran, Lockheed Martin
Jerry Gross, Country wide Home Loans, Inc.
Lou Harm, Burson-Marsteller
Chris John, Resource Financial Group
Cindy Johnson, Texas Instruments
Barbara Kachelski, Credit Union Executives Society
Debra Kaplan, General Electric Information Services
Gary Kayye, Extron Electronics
Jody Kramer, Netscape Communications Corporation
Ed Landt, Minvalco
Steven Neathery, R.E. Michel Corp.
Peggy Odem, American Productivity & Quality Center
Dennis Passovoy, Amicus Networks

Bob Peck, Hewlett Packard
Alan Powell, American Productivity & Quality Center
Michael Sanders, Commerce Bank
Neil Schmitt, Hewlett Packard
Mark Takahama, Wintronix, Inc.
Steve Telleen, Silicon Valley Intranet Partners
Edward D. Withee, PE, Manufacturing Applications Experts
Stan Witkowski, Prudential Securities
Susan Wood, Financial Services Corporation
Tom Vassos, IBM
Ann Yakimovicz, Columbia Quantum Innovations, Inc.

We'd like to thank the other writers and journalist who are out there. The folks writing for *Fortune, Business Week, Industry Week,* and *Information Week,* and all the other weeks and months and dailies. They gave us ideas for people to call and places to look. They gave us some of the facts that you'll find in this book. And they helped us document the excitement, the success, and the obstacles.

This was not the first book for either one of us. Between us, in fact, we've done almost 20. This time, though, we had something special going for us—a great editor. Noah Shachtman, our editor at Van Nostrand Reinhold, conceived the project and brought it to us as a possibility. He helped us shape the initial idea and pushed us on schedule. And every time we sent him some work, he was supportive and told us how good it was, and then suggested eight or ten ways it might get just a little bit better.

Again, and again, Noah held our feet to the fire. The results are four blistered feet and a much better book. If you appreciate the specifics in many of the examples you read here, he merits your thanks as well as he does ours.

There are also personal thanks to be done. For Wally there's family, my wife Kaye, my daughters Debbie and Di, my son Dave, and my grandson Teddy. They, my father, and his wife put up with a great deal of "Wally won't be here today, he's working on the book." Sandra and Angel, who shared our home for much of the time that this was being written and who suffered many of the trials of family without having the same last name, deserve thanks too.

For Jeff there's family, my life partner Michelle and my two sons Jared and Justin. There's my business partner in The Expertise Center Web site, Ken Braly. All of whom supported me by giving me advice and encouragement and allowing me to not spend as much time with them as they might have wanted or needed while I worked on this book. There is also a special thanks to Suzanne Anthony, the Public Relations Manager at Netscape Communications Corp., for her support, guidance, and direction in finding our way around Netscape's Web site with all it's valuable information resources and for referring us to contacts within many of Netscape's customers and business partners who supplied many of the practical business challenges, strategies, solutions, and lessons learned from their experience using Net technology.

Finally, from both of us, thanks to our readers of this and other books, and our clients who make it possible for us to do what we think is exciting and meaningful work. We appreciate you all more than you know.

CONTENTS

Foreword   xv

Introduction   xvii

1   THE TACTICS ACTION PLANNING SYSTEM   1

The Big Picture
Where Do You Start?
WALLY AND JEFF'S QUICK STRATEGY ANALYSIS
Question 1: What's Your Strategy?
Question 2: What Are Your Key Business Processes?
Question 3: Who Are Your Key Suppliers?
Question 4: Who Are Your Customers?
Question 5: Who Are Your Partners?
From Answers to Action
THE TACTICS ACTION PLANNING SYSTEM

2   PRODUCT DEVELOPMENT   17

CRITICAL CHALLENGES OF PRODUCT
    DEVELOPMENT
SOLUTIONS: BUILDING A RICH SOURCE
    OF PRODUCT DEVELOPMENT IDEAS
Start with Your Own Information
Small Publishers Share Ideas with a Mailing List
Using the Net for Surveys
A New Way to Design Quickly
Boeing Internal Web
TACTICS—TRANSFORMING STRATEGY INTO
    RESULTS-ORIENTED ACTIONS
WALLY AND JEFF'S PRODUCT DEVELOPMENT
    LESSONS LEARNED

**3   MANUFACTURING AND QUALITY
       ASSURANCE   37**

CRITICAL CHALLENGES TO MANUFACTURING
Customer Responsiveness
Quality
Agility
Where Are We Now?
TACTICS
WALLY AND JEFF'S MANUFACTURING AND
    QUALITY ASSURANCE LESSONS LEARNED

4   **ADMINISTRATION**   61
CORE ADMINISTRATIVE CHALLENGES THAT
    ONLINE TOOLS CAN SOLVE
SOLUTIONS: COST-REDUCTION BENEFITS OF
    USING INTERNET TECHNOLOGY
Cutting Costs in Basic Administration
Snapshots of Administrative Operations Online
Cutting Employee Benefit Costs Using the Web
Net Technology for Investor Relations
Cutting Purchasing Costs Online
How to Access $1 Billion in Trade without Leaving
    Your Desk
TACTICS
WALLY AND JEFF'S ADMINISTRATION LESSONS
    LEARNED

5   **RECRUITING AND TRAINING**   87
CRITICAL CHALLENGES OF RECRUITING AND
    TRAINING
SOLUTIONS
Columbia/HCA Healthcare Corporation Meets a
    Huge Recruiting Challenge
Online Recruiting—A Growing Phenomenon
Using the Net for Training
Computer-based Courses Online
Training as a Competitive Strategy
TACTICS
WALLY AND JEFF'S RECRUITING AND TRAINING
    LESSONS LEARNED

6   **ENHANCING SALES EFFECTIVENESS**   111
CRITICAL CHALLENGES OF ENHANCING SALES
    EFFECTIVENESS
SOLUTIONS

Starting From a Green Screen
Getting Account Information Where and When
    It's Usable
Providing Information to Set Up Retail Sales
TACTICS
WALLY AND JEFF'S ENHANCING SALES FORCE
    EFFECTIVENESS LESSONS LEARNED

7   ENHANCING SERVICE DELIVERY   137

CRITICAL CHALLENGES IN ENHANCING SERVICE
    DELIVERY
SOLUTIONS
Mortgage Services via Extensive Net Systems
A Credit Union in Front of the Pack
Leveraging Knowledge Using the Net
TACTICS
WALLY AND JEFF'S ENHANCING SERVICE
    DELIVERY LESSONS LEARNED

8   FULFILLMENT AND DISTRIBUTION   155

CRITICAL CHALLENGES OF FULFILLMENT AND
    DISTRIBUTION
SOLUTIONS: A LOOK AT THE WHOLE SUPPLY
    CHAIN
Potential Relationships and New Efficiencies
Getting Lower Prices
Bringing EDI to the Web
Improving Relationships with Wholesale
    Distributors
Outsourcing Distribution and Fulfillment Services
Supply-Chain Partners
Knowing Your Customers and How They Buy
Integrated Solutions
TACTICS
WALLY AND JEFF'S FULFILLMENT AND
    DISTRIBUTION LESSONS LEARNED

9   CUSTOMER SERVICE   175

CRITICAL CHALLENGES OF PROVIDING
    HIGH-QUALITY CUSTOMER SERVICE
SOLUTIONS
Making Hay Out of Customer Complaints
Saving Call Center Costs

Adding Enhanced Value in Securities
Customer Service on the Web
What Is the Process for Delivering Customer
    Service Using the Net?
An Extended Intranet with a National Network
    of Financial Representatives
How Smaller Companies Provide Customer Service
Enhancing Customer Responsiveness with a Large
    Dealer Network
Smaller Companies Can Use Mailbots, Too
TACTICS
WALLY AND JEFF'S CUSTOMER SERVICE
    LESSONS LEARNED

10   LEADERSHIP   199
CRITICAL CHALLENGES OF LEADERSHIP
SOLUTIONS: CHALLENGES OF THE
    AEROSPACE INDUSTRY
A Virtual Open-Door Policy
Boosting Profit Margins as a Core Business Strategy
An Extranet for More Effective Partnership
Net Seminars for Education, Training, and
    Communication
Evolving Uses of the Net
The Internet as a Strategic Planning Tool
TACTICS
WALLY AND JEFF'S LEADERSHIP LESSONS
    LEARNED

**11   MAKING THIS HAPPEN IN YOUR
           ORGANIZATION   227**
There Are Lots of Ways These Projects
    Get Started
The Process

APPENDIX A   RESOURCES   249

APPENDIX B   PRECURSOR TECHNOLOGIES   253

APPENDIX C   SALES   263

GLOSSARY   269

INDEX   279

FOREWORD

At Netscape, we talk about the Networked Enterprise—a seamless business environment that enfolds employees, partners, and customers in a web of information. Wally Bock and Jeff Senné have written the business professional's guidebook about the practical strategies that drive this new enterprise.

We've seen companies that share this vision achieve astonishing results. On average, they've achieved returns on investment of over 1500%—spectacular by any standard. Many of those companies are our customers, and you'll learn more about them and how they did it on these pages.

But you'll find a lot more. This is not just another Internet book. It's not even another technology book. It's a business guide. The authors are businesspeople who care about business results—just as you do. From the moment they contacted us for help with research on the book, they asked the kinds of questions our customers ask. Instead of technical updates on the latest software, they asked for real-world examples of companies that have raised profits using the Net. That's because Bock and Senné know that the value of this technology is determined by how businesses can cut their costs and enhance their operations online to be more competitive in today's tough global marketplace.

What you'll find in this book is the result of research into the experience of over a hundred businesses, from small entrepreneurial and medium-sized businesses to Fortune 500 companies. You'll also find the results of the years that Bock and Senne have spent running their companies and consulting with other businesses.

They told us they got started on this project because they couldn't find a good book that they could recommend to clients and their audiences about how business could use the Net. Now they've written it and it's packed with:

- Facts about how companies are using the Net for profit.

- Ways that businesses are forging profit-building links of information all along their value chains.

- Details about how companies integrated this technology into the business and used it to support their strategic goals.

- Advice from the trenches about what works and what doesn't.

- Recommendations about how you can make this work for you.

The outcome is more than an interesting book; from finance to manufacturing, training to customer service, *Net Income* is an operating manual for producing results.

Very simply, this is an excellent book about how you, in your business, can create a Networked Enterprise and use it to increase your net income.

Read it. Learn the lessons Bock and Senné have to teach. And I hope you'll enjoy the same great returns on investment that many of our customers have already achieved.

James L. Barksdale
President and Chief Executive Officer
Netscape Communications Corporation

WHY READ ANOTHER BUSINESS BOOK ON THE INTERNET?

Does your business need to be on the Web? A group of successful owners and managers of fruit-growing and -packing companies didn't think so. They were doing quite well, thank you, without the Web.

One of the authors, Wally Bock, was speaking at one of their conferences. During a social event the day before his speech, one of the owners challenged the idea that the Net or Web could do anything for his business.

"All I'm going to get from this Net and Web thing you're talking about is a bunch of people who want to buy a couple of peaches at a time. I'm not interested in that. I'm not even interested in selling a case of peaches. What I want to do is sell truckloads of peaches. And I know how to do that using my salespeople and the relationships we've built up over a couple of generations."

As far as it went, that business owner was right. He knew his business well; he knew it was based on sales, transaction, and service relationships built up over the years. But he was looking for a way to make *more* profit from that basic business. And Wally showed him and the other owners and managers how the Net and the Web could work for them. He asked one business owner, "Would it help you to save money on as many of those orders as possible by saving on the order-processing cost?" It would. That could run from around $5 to $20 per order, depending on whether the order coming in over the Net replaces a mail or phone order and how much rekeying of information is saved after the initial order entry.

Would it help the sales representatives in the field to have certain kinds of specific information immediately available? It would. It's almost impossible to quantify the value of better decisions and presentations, but most people who've done direct sales work would agree that salespeople with good and timely information about customers, products, and offers make more and bigger sales.

Would it help if customers could get information about special situations or offers without tying up customer service people on the phone? The customers would like that a lot because they could do things on their own. The company would like that a lot because they'd get more information shared with the right people without incurring additional costs.

Using the Web, each of these three suggestions could save money and increase revenues for the fruit produce owners and managers. Using the Web, you and your business can do the same.

This book is a practical business manual that will show you—whether you're concerned with a large business or a small one—where to find the hidden profits in Internet income. Those profits are in product development and administration, in manufacturing and marketing, in customer service and human resources—in every process and function of modern business.

We have researched hundreds of businesses in preparing this book for you. Here are hundreds of solid examples, advice, tips, strategies, tools, and tactics from leading-edge businesses that are optimizing their everyday business activities with Net/Web technology and related technology. They are improving their net income.

SNAPSHOTS FROM CASE STUDIES OF BUSINESSES USING NET TECHNOLOGY

Our research shows lots of bottom-line reasons why the business community is so interested in the Internet and World Wide Web. There's lots of money to be made from implementing a *Networked Enterprise* strategy in conducting business. Here are just a few examples.

- Columbia/HCA Healthcare Corporation saves $6000 per physician every time it delivers training over the Net instead of sending the doctor away to a conference.

- Boeing saves relocation costs for an entire unit by bringing the members together in virtual space.

- Liberty Mutual reduces its number of purchase orders from 17,000 per year to 8000 while increasing the amount of maintenance supplies ordered from preferred vendors.

- Countrywide Home Loans cuts communications costs from seven figures per year to five figures by moving from fax and phone to the Net.

- McDonnell Douglas covers the cost of operating its intranet from the savings on its automated bidding system.

- An executive at NASA saves four hours a week because administrative functions can be handled automatically over the Net.

- Booz-Allen & Hamilton connects all its partners to a sophisticated knowledge base that allows them to be more productive more quickly.

- An engineer at Tektronix can find a data sheet from National Semiconductor in seconds rather than having someone search for it through a 16,000-square-foot warehouse filled with file cabinets.

- A salesperson for Hewlett-Packard prepares for a sales call with a computer system that provides suggestions on presentation as well as product and customer information.

- Heineken USA cuts its order cycle time from 10–12 weeks to 4–6 weeks.

- General Electric cuts its average purchasing cycle from 14 to 7 days.

These companies, as well as many others you'll meet in these pages, are using Net and Web technology as one of the tools to improve their net income.

If all that's true, why have you read so many articles saying that the Web isn't a place to do business or that electronic commerce is still a year or two away? We think it's because most of those articles, books, and news stories focus on only part of the business equation.

Take one of our clients—let's call him Gary. Gary told Wally, "Our Web site really isn't helping us all that much." The site was taking an increasing number of orders a day—an average of 32 orders at an average order size of $130—with revenue coming off the site a bit over $1 million a year. But Gary thought that probably half to two-thirds of those orders would have been received via mail or catalog sales. "It's not bad," Gary said, "and we're making a profit on the site, but it's not really what I'd hoped for."

But there's more to profit than just sales. There's also the costs saved by having those sales on the Web and tied to an internal network. The exciting part of doing business on the Net is seeing the profit jump when cost goes down and revenue goes up at the same time.

Gary's order-processing cost for a phone-in catalog order is about $16. Phoned in, those 32 orders a day would cost $500; $2500 per week; $133,000 per year. The cost to process those orders through the Web site and into the network? About $2. That's $16,640 a year, and a direct and immediate saving of over $100,000 a year.

That's Net and Web economics: the possibility of increased sales and, more important, the increased profit on all those sales. The promise of cost reductions on administrative services that go directly to the bottom line.

In the excitement of a new technology, it's easy to forget the business basics. Traditional business basics hold the key to how you can increase profits by using Net technology.

The basic equation from Business 101 is

Profit = Revenue − Expenses.

With an equation like that, there are two ways to make profits go up: Increase revenue or decrease expenses.

When Gary was looking at whether his Web site was helping the business, he was looking only at building profit by making revenue go up. But the real profit builder for his company was in making expenses go down. Gary's company would have had to make millions in sales to earn the $100,000 profit generated just by those cost savings.

So just what is the Internet and what is the Web, and how can they earn you more revenue and cut your expenses?

KEY DEFINITIONS OF NET TECHNOLOGY

The Internet is a worldwide collection of computers, the links between them, and agreements about how information is going to move over those links.

The World Wide Web is the point-and-click multimedia part of the Internet. It's the part you get to with a program called a *browser*.

Those two, the Internet and the World Wide Web, are the public face of IP, or Internet Protocol, technology. It's the part of the Net you use when you send e-mail to someone at another company or a friend on another continent. It's the part of the Net or the Web you use when you visit a Web site to look for good travel fares for your next trip. The public face of the Web widens the range of a business's marketing, sales, and advertising at very low cost.

Then there's the private face of the Web created by an intranet. This is a miniature Web site inside your company, protected from outsiders by what's called a firewall. An intranet enhances the efficiency of your internal business operations.

The next step, an extranet, extends your local intranet out to your key business partners, suppliers, and customers.

These are the key elements you use to boost your net income.

ACTION STRATEGIES: USING NET TECHNOLOGY TO BOOST PROFITS AND ENHANCE OPERATIONS

The action strategies outlined here give you an idea of some of the ways the Internet, Web, intranets, and extranets can build your business into a "networked enterprise" and use this twenty-first century technology to improve your bottom line now.

1. BUILDING A PUBLIC WEB SITE FOR MARKETING, SALES, AND ADVERTISING

This is how many companies start on the Net, and it's a strategy that can provide some profitable results.

The Net and Web can be a way for a business to extend its reach. That's what a small hot-sauce retailer in Pasadena is doing. The store is called Hot, Hot, Hot, and it uses its Web site to sell hot sauce to customers who live far beyond easy driving distance. Web sales now account for a third of the store's business and are growing at a rate more than double either walk-in or catalog sales.

The Net and Web can be a way for a business to provide more detailed information about products than would be feasible in a print catalog and, at the same time, make it possible for customers to easily order items as they move through the site. That's what Lands' End does with its site.

The public Web can help boost sales at a retail location. That's what companies like Saturn, Goodyear, and Wal-Mart do with their store locators. And that's not the whole story. Consider the following:

> The marketing cost for Hot, Hot, Hot's Web sales is 5% of sales compared to 22% for catalog sales. That's direct bottom-line impact.

> The order-processing cost for an order placed on the Web is about 70% less than handling an 800-number order. But taking orders on the Web also frees up order takers to do other work for your business.

> For retail stores like a Saturn dealership, Goodyear, and Wal-Mart, the public Web eliminates lots and lots of printing and postage and the need for some of the telephone staff.

This is the public face of the Web, and it's been written about a lot. Direct sales to consumers are important but, right now, they're not where the big profits are. If you'd like more information on direct sales, see Appendix A. But now let's step into the area where the big profits from Net and Web technology happen. They happen when the technology is used inside your business to make it more profitable and when you use the technology to connect your business more effectively to the outside world.

2. BUILDING AN INTRANET

Take Net and Web technology, bring it inside your firewall, and you have an intranet. Once you do that, you can reap some profit-building rewards.

Basic administrative information, like the employee phone directory, can be totally current without any of the cost of printing updates. The same is true for product specification sheets, production and shipping schedules, benefits information, company calendars, and a host of other information that is frequently updated.

Any company—large or small—that requires forms to be filled in is a natural for an intranet: expense reports, travel advance requests, simple purchase order processes, and order-tracking requests. Consider also the documentation that needs to be maintained on quality assurance, emergency procedures, nonroutine administrative functions (such as bringing in temporary staff). Having those items available on the intranet makes everyone more effective.

Once again, that's not the whole story. Consider this:

There are immediate savings in printing and postage. There are savings in people's time. Personnel-benefits specialists, purchasing agents, and others with specialized knowledge can use their knowledge, skills, and abilities to deal with the situations that really require their higher-level skills. And clerical costs drop.

There are technology savings because the Web was developed to manage and link lots of information across a number of different computer platforms. If your company has different computer systems, an intranet will link them easily as long as you've already got them networked.

International Data Corporation, a consulting and research firm based in Framingham, Massachusetts, has studied the return on investment to companies that have implemented an intranet. The result: The average ROI is in excess of 1000% a year. Payback periods range from 6 to 12 weeks.

There are several factors pushing these numbers upward. The

first, and probably the most important, is that productivity gains are really enormous. The tangible benefits of turning labor-intensive work over to an automated process quickly and easily has immediate and powerful benefits.

Setup costs for intranets are far lower than those for other kinds of business systems. Most of the companies setting up intranets are not buying new equipment to make the intranet run. In companies used to client/server computing, the only additional cost may be for a site license for a browser, such as Netscape. And some browsers, such as Microsoft Explorer, are free and may already be on desktops.

Training costs are minimal. Many of your people are already familiar with browsers from having browsed the Internet on their own. And the technology of the Web, hyperlinking, is brain-friendly. In a well-designed intranet or public Web site, hyperlinking lets users follow their association of ideas to find the answer they want. The only additional training that needs to be provided has to do with the rules and resources on the intranet. And that can be distributed—how else?—over the intranet itself.

Intranets are such a fast-growing and powerful tool that Zona Research has forecast that the market for intranet servers is going to leap from about $456 million in 1995 to over $4 billion in 1997. And Forrester Research is predicting that, by the turn of the century, intranet servers will outsell Internet servers by 10 to 1.

OK, who's doing this? Research by several different companies indicates that, by the end of 1997, better than 90% of the Fortune 1000 companies are likely to have an intranet in place. They're doing it for all the reasons we've cited: high return on investment, easy setup, low cost, quick payback, powerful results to the bottom line. But you don't have to be a Fortune 1000 company to use this technology.

One of the authors of this book runs a small niche publishing firm in Northern California. Some of the people who work for him are located in northern California but some live in other parts of the country. Files routinely move back and forth between northern California and a production worker in Kentucky. They also move between the different members of the company, no matter where they happen to be, via e-mail and attached files.

As you read this book, keep that principle in mind. This technology is so cost-effective and so easy to use that it is accessible to, and will benefit, businesses of any size.

Chapters 3–7, and 10 will give you more examples of companies such as Schlumberger, Lockheed Martin and Eli Lily, that are using intranets to boost their net income.

3. CREATING AN EXTRANET

An extranet is the place where the Internet and your intranet come together in an external network. It's the way your company reaches out to people who don't work for you but who are key players as business partners or suppliers.

It's also a way to provide added service to your customers. You can, for example, give key customers a way to check on their orders, which are already in your order-processing system and available to your people through the intranet. Giving your key customers access to that information, permits them to check on orders without delay and without incurring any labor costs to you.

On December 3, 1996, Jim Barksdale, president and CEO of Netscape Communications, in his regular Web site column, "The Main Thing," laid out the reasons why businesses are turning to extranets now.

Companies used to create systems with the idea that they were building them for inside the business, for whatever use the application had—improving employee productivity, sharing data, while updating human resources information, for example. Then they would build other applications for use outside the business—either products for their customers or products to let the company communicate better with vendors.

Open Internet software changes that whole communications paradigm. ... Companies can't be sure anymore about who they might want to access these applications five years from now. So they might as well build them for the broadest possible connectivity—namely, the Internet. ...

Look at the systems you're building and ask, "What if partners, customers, or prospects outside the firewall could tap into this?" ... You might ... find that people want to get more information and buy more of your products. I'm seeing these kinds of discoveries in every industry: from software to financial services, from transportation to insurance to pharmaceuticals.

Barksdale pretty much sums up why this technology is so powerful. It works on just about any platform, it uses software that people are used to and comfortable with, it provides tools that are easy to learn and to use, and it lets people go about doing business in ways that are comfortable for them and profitable for their companies.

All this sharing of information fits in with the major trends in corporate strategy over the last 15 years. Terms like *outsourcing, partnering, strategic alliances, demand-driven, lean,* and *agile* are probably familiar to you by now. As companies have become more lean, more agile, and more demand-driven, we've begun to create strategic alliances, channel partners, and value chains.

Extranets link these together so that business can communicate effectively from either side of a relationship. This is one of the most powerful business ideas of the century.

Chapters 4–6, 8, and 10 illustrate how companies such as Financial Services Corporation and Marshall industries are using extranets to increase net income.

4. CREATING A NETWORKED ENTERPRISE

Beyond the basic public Web site, the intranet, and the extranet, is the concept that Marc Andreessen, the creator of Netscape, calls this concept the Networked Enterprise. Here's how he describes it:

The Networked Enterprise vision comprises one seamless network, extending the corporate intranet to all the entities a company does business with—consumers, business customers, prospects, suppliers, distributors, resellers, partners, consultants, contractors, and anyone else.

The Networked Enterprise provides two primary benefits:

- By creating new types of services, businesses can engage customers in a direct interactive relationship that results in customers getting precisely what they want when they want it, resulting in stronger customer relationships.

- By taking the entire product design process online—drawing partners and customers into the process and removing the traditional communication barriers that prevent rapid product design and creation—companies can bring products and services to market far more quickly.

Because of the very nature of their industry, aerospace companies are excellent leading indicators of what some kinds of networked enterprises will look like. You can see what Boeing is doing in Chapters 2, 4, and 5; Lockheed Martin in Chapters 4–6 and 10; McDonnell Douglas in Chapters 3 and 4. Stanford Federal Credit Union presents a somewhat different model in Chapter 7.

GREAT! BUT DO I REALLY NEED AN INTRANET OR EXTRANET TO GET THESE RESULTS?

The short answer is, "No, but ..."

You can avoid building an intranet or extranet by cobbling together a number of older, so-called *precursor,* technologies like Electronic Data Interchange, Groupware, and Value-Added Networks. While that method can work, it's usually more expensive and more problem-prone, because the systems are made up of several different technologies, with no common bridge readily available. An intranet or extranet can be the common screen and connection to use many different pieces of hardware and software.

You can also get around an intranet/extranet by developing a special proprietary system. One that's gained "near-cult status" in parts of the corporate world, at least according to *The Wall Street Journal,* is R/3, a comprehensive set of application programs developed by the German company SAP AG. There are two major problems though. First, such systems cost a lot up front and need new software, at the very least. More important, using most of these systems requires changing the way your company works to fit the software. Almost always, it means lots of training and learning time. Proprietary systems can be the right solution for some businesses. We think they're best suited to companies with strong central direction, whose basic business processes are likely to be stable for a long time.

We think a better answer to the question is Yes. The Web, intranets, and extranets are simple, cost-effective ways of achieving the same goals of improving profits in ways that allow a business to take advantage of the technologies that will lead it into the twenty-first century.

That's true even if you find that proprietary systems are necessary for some parts of your business. We find companies like Commerce Bank designing a system to use a Web browser to access multiple proprietary system files more efficiently. It's true even if you're using groupware systems like Lotus Notes or EDI since these, increasingly, can work with your intranet and extranet.

HOW THIS BOOK IS ORGANIZED

We've tried to organize this book in a way that will make it most productive for you. And we've supported it with a Web site where you can get more and updated information.

In the next chapter, we'll give you a quick overview of how to think about this technology and how you can boost your profits with it. We'll show you how to tie it to your business strategy. To help you do that, we'll introduce you to a simple system we've used with clients for this. We call it TACTICS. The key phrases are:

> Think links
>
> Automate
>
> Customize
>
> Transform
>
> Inside/Outside
>
> Core functions/Big payoffs
>
> Start now

We've organized the book around business functions for two reasons. First, most of you work within a particular specialty or whose career has developed through a specialty. You're most likely to start with the things you know best and most likely to apply ideas effectively in areas you know well. The second reason is that most businesses have a function or two that is their core competency. For industrial distributors, distribution and fulfillment are core competencies; for manufacturers, sales and customer service are core competencies.

Now, after you've checked the functions you're familiar with, we suggest that you look at all the chapters. That's because businesses don't come in functional silos despite some of the organizational charts that lead you to think that way. Instead, businesses are made up of an interrelationship of functions. What you do in distribution affects what happens in administration and in finance. And what the sales force does affects product development just as manufacturing does.

The core business function chapters in this book are:

Chapter 2	Product Development
Chapter 3	Manufacturing and Quality Assurance
Chapter 4	Administration
Chapter 5	Recruiting and Training
Chapter 6	Enhancing Sales Force Effectiveness
Chapter 7	Enhancing Service Delivery
Chapter 8	Fulfillment and Distribution
Chapter 9	Customer Service
Chapter 10	Leadership

Each functional chapter has four sections:

"Critical Challenges" lays out some of the key issues in the chapter's functional area.

"Solutions" covers the ways businesses today are meeting those challenges using Net and Web technology.

"Tactics" includes our comments about how our four basic tactics were applied by the companies we talk about.

"Lessons Learned" isolates the key learning and application points that we see arising from the solutions.

Chapter 11 is designed to help you start, wherever you are right now, to develop an action plan to turn the ideas you've gotten from this book into online strategies, tactics, and actions that improve your business's bottom line.

The Appendixes include discussions of direct selling on the Net and precursor technologies (EDI, groupware), a resource list, and a glossary.

Whatever kind or size of business you're in, you're going to want to find ways to use this technology effectively. As one of the authors says in his speeches, "If you want to make the trip, you've got to get on the ship." If you want to use this technology and all the benefits it can give you, you have to get started. The next chapter will give you tools to get started, and then we'll show you what others have done and why it works.

CHAPTER 1

THE TACTICS ACTION PLANNING SYSTEM

This chapter is about the point at which strategy and technology come together. It's about the principles you'll use to apply and adapt the lessons and examples you'll find in this book to build your bottom line.

THE BIG PICTURE

Let's survey the terrain for a moment.

Just a couple years ago, businesses latched onto the open technology of the Internet and the brainpower-leveraging vigor of hyperlinks and the Web, and launched a revolution. Part of the reason why that revolution is so incredibly powerful is that its strengths—efficiency, sharing between different groups, information primacy, and networking—match up almost exactly with the most effective strategic ideas of the decade.

Now, let's look at how this revolution fits into the best thinking about business strategy and where it fits into the best things we know about the development of technology.

Consider the following from Michael Porter's classic, *Competitive Strategy*: "Every firm competing in an industry has a competitive strategy, whether explicit or implicit. This strategy may have been developed explicitly through a planning process, or it may have evolved implicitly through the activities of the various functional departments of the firm."

Whatever your strategy is, you probably think about it differently than you did 10, 15, or 20 years ago. Here are the overall driving forces generating today's business strategies:

> Driving Force 1: Striving for leanness and efficiency
>
> Driving Force 2: Blurring the lines at organizational boundaries
>
> Driving Force 3: Seeing the organization as a living system that is part of a larger, living, networked system.

DRIVING FORCE 1: STRIVING FOR LEANNESS AND EFFICIENCY

One of the most visible trends in business strategy is toward leanness and efficiency. Books, journals, boardrooms, and casual business conversation crackle with phrases like *reengineering, efficient consumer response, lean manufacturing, reduced cycle time, agile manufacturing* and others that point you toward a lean and efficient organization. Net/Web technology can help you make your business leaner and more efficient.

Follow the lead of companies like Heineken, whose net ordering system (see Chapter 8) chopped its order cycle time in half. Look at how Columbia/HCA Healthcare and Sheraton (Chapter 5) are streamlining training delivery by making some materials available online when and as they're needed.

DRIVING FORCE 2: BLURRING LINES AT ORGANIZATIONAL BOUNDARIES

There's a clear trend toward blurring lines at the boundaries of the organization. You hear terms like *strategic alliances* and *virtual organizations*. The idea is to think about your business as more than just the people inside your office or factory or warehouse walls.

For example, Resource Financial Group (Chapter 4) offers the service of a virtual employee benefit department to its clients. When employees of a client company use the Net to check benefits provided by RFC, it's just as though they were connecting with an in-house department.

The consulting firm Braxton Associates has done research into strategic alliances. It shows "a doubling in the number of alliances from the late 1970s to the early 1980s, followed by another doubling as the 1980s came to a close. Companies large and small now incorporate alliances as a core strategy."

Outsourcing has been common for years in areas such as payroll processing. Lately, the idea has been extended to include any area of business that's strategically important but not a core competency. That's what leads a chemical company like DuPont, with plenty of resources, to contract with Computer Services Corporation to run DuPont's computer operations for $3 billion over the next 10 years.

Net/Web technology can help you outsource the functions that make sense while maintaining efficiency. In Chapter 5, check out how Financial Services University offers to handle the detailed but important tasks of tracking certification and providing needed training for securities dealers. Look at how manufacturers, such as Johnson Controls (Chapter 8) develop a strategy to use the Net/Web to forge powerful partnerships with key distributors.

For years, the aircraft industry has been a place of joint projects. Boeing's new aircraft, the 777, for example, allocated 65% of its costs to companies other than Boeing. McDonnell Douglas uses the Net/Web to move critical information to and from partners in its projects (see Chapter 3). Different partners can use the Net to link up on projects and cut development times just as they do with the Darwin system for aerospace projects described in Chapter 2.

Both Lockheed Martin (Chapter 10) and Boeing (Chapter 4) use the Net/Web as part of their key strategy for helping to integrate newly merged companies.

DRIVING FORCE 3: SEEING THE ORGANIZATION AS A LIVING SYSTEM

In the last few years, effective companies have begun to notice how organizational charts that divide their organization into functional silos can hamper efficiency. One friend of ours refers to these as stovepipe organizations, in which information and requests travel up one stovepipe and move over to another stovepipe to travel down to the same level at which they started but in a different part of the company. But stovepipes slow down the flow of information, get in the way of learning, create unnecessary work, and block the natural, informal interfunctional cooperation that is a key advantage in many small and well-run businesses.

To be effective, organizations need to learn. They learn from inside sources as one person taps the knowledge of another for greater effectiveness. That helps the organization's operation to stay lean and efficient. Organizations also learn from outside sources. That's far easier when you see some outside sources as partners—when the lines blur at your organizational boundary.

In both cases, networks help organizations learn. Networks share data, information, and knowledge. And, through that sharing, they help learning—both organizational learning and individual learning—to happen.

Booz-Allen & Hamilton is a leader in this area with the development of their extensive knowledge base (see Chapter 7). Like many other firms, Booz-Allen & Hamilton realizes that it needs to make the learning of individual members of its firm available to other members. Its intranet, Knowledge On-Line (KOL), is the way it moves from individual learning to organizational learning. Members of the firm can quickly find information to help them with projects, as well as identify other members of the firm who have knowledge that might be helpful.

Booz-Allen & Hamilton's intranet deals with corporate knowledge and learning. For Johnson Controls, the strategy is a bit different. Johnson Controls is looking for ways to make its distributors more effective. That's because distributors have the knowledge of local markets and contractors that helps them make good recommendations of Johnson's products. Johnson Controls' strategy is to use an extranet to help its distributors increase their effective knowledge by letting them check order status, stocking, and pricing easily and quickly (see Chapter 8). Johnson Controls sees the distributors as partners with specialized local knowledge.

Information and knowledge are strategic resources. The information in your company resides in people—in their files, their databases, and their heads. Those people are both inside your organization and part of your alliances and partnerships. Technology is what gets the information and knowledge out of people's heads and files and databases and out where everyone can use it and where it can enhance your bottom line.

Financial Services Corporation (Chapter 4) is a good example of sharing. Its trading desk helps keep people aware of key rates, and a private chat room for field associates lets them share strategies that work.

Networks help learning. The idea of the learning organization is just one way we've started to shift our business thinking from an engineering, or mechanical, model toward a biological, or ecological, model.

The mechanical model has been the key organizational model since the late 19th century. And it works well for organizations that don't change a lot. It works well for organizations with those functional silos and stovepipes. It works well when speed and reaction time are not critical.

But, in today's demanding, hypercompetitive business environment, the biological model simply makes more sense. The biological model treats organizations and markets as a collection of interrelated parts, each of which can act independently. It sees information flows in and between organizations much like the flow of nutrients in the biological world. And it sees parts of organizations and people acting with clear purpose, direction, and choice, just as living organisms do.

We think you'll find it helpful to start thinking of your organization as a living thing made up of parts that work together by sharing information nutrients with each other. Start to think of your organization and industry as a system of interrelated parts and you'll find that information flows become keys to greater profitability.

WHERE DO YOU START?

First, take a look at Figure 1.1 to see how this networking thinking works.

YOUR BUSINESS'S ENVIRONMENT AND VALUE CHAIN

Here, you'll see how your business is an entire process going from the goods you receive from suppliers to what you provide to your customers. The diagram also shows your key partners. Take a minute to make any notes you want to about how that process works. What goods and information flow along that chain? What goods and information flow from your partners to you? From your partners to your customers?

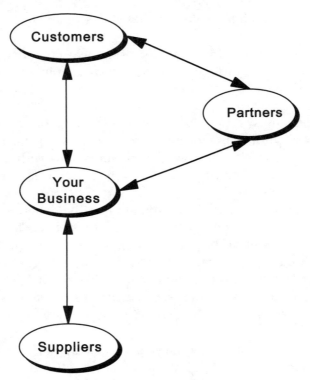

Figure 1.1 The system of interrelated parts of your company.

Those flows of goods and information are what we're going to try to improve with the Net and Web technology we talk about in this book. These are the same kinds of flows to which the successful companies we've profiled have applied their technology. You may want to sketch a version of this diagram for your company.

FROM PROCESS TO STRATEGY

Now, look at the strategy of your business. Ask yourself, What are your company's strategic objectives? Then look for ways to use Net and Web technology to achieve the objectives that improve net income.

Here's an example from Tod Fetherling, director of interactive marketing at Columbia/HCA Healthcare: "We just want to strengthen our relationship with our vendors and allow the clinicians who are actually in the day-to-day patient care to have access to the best information about the tools that they're using to deliver quality patient care."

Or another from Susan Wood, marketing manager for Business Edge, Financial Services Corporation: "One of the goals that marketing has is retention.... Well, we retain our field associates and we really do think of them as associates as opposed to customers in many respects. Well, we try to give them the very best service that they can get. If I'm a salesperson, I need to work when I need to work. That means having information available when I need it; that means having information in a format that's easy for me to understand."

WALLY AND JEFF'S QUICK STRATEGY ANALYSIS

We're going to introduce you to a process that we've used with our clients to help them utilize this technology most effectively. We're going to ask you to answer six key questions for your business. Then, we'll show you the TACTICS that we've developed for applying Net and Web technology to achieve business objectives.

QUESTION 1: WHAT'S YOUR STRATEGY?

To borrow Peter Drucker's question, "What business are you in?" You may find this in your vision and mission statements or in a formal strategy document. Or, if you haven't got a formal strategy to refer to, take a minute to think about what your company does. Ask yourself:

What are my company's strategic objectives or goals?

Do I sell books or information?

Do I make a product or perform a service?

Who are my customers?

How do they use my product or service?

Who are my competitors? Why would my customer buy from them?

Why do my customers buy from me instead?

QUESTION 2: WHAT ARE YOUR KEY BUSINESS PROCESSES?

A business process is a set of actions, usually taken in sequence, to achieve a desired result. There are hundreds of processes in any business, but most businesses have two or three core processes.

A core process is one that you must do well if your company is to succeed. Most business people we've worked with know what these processes are for their companies, but they've never explicitly identified them. That means that, after we've done this exercise in a consulting process, clients usually say, "Of course...." But having those processes explicitly identified, agreed on, and clearly stated will help you use Net/Web technology more effectively to improve them. Ask yourself the following questions:

What things must any business in my industry do well in order to succeed?

What are our core competencies?

What do we do especially well that helps us succeed?

For a company like Marshall Industries (see Chapter 10), a distributor of electronic components, a core process is the one that begins with taking an order and continues through processing to timely delivery. Marshall uses a combination of its public Web site, intranet, and extranet to make that process as efficient as possible.

For Texas Instruments, one core process is wafer fabrication—the making of chips. By using the Net to share best practices, TI was able to make that process so much more effective that it could avoid building new plants, as you'll see in Chapter 3.

IBM has identified customer service as one of its core processes. In Chapter 9, you'll get an idea of how IBM is constantly working to improve that process.

You may find it helpful to consider the diagram in Figure 1.2 and to draw a similar one for your company.

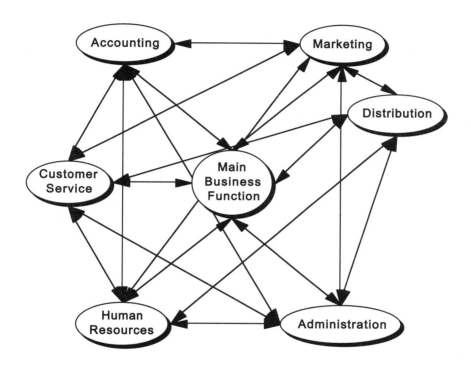

Figure 1.2

Normally, the core processes are the ones that would go inside the area labeled "main business function."

There are other important processes you should identify, too. Ask yourself the following questions:

> What are important support processes? IBM's customer service call handling is an example.

What processes are used most often? Liberty Mutual identified the process of purchasing maintenance, repair, and office supplies as one of those. Then, use the Web (Chapter 4) to cut costs and make the process more effective.

QUESTION 3: WHO ARE YOUR KEY SUPPLIERS?

For people in manufacturing industries, that's usually a pretty easy question to answer. They just look at the list of companies they bought materials from. For consultants, suppliers may provide ideas and information. All businesses generally have suppliers who produce office supplies or basic support equipment.

Tektronix (Chapter 2) has National Semiconductor as a supplier and uses the Web to gather key information quickly about the components National (and other companies) supply.

Marshall Industries (Chapter 10) sits in the middle of the supply chain. Marshall's customers buy parts manufactured by someone else. Marshall uses the Net/Web to reach back along the chain to check part specifications from its suppliers.

For Booz-Allen & Hamilton, the situation is a little different. Information and knowledge are the keys here. Some suppliers of these, such as database providers and publications, are outside the firm. But other key suppliers are inside the firm such as partners and reports. The Knowledge On-line system (see Chapter 7) helps members of the firm find internal information and experts that supply knowledge and information.

QUESTION 4: WHO ARE YOUR CUSTOMERS?

We usually ask our clients to identify, specifically, their most important customers. And that's what we'll ask you to do. Think about specific customers because that usually gives you the best idea about who actually buys what you're selling.

National Semiconductor (see Chapter 2) recognizes that it has two kinds of buyers inside each customer company. Purchasing agents actually make the purchase, but the decision about what to buy is made by the design engineer who specifies products. So National uses the Net and the Web to make both these jobs easier.

QUESTION 5: WHO ARE YOUR PARTNERS?

> Who are the people outside your business that help you achieve your business objectives?
>
> Who do you have formal joint venture or partnership agreements with?
>
> Who do you have an informal relationship with?
>
> Who are the people who regularly refer customers or suppliers to you?
>
> Whose products are used in conjunction with yours?

Johnson Controls (Chapter 8) is developing a strategy around key channel partners. InfoTest (Chapter 3) is developing sophisticated ways to use the net to support wide-area sharing among multiple enterprises. General Electric (Chapters 4 and 8) and Industry.net (Chapter 4) are developing networks where partners can find and work with each other.

FROM ANSWERS TO ACTION

If you take a look at the key processes you've defined in your strategic analysis, you'll find that, within your business, key flows of information and goods make up your core business processes. And there are key flows of information and goods between your business relationships and value chain. Revisit Figures 1.1 and 1.2 or your own versions of them.

What you want to do is to take your key processes and key relationships and use Net and Web technology to develop tactics that support your strategy, to develop tactics that transform your vision into action, whether you're a small, local business or a global giant. The way you'll do that is to apply the seven key TACTICS, which we have found to be effective.

THE TACTICS ACTION PLANNING SYSTEM

TACTICS stands for:

> **T**hink links
>
> **A**utomate
>
> **C**ustomize
>
> **T**ransform
>
> **I**nside/Outside
>
> **C**ore functions/Big payoffs
>
> **S**tart now

THINK LINKS

Think links because links are power. The power of your brain, according to brain researcher Bill Calvin, is its ability to make connections, to make links. The power of the Web and all the technology that surrounds it is the ability to link information, ideas, and people. You'll use this technology effectively if you think about links. But how?

Look inside your company. Booz-Allen & Hamilton (Chapter 7) looked there for ways to link various centers of knowledge important to the firm's success. Texas Instruments (Chapter 3) linked people worldwide to share Best Practices.

Look at your value chain. Marshall Industries (Chapter 10) sees itself in the middle of such a chain, providing services to both its suppliers and its customers by using Net/Web technology.

Look at your partners and alliances. Lockheed Martin shows how this works with the usual multicompany team in what they call Generic Project X in Chapter 10 and how Net technology can help things run better.

AUTOMATE

Automate for efficiency. There are simple information-sharing processes that are probably being done right now in your company that you'll want to automate with Internet technology.

Automate situations in which you've got one human being reading to another human being, sometimes off a computer screen. The best-known example of this is Federal Express's package tracking (see Chapter 9).

Automate situations in which a human being consistently takes the same sheet of paper or brochure and puts it in an envelope for mailing. National Semiconductor (Chapter 2) delivers high value to its customers while cutting costs by making detailed technical and pricing information available over the Net.

Automate information retrieval so that the people who need information can get information when they need it without having to involve others. Westinghouse, for example, on its intranet posts the company policy for hiring part-time employees. Resource Financial Group is a virtual employee benefits department for many companies, whose employees can simply go to the Web to check their own medical insurance deductibles, the list of doctors in their medical plan or the terms of their life insurance (see Chapter 4).

CUSTOMIZE

You can gain competitive advantage by using technology to help you customize, so that your customers and partners get what they want when they want it.

Several studies have indicated that what people really want when they buy a car is to be able to browse and find out information without having a salesperson hanging over them. That's exactly what successful automotive Web sites, such as Saturn's, do. They allow customers to find out lots of information about different models; they offer all kinds of technical specifications, information on pricing, reviews from automotive magazines, and a variety of other options. They let people sort out their own custom answer to their questions about a vehicle.

People also want solutions on their time and terms, not necessarily on yours. Consider a Ford engineer laboring late at night on a design project. Using Ford's internal information system, that engineer can grab a part drawing that's necessary to the engineer's project right then and there—no filing a report and waiting until the next day; no going home frustrated just when the creative juices are starting to flow (see Chapter 2).

Customize, so that people can get things the way they want them. That's why loan calculators are great on bank and credit union sites like the one for Stanford Federal Credit Union (Chapter 7). They allow customers and business partners to check out several solutions until they find the one that's right for them. In the next few years, you're going to see lots of effective ways to use technology to give people custom answers using intelligent agents, sophisticated databases, and on-the-fly Internet and intranet applications.

TRANSFORM

Use technology to transform data and raw facts into information: data with context. Employees checking on their 401(k) plan, for example, not only can find out how the plan is doing but can also compare performance against other measures and indices. That's transforming data into information. You'll see other, similar examples in Chapter 4.

Transform information into knowledge: information with guidance. The knowledge that's embedded in a sophisticated system like the one at Booz-Allen & Hamilton can give newer consultants an idea of what works in different situations and can get them up to speed on specific industry applications faster and more effectively (see Chapter 7).

Transform connections into relationships. Those links you've thought about and forged are ways to make connections. Relationships are built up over time from lots of connections. When we only had the physical world and paper to make those relationships happen, the effort and expense required to make lots of connections could be a barrier. Making and keeping connections is easier and costs less in the digital world. Johnson Controls' strategy (Chapter 8) concentrates on relationships with its key distributors. Marshall Industries (Chapters 5 and 10) uses quality information and training contacts to build relationships.

INSIDE/OUTSIDE

Apply this technology inside your business. Setting up an internal net, or intranet, is a powerful way to move information around inside your business and make people more effective and efficient. Where can you set up links, automate process, or connect customized information resources for your internal customers? What kinds of information can you gather from the public Net or Web about your competition and your prospects?

Look outside your business as well. What kinds of information do your customers, business partners, suppliers, strategic alliances, and outside and remote sales force need to be effective? How can you give them that information using this technology? How can you help them get information from other sources?

Now, look at how the inside of your business and the outside come together. This is where efficiency and effectiveness meet as you make available to selected companies and individuals outside your organization information from inside your organization. Is there information your suppliers could use to serve you better, information that they can get on their own from your network? Can your customers get information from your system that might help them buy more or buy more easily?

As they told you back in kindergarten when you learned to cross the street, "Look both ways." Look along the information flows inside and outside your business to determine good places to apply Net and Web technology.

CORE FUNCTIONS/BIG PAYOFFS

Core functions, or core competencies, are those that matter most to your company. Earlier, we asked you to think of them as your key business processes. This is a way to decide where to start by determining which functions, if made more effective, will have the biggest impact on your business. That's what Schlumberger (Chapter 3) did by identifying the process of maintaining ISO 9000 documentation as a key process and then moving that process to the Web.

Then look for the places where there may be big payoffs. We've been at this long enough now to be able to identify a generic class of situations that are likely to give you a big payoff. Those are the situations that have lots of information sharing. One of the biggest quick payoffs we came across was Countrywide Home Loans' replacement of fax with e-mail, which is described in Chapter 4.

Be sure to apply the 80/20 Rule when developing your networked enterprise: Look for those 20% connections of people and information that will yield you the 80% results you want to achieve your company's strategic goals.

START NOW

If you're not among the better than 90% of Fortune 1000 companies that said they plan to have an intranet up and running by the end of 1997, now's a good time to start. If you already have an intranet, look at the ways you can make it more effective. These companies are finding ways to use their public Web sites as part of an overall strategy to make their businesses more effective. If your company's Web site hasn't incorporated net technology as a key action in your strategic business plan, now is a good time to start.

A key rule for starting now: Whatever your strategy, your technology, your readiness, you can start from exactly where you are. This book is designed to help you get off the dime, get started, and turn that dime into dollars.

As you move through the functional chapters in this book and think about how this relates to your business situation, think about how you can customize and use the strategies and action steps in each tactic contained in the TACTICS Action Planning System. Think links, Automate, Customize, Transform, Inside/Outside, Core functions/Big payoffs and Start now on your way to better operations and bigger profits.

CHAPTER 2

PRODUCT DEVELOPMENT

In February 1996, Alex Trotman, chairman and CEO of Ford, spoke to the National Automobile Dealers Association and laid out his vision of the future. He talked about the movement toward a shrinking, "borderless" world with the opening of lots of new markets. At the same time, he said, the information revolution is creating customers who are more knowledgeable and more sophisticated than ever before and less loyal to a specific brand. "… the bottom line of the revolution will be intense competition for the customer," Trotman said. "Customers don't want fewer features, they want more."

Product development has always been critical to meet market demands. What you want is the best possible product to fill the customers' needs. To be effective, you have to know what's wanted and then develop it. That's never been easy and, in the last few years, it's gotten harder.

In addition to just meeting market demands, there's a greater requirement to develop more complex products in an increasingly regulated environment. The competition's moving too. And speed to market has become a critical way to add value.

If that isn't enough, the product that we develop often turns out to be more than one product. We're finding it necessary to develop

17

different products for different markets in different parts of the world. The challenge of product development today also involves building good, effective teamwork across geographical boundaries.

CRITICAL CHALLENGES OF PRODUCT DEVELOPMENT

Although Trotman was talking about the automotive business, his remarks really could relate to any company that has to develop products for today's hypercompetitive global markets. What are the key challenges?

There are four primary challenges you can solve with Internet technology. They are:

1. To build a better product that meets and exceeds your customers' expectations;
2. To build it faster than your competition;
3. To build it less expensively while still maintaining high quality;
4. To build a productive project team of cross-functional experts (both internal—from various departments of your company—and external—business partners, suppliers, and customers) that often have to work across geographical boundaries.

The first critical challenge is to build better, more sophisticated products. The technology is certainly there to provide them, but it raises both the stakes and the level of difficulty for those who have to design the new products. An important aspect of this challenge is to get timely feedback from customers that enables you consistently to stay ahead of your customers' expectations with new and different products and services.

The second critical challenge is to do it faster. Engineers responding to the *Design News* Career Survey, for example, overwhelmingly (79%) said that they had less time to design products than they did five years ago. And 17% of the engineers responding said that design cycles were only about half as long as they used to be. Indeed, bringing products to market quickly has become one of the key competitive challenges of the '90s, and it doesn't promise to get any easier. Basically, the idea is to be able to hit the market window of opportunity with all your functional departments aligned for a productive and timely product launch. You can hear the importance of timing in the language of product development, in terms like *rapid prototyping* and *improved speed to market.* In fact, speed to market has become one of the key differentiators. All the customization in the world won't do you any good if your product comes out later than your competition's.

The third critical challenge is to do things less expensively. That's the basic challenge of competitive business. Build a better mousetrap, but build it for less than your competition.

The fourth critical challenge is to build a productive project team of cross-functional experts (both internal—from various departments of your company—and external—business partners, suppliers, and customers) that often have to work across geographical boundaries. When you're trying to produce the right product as rapidly as possible for less cost, two things that get in your way are geography and time. The synergy of a well-built team brings to the product development process two powerful ingredients that, when combined and properly focused, will find solutions to achieving any goal. Those ingredients are a variety of expertise and creative brain power.

In manufacturing, the buzzword is often lean, but *lean manufacturing* has to start way back before the factory floor. It has to start in product development, by, for instance, finding ways to integrate the entire product design process with other operations. When we can get more efficient all along the chain, we can drive costs down and make more money.

The professional responses to all the modern strategic thinking in manufacturing have some familiar names. Terms such as *concurrent engineering* and *reduced cycle time* refer to approaches and objectives. And other terms such as *rapid prototyping* relate to the idea of specific techniques for doing things faster, more efficiently, and in a more integrated way.

Underlying all this is attitude. If you start with the idea that there is a way to do things faster, more effectively, and less expensively, you're likely to find it. That leads you to simple ways to get the job done by using computer solutions and Net technology.

SOLUTIONS: BUILDING A RICH SOURCE OF PRODUCT DEVELOPMENT IDEAS

Let's take a look at our design process in the entire product development continuum. The continuum starts with figuring out what ideas to develop. In traditional business, the ideas about what products ought to be developed have come from three primary sources: from customers; from people who have direct contact with customers, such as customer service representatives, salespeople, and repair staff; and from designers. In all those cases, the basic functions revolve around gathering information and analyzing it for product development possibilities.

START WITH YOUR OWN INFORMATION

The Net and Web can help here. One place to start is your internal sources. Complaint, repair, and service databases can easily and quickly be mined for ideas about what aspects of current products your customers would like to see changed. The databases and information sharing you use for customer service (see Chapter 9) and enhancing sales (Chapter 6) are excellent sources of product development ideas.

Intranet and e-mail make it easy to gather and consolidate good ideas from field sales representatives, inside salespeople, and others who have direct contact with customers.

Use the company's Web site and monitor Web activity to gather information for product development. Monitor your logs to see what kinds of things people want information about and which products generate the most information requests. Consider adding a question on product pages like: "What feature would you most like to see us add to this product." This is another form of front-line information that can supplement what you're hearing from sales and customer service.

This can have two direct benefits. On the product development side, visitors searching for a feature that doesn't exist can generate a good product development idea. But there can also be an effect on the sales side. Sometimes visitors will use different terminology to look for a feature that already exists. That can give salespeople a clue to the language to use in presenting the product.

SMALL PUBLISHERS SHARE IDEAS WITH A MAILING LIST

Small companies benefit even more from the Net to generate ideas. The Publishers Marketing Association represents small press publishers. Most of them are very small, and many have no staff at all beyond the founder, who may be working part-time. The Publishers Marketing Association mailing list, PMA-L, provides a way for participants to check ideas out with each other. A recent look at two days' worth of posting found questions and advice related to titles, marketing, public relations, production, printer selection, and a host of other topics. These small publishers get to use the mailing list to check out ideas with others like themselves, some of whom might not be reachable otherwise. Dan Poynter and Tom and Marilyn Ross, authors of definitive books on self-publishing, regularly participate in the list. Top authors like Herman Holtz stop by as well. The result is a place to test ideas that is richer than any single participant could probably muster, even if that person had a much larger organization.

USING THE NET FOR SURVEYS

Surveys on your Web site directed at finding ways to serve your customers better can also be mined for product ideas. A single question, such as "What's the most important thing to you about a product like this?" can provide a wealth of answers that lead you to what customers want from your products.

According to a *Web Week* article, the Council of American Survey Research Organizations says that 81% of corporate executives expect to conduct the same amount or more online research in the next five years. In a late 1996 poll of 300 executives from Fortune 2000 companies, 87% of respondents thought that Web surveys were useful. Why? The primary reasons are that Web surveys are easy to put together quickly and have wide geographic reach. You can set up an online focus group project and complete it in days, not the weeks you often need for similar projects in the physical world.

Be careful, though. Web surveys aren't good for every product or service. Make sure that the demographics you're getting are right for your product. And don't expect statistically valid samples. These are not likely to be possible in a Web survey.

We've seen companies doing several things to make Web surveys more effective. First, they're using them in conjunction with other surveys. One marketing executive told us, "I find that a quick Web or e-mail survey of our best users is a great way to shorten the time it takes me to develop the full survey that we'll do by mail or telephone." Also, a lot of findings from major research firms like FIND/SVP are available from their Web sites.

We also see a growing industry specializing in online market research. Firms like Nielsen and the NPD Group are adding this to their toolkits. In fact, NPD has an Online Research Division. They use a prerecruited panel to put together samples for individual client projects. And there are companies springing up all over that do only online research. These companies can be easily found on the Web by using one of the many popular search engines, such as C/Net Search at www.search.com, or Excite at www.excite.com.

Once you have the ideas, you have to get your design engineers to work on models and prototypes. You want to build fast and build cheap. Here the Net really comes into its own.

A New Way to Design Quickly

The convergence of attitude and technology is giving companies a way to design products that can produce effective designs quickly while helping to drive both development and manufacturing costs down.

Collaboration is a key to effective product development. The Net lets companies form teams that are not in the same geographical space and whose members don't need to travel for a lot of their work. Sharing work and ideas over the Net can help make that happen.

We're also seeing the development of design tools that facilitate collaboration on the Net, through either an internal or Internet connection. A simple example is the online version of the whiteboard. Physical whiteboards have been used for years to help groups meeting in physical space capture ideas and link them. Similar tools are available in cyberspace. Figure 2.1 shows a whiteboard product designed for use over the Net. This particular one comes from the XtX Internet Communications Suite from Wintronix Inc., based in Santa Clara, California. It's part of a software package that includes several collaboration tools, including chat and audiovisual recording in addition to the whiteboard.

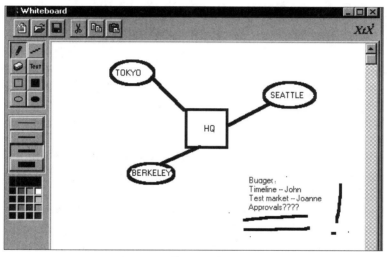

Figure 2.1

And makers of computer-aided-design (CAD) products, such as Intergraph and Autodesk, are taking their products to the Net/Web. Both are developing hotlinkable vector files that will let designers link drawings and drawing elements as easily as they now link text.

Collaborating, sharing ideas, and linking different systems and locations are reasons why many manufacturing firms are using intranets and extranets as part of their product development solution. Automotive and aviation companies appear to be at the forefront.

At General Motors, the Powertrain Control Center coordinates the work of over 300 engineers around the world using GM's intranet. In addition to the collaboration itself, an additional benefit is that documentation on policies, decisions, and project status is more likely to be current and up-to-date.

General Motors engineers used to use paper documents that were distributed through the internal mail system. The next move, in 1994, was to a Unix-based file server. That improved speed but didn't deal with coordination issues. The intranet sharing version lets GM engineers get to information using a standard Netscape browser.

General Motors is not alone in this. According to the *Wall Street Journal,* Chrysler has spent about $750,000 developing the engineering part of its intranet. For Chrysler, the main goal is to link systems that used to work in isolation. There's a Roadmap page that lets engineers find a variety of information from product manuals, government regulations, and other sources. They can also click in to Chrysler's engineering software system.

What if your product development partners are outside your company? Then you've got two options if you want to make use of Net/Web collaboration. You can access your partners through your extranet, or you can create a shared space that anyone can reach through the Internet.

The extranet method is used a lot. The major downside is that you have to pay a lot of attention to segregating proprietary information so that trade secrets are not available to unauthorized partners.

For that reason, several companies are preparing to move collaboration outside their own firewalls. That's part of the idea behind Darwin, a collaborative aeronautical design system based at NASA Ames Research Center at Moffett Field, California. Using Darwin, an engineer can analyze wind tunnel or flight data in real time as it comes in from the test location, collaborate with partners in still other locations on the analysis, and check data against NASA's supercomputer databases. Darwin cost NASA $500,000 to develop, and NASA is responsible for security and for segregating the data for different partners. Using Darwin can really cut down on the time it takes for the initial phase of airplane development. Testing and analysis savings can be large. One wind tunnel hour saved, for example, is worth about $5000.

One company that is using Darwin to reduce design cycles on commercial aircraft is Boeing in Seattle, Washington. In fact, Boeing is using Net and Web technology in all phases of business with one of the world's most extensive and ambitious intranets.

BOEING INTERNAL WEB

Boeing is one of the world's biggest companies, with 147,000 employees worldwide and revenues of $22.7 billion in 1996. Boeing's challenge is to coordinate a huge number of people doing complex tasks that result in the design and construction of one of the most complex products in the world—commercial (70% of revenue) and military (30% of revenue) aircraft.

Consider the Commercial Airplane Group. It produces airplanes in five basic families. Each one may include more than a million parts. The design and manufacturing processes are about as complex as it gets.

To help pull everything together, Boeing has developed a worldwide intranet called Boeing Internal Web. At the end of 1996, there were about 80,000 employees on it, with new users hooking up at the rate of about 500 per week. There are over 400 internal Web sites with thousands of pages.

The intranet was set up with three primary goals: save money, reduce cycle time, and facilitate the integration of new business units from mergers and acquisitions. *Information Week* quotes Srivats Sampath, Netscape's Communications VP: "Boeing is the biggest [corporate intranet] ... Boeing is one of the leading companies to see the benefits of standards-based computing and is ahead of the pack in truly leveraging that benefit."

So, how's it working? To some extent, it's a work in progress. Independent groups are working to move hundreds of business processes to the Web. Several of those processes are product development.

The impact of design process on manufacturing cost can be substantial. Boeing is using computer-aided, three-dimensional, interactive applications (CATIA) and the Net to hook product development to manufacturing. The design software is linked to manufacturing software, with instructions about machining individual parts, sometimes with the addition of small drilled reference holes. When it comes time to put things together, assemblers line up the reference holes and join parts with rivets.

What's that worth? Paul H. Nisbet is president of JAR Research, an aerospace research firm. The *Los Angeles Times* quotes him as estimating that the switch to these design and manufacturing technologies could save $15 million on building a single 747.

With a company the size of Boeing, you'd expect some top management direction to get employees onboard; and the direction is there. In 1995, Boeing adopted a corporate policy that makes the Internal Web the primary means for sharing information. And Boeing people are doing just that, sharing information about parts, projects, and human resources and, of course, sharing news. But, in one key group, the intranet is more than something they use; it defines the way they work.

In November 1995, Boeing set up the Wing Responsibility Center (WRC) which consolidated management of wing responsibility centers and related activities in three locations. The center is responsible for wings, tails, and rudders. In most companies, you'd have to move a lot of people to achieve such consolidation. But Boeing elected to use the Internal Web to bring people together in virtual space. That has both monetary and intangible benefits. Whenever someone is moved, they have a period where productivity is down. Family and work life are both disrupted. Staying in the same house and neighborhood avoids that. And cost? Five thousand people work for the WRC. The cost of relocating a large number of them would certainly be in the millions. To relocate only 2500 at an average cost of $6000, the amount would be $15 million.

Boeing is using the intranet to design planes, link design to manufacturing, and manage a great variety of business functions and processes. As with other companies moving to the Net/Web for all or part of their development process, the Boeing Internal Web is changing the way those processes are carried out.

GETTING A DRAWING WHEN IT'S NEEDED

Let's say an engineer needs a part drawing. In the pre-Net world, the engineer would have to fill out a request form and send it to the department that's responsible for engineering drawings. If that drawing was critical to our engineer's process, the engineer might have put the form in the out basket and then headed home for the night, losing creative momentum. Then, he or she would have to wait days and perhaps weeks to get the drawing, another break in the process.

But, in the Net world, those drawings can be available right away. Ford is working on a massive project to make all 26 million of its technical drawings available online. Understand, now, that those drawings go all the way back to the Model T. The initial prototype system with about three-quarters of a million drawings is projected to be up in 1997.

With that kind of database available, an engineer can grab the drawing that's needed right away. And that's going to be facilitated by systems that index drawings effectively and develop common standards for sharing them across the Net and across different systems.

Drawings aren't the only thing that might be needed in a late-night designing session. One of the things that product designers need most is information—about what other people have done or about certain materials characteristics or about which particular product from which particular vendor might best fit the spec sheet.

Manufacturers of products that might be components for the product being designed aren't left out either. If our engineer is looking for plastics, he or she might check out the materials specifications found on the Web sites for GE Plastics or Allied Signal Plastics.

Tektronix (Beaverton, OR) publishes a daily Web-based online resource manual, called Netbook. Netbook looks on the screen like a spiral notebook and contains links to press announcements from inside and outside the company about relevant engineering topics or products.

A LIBRARY OF SPEC SHEETS ONLINE

National Semiconductor is another supplier that makes information about its products readily available to engineers. The company offers over 30,000 parts to various manufacturers. Each of those parts has a spec sheet that may be up to 40 pages in length. In pre-Net days, companies such as Tektronix that buy from National Semiconductor would store those technical specification sheets in file cabinets ranked row on row in a 16,000-square-foot area. An engineer could spend weeks searching those files for the spec sheet he or she wanted. Of course, the engineer could always request them from the manufacturer, but that would normally take a week or more as well. In the Net world, it's different.

Now, an engineer at Tektronix can find the spec sheet quickly and get it almost instantly from National Semiconductor's Web site. Providing good information to design engineers in an easy-to-access and easy-to-use format is part of National Semiconductor's strategy for becoming a preferred supplier. But the benefits don't end there. That all this is digitized means that engineers can cross-reference every data sheet at National that contains a particular topic—something that would have been impossible to do manually.

And the engineers at both ends don't have to worry about what kind of computer the other company or function has because Internet and Web technologies are used and support is cross-platform and transparent to the user.

On National's site, engineers "enter parameters that describe their design problem," according to Webmaster Klaus Schulz. Then the search engine goes to work. The site gets over 1 million hits a week and delivers as many as 6000 data sheets a day.

Why is this an especially good site? According to Mike Mayer, a design engineer quoted in *Web Week,* the site is easy to get to and use, and the data sheets are complete, including prices.

NATIONAL SEMICONDUCTOR ENHANCES EMPLOYEE COLLABORATION, INNOVATION, AND EFFICIENCY

National Semiconductor's excellent site for design engineers on the public Web is backed by an effective intranet to get its own products to market quickly and profitably. "We're trying to make it easier to connect our employees to knowledge. We want to help our employees be more innovative. And we are also trying to reduce the cycle time of all processes," according to National's Tom Stuart.

Part of the reason for setting up an intranet to do this is that it simply makes things easier. "It gets more difficult to distribute new applications with more and more versions of operating systems and variations of desktop platforms. The logistics of upgrading people to the latest version of client software can be overwhelming," Stuart says.

"When employees have Netscape, it eliminates the need to distribute client software," he says. "You can have one application on the server side and you don't have to worry about distributing three different versions of an application. The software works with what they have. To have one tool that users on all three platforms can access equally well is very powerful."

Having information right when they need it and being able to try things out lead to greater creativity. According to Stuart the software makes people more comfortable exploring new ideas. "That's contagious. People are experimenting and not taking things for granted."

NEWSGROUPS AND E-MAIL DISCUSSION GROUPS AS INFORMATION SOURCES

There's also an information source for engineers and designers that's a bit of a mixed blessing. Engineering newsgroups and mailing lists are great ways for engineers to connect with each other. That makes them a good source of ideas and information. The problem comes from the possibility of leaks of sensitive information.

There are other resources available to engineers right now. Professional and engineering societies, like the American Iron and Steel Institute or the Society of Automotive Engineers, provide a wealth of insightful technical information on their Web sites. The same is true for important educational, material science, and design institutions, like MIT and Princeton in the United States and the Design Institute in Delft, The Netherlands. All this is comprehensive, reliable technical information available over the Net with a mouse click or two, at any hour of the day or night.

So the designers and engineers bring together a lot of information, use it in digital form, and share it with colleagues and partners around the world and across time zones. But there's more to the product development process.

Jonathan Warren is an engineer with Millipore. Millipore manufactures filtration systems and purification systems for a variety of industries. Jonathan's job is to design sophisticated filtration systems for customers in the pharmaceutical and biotechnical fields.

He found that one problem was that the people he was designing for couldn't visualize the systems he was designing well enough to give him good feedback. Well, if the problem cannot be visualized from engineering drawings, then perhaps what's needed is a picture of the product. And that's what Jonathan, assisted by information systems staff from Millipore, set out to provide.

Together, they developed a system that allows Warren to post pictures of his work in process where customers can see it. That happens to be on a password-protected portion of Millipore's public Web site. The result is that drawings that Jonathan produces with sophisticated design software can be viewed by customers with standard Web browsers and a 28.8 modem.

Once the product development and design are done, the next step is to move rapidly into manufacturing. Again, the Net makes this possible because the same tools that allowed collaboration and information sharing during the design process enable companies to port information, drawings, and systems over to the manufacturing side. And, because manufacturing has been involved early in the design and review processes, a product under development should be able to move directly into manufacturing rather than going through a costly and time-consuming test period.

TACTICS—TRANSFORMING STRATEGY INTO RESULTS-ORIENTED ACTIONS

Let's look at our TACTICS and how they're going to apply to product development.

THINK LINKS

As you think links, look for ways to integrate your product development activities by hooking up people who are involved in the design, the use of the design, and ultimately the purchase of the design.

AUTOMATE

Look for automation possibilities that enable you to move critical information around quickly and also to conduct trials in a virtual environment rather than a real one.

CUSTOMIZE

Use the power of the Net to help your engineers and other designers draw together information quickly so that they can spend more time on customizing design and less time on information gathering. For example, Netscape reports that Olivetti, to foster innovation and streamline processes at their R&D laboratories, is running Netscape Communications Server software on an Olivetti SNX Intel-based multiprocessor system that is running Microsoft Windows NT. Olivetti's researchers use the intranet to access a wealth of product development information, debate topics in dedicated discussion areas, and share experiences and project results with colleagues.

TRANSFORM

Look for ways to make the wisdom of successful products—yours and others'—available to those designing new products. The efforts to meet these challenges don't involve only the Web or the Net, but the Web and Net become ways to connect them. Since we're talking about computer-aided design (CAD), computer-aided manufacturing (CAM), and computer-aided engineering (CAE), we're now moving toward using the communication and linking power inherent in the Net and Web technologies to get even more effective.

INSIDE/OUTSIDE

Inside/Outside in product development means collaboration among all the partners. Look for ways to bring together the people, processes, and information you need from a variety of sources using the Net instead of trains, planes, and automobiles. The Net provides the links, and the browser provides the common interface. That's why the Net and its effective tools, such as virtual teams, can help you be more effective. Look for ways to gather expertise and concentrate it where it's needed. For example, Olivetti's R&D organization is using a Netscape-based intranet to create a single virtual laboratory that links together Olivetti's research laboratories located throughout Italy and abroad.

CORE BENEFITS/BIG PAYOFFS

Here, core benefits/big payoffs come from lots of timely information, lots of sources of ideas and reaction, and lots of trials. Those three factors make for faster and better product design.

START NOW

Start now by looking for a way to use the Net/Web to bring together lots of information, including that from outside suppliers and partners. Find ways to get feedback. And consider using the Net for virtual product testing as Deere has done, using e-mail and secure sites as a way to share developing product ideas with your customers and partners, and using the Net to provide new ways to collaborate on design issues, including virtual design teams, or to implement surveys and feedback mechanisms on a public Web site as a continuing source of product ideas. Some other engineering applications of the product development process you might want to start with are as follows:

- Create project newsgroups or e-mail discussion LISTSERVs to promote and facilitate brainstorming and communications within product development teams.

- Make available engineering reference information, such as design guides, engineering reference manuals, and engineering materials available via hyperlinked Web pages.

- Publish information about engineering projects, such as schedules, action plans, progress reports, product specifications, design ideas, and team member contact information.

- Set up an extranet on which you make available newsgroup communities of expertise, where project members can ask questions and discuss topics from a panel of experts or review product design and development ideas.

- Publish a FAQ (frequently asked questions) for best practices and procedures used by virtual teams on the Net.

WALLY AND JEFF'S PRODUCT DEVELOPMENT LESSONS LEARNED

1. Effective, efficient, rapid product development starts with attitude. If you go into the process believing that you can develop rapidly and effectively, you're very likely to do so. The companies that do well at this seem to be asking "how" questions instead of "can we" questions about product development.

2. Use all the tools. Use an intranet/extranet system combined with e-mail, newsgroups, discussion forums, whiteboards, and videoconferencing, working with design teams to develop different products for different markets in different parts of the world. The people we saw succeeding here didn't use just one tool; they used lots of them.

3. Build on the technologies already available. Product development on the Net would be much less effective if it were not for the CAD, CAM, and CAE systems already in place. And it would be much less effective, efficient, and profitable without the efforts of key vendors of those technologies to make their systems Net-capable and available. Expect that those technologies, techniques,

and programs that aren't Web-capable or Web-compatible now will be made that way in short order.

4. Geography is not a boundary or a bar. Look for ways to bring together the people, processes, and information you need from a variety of sources using the Net instead of trains, planes, and automobiles. Look for ways to gather expertise and concentrate it where it's needed. Virtual space is in people's heads. The Net and Web technologies deliver data, information, and knowledge to that space.

5. The key words in making this process happen seem to be information and collaboration. The sheer engineering advantage of being able to deliver mounds of relevant information to the desktop in seconds and then to deploy it effectively is one of the keys to effective product development using the Net. Keep seeking new information sources inside and outside your organization. For product development efforts, pay special attention to the information contributions of vendors and professional associations.

6. Continue seeking collaboration at all stages. That includes links and connections with customers and clients. It includes feedback and analysis from front-line people within the company and from those outside the company who are partners in the business and product development process. Use the intranet to link information from sales and customer service to the product development process.

7. In the companies we reviewed, we saw constant struggles to balance open sharing and security, an especially thorny problem in product development. Clearly each industry and situation will be a bit different, but we found lots of people who had only one answer. Some chose the "share it" answer and used that almost all the time. Others came down consistently on the "keep it confidential" end of the spectrum. The best advice we've heard comes from a computer security expert:

"On security questions, formula answers don't work. Remember that you should always engage your brain before you put your mouth in gear."

8. Use this technology to move quickly to situations where you get feedback on your ideas. This can be product testing in virtual space, gathering data from field tests, or just using e-mail or surveys to get user feedback. Good, timely feedback, properly used, is a key to great product development.

Chapter 3

MANUFACTURING AND QUALITY ASSURANCE

Manufacturing used to be simple. In what's been called the craft era, manufacturing involved a collection of skilled workers who took a collection of approximately right parts and worked them so that they'd fit together to make something bigger and more complex—like a car.

Technological limitations were the key. In the late 19th century, metal-cutting tools couldn't work hardened steel. So you machined first, then heat-treated, and then machined again. That placed technological limitations on what you made and how fast you could make it, but the big limitations on production involved how companies thought about and designed production systems.

The man who moved manufacturing from the craft era to the mass era was Henry Ford. He didn't invent the key technologies that made mass production possible. Instead he used them, as manufacturers today are using Net technology, to create a more efficient production system. And he got some spectacular results.

Ford insisted that the same gauging system be used for all parts. He utilized state-of-the-art metal-cutting technology that allowed him to cut hardened metals. Perhaps most importantly, he established a production system (a production line) to replace the individual craftsmen (called *fitters*) who had assembled each car.

By using these techniques together at the Highland Park plant, Ford was able to achieve a 90% productivity improvement in the year 1913–1914. Like today's manufacturing innovators, Ford took advantage of available technology and changed the system in which production happened.

Manufacturing today is in the middle of another transition, this time from the mass era to the lean era. In the mass era, the challenges were pretty simple—go for capacity utilization and economies of scale. But a new era brings new challenges.

CRITICAL CHALLENGES TO MANUFACTURING

Lean manufacturing has been defined as "a production approach using multiskilled workers, highly flexible machines, and very adaptable organizations and procedures to manufacture an increasing variety of products while continually decreasing costs." So, essentially, *lean* means using less of just about everything than is used in mass production and using it more flexibly. The lean approach includes many other concepts such as Just-In-Time manufacturing and Total Quality Management.

Every year, for their Best Plants competition, *Industry Week* magazine looks for the manufacturing facilities that are meeting today's challenges. In his book, *America's Best:* Industry Week's *Guide to World Class Manufacturing Plants,* Theodore Kinni describes three core competencies for manufacturing facilities to master:

- customer responsiveness

- quality

- agility

Today's top manufacturers are doing a number of things to meet the challenges. They're involving and empowering their workers. They're looking at the entire value chain, from suppliers all the way to end users. They're linking product development and production earlier and more tightly. And they're using Networks to leverage their knowledge and share information.

CUSTOMER RESPONSIVENESS

Lots of the work of responding to customer needs and wants is handled by the product development process we discussed in Chapter 2, but manufacturing and product development are overlapping more and more.

Customization is clearly the wave of the future. Already, companies that manufacture by assembling components made by others are offering custom solutions. A good example is Dell Computer Corporation, which offers both individual and corporate buyers the chance to design their own systems at the Dell public Web site. Dell then assembles the systems and ships them.

That's the way things are going for much larger projects, too. Chrysler has been quoted in the *Economist* as predicting that, within five years, a quarter of all their cars will be sold over the Net. That will involve lots of custom orders that will be put together at an assembly plant.

But what about meeting a customer request for a custom version of an existing product. Lots of companies already do this—with response time measured in weeks or months. In the mile-high city of Denver, though, representatives from more than 30 top corporations think it should take only a few days. InfoTest International, a private, nonprofit consortium founded in 1993, has been involved in pushing the limits of how information technology can support mission-critical business processes. One key current project is the Enhanced Product Realization (EPR) project, which is testing how the public Internet can let enterprises work together on ways to meet customer demands quickly and profitably. In November 1996, EPR ran a simulation of how a group of companies would respond to a customer request for a key product modification and produce and deliver the modification in five days. Here's how it all looked.

On day one, a large farm operation contacts Caterpillar about modifying part of a Caterpillar Challenger tractor so that it can operate in different soil conditions. The contact is made through the local Caterpillar dealer, who alerts the company.

At Caterpillar, a project is started. This involves setting up the appropriate files on the Network, notifying members of the project team, and gathering information. A late-afternoon electronic conference brings together team members from a number of specialties and locations.

The next day includes conferences, communication, and planning, during which the decision is made that a new component should be designed. The design is started and concluded on the third day.

Day four sees the hand-off to the supplier who will actually make the part, in this case, a casting that will replace the one on the current tractor. On day five, final machining is complete and the casting is shipped to the customer.

In this trial, the Internet and its technologies enable collaboration and responsiveness that would not be possible any other way. Other technologies play a role as well, like desktop videoconferencing, sophisticated design software, and such, but the key enabler is the Net, closing the gaps between participants and spanning geography.

What's been learned from the trial? Troy Eid, COO of InfoTest International, points out that the most important thing is that the Internet and supporting technology make it possible to conceive, test, and actually bring off a five-day turnaround on a custom product modification.

Is this the real world? Yes and no. Yes, in the sense that similar projects on smaller scales are already happening in thousands of places. No, in the sense of the size and complexity of the project, given today's realities.

First, most companies do not have the need or the technology to bring this together. Second, InfoTest is an artificial environment. Security concerns are pretty well avoided by having the systems used by participants located outside the firewalls of the participating companies.

Now that the consortium knows that the basic concept works, Eid says that the next step is to tackle the security issue. Since the completion of the November 1996 trial, that's where most of the emphasis has been. There also needs to be work done on developing how technologies like video and whiteboarding might work over the public Internet.

For now, InfoTest International is showing the way in a couple of key areas. First, the Enhanced Product Realization project demonstrates some of the things that can be done with the current technology. It's a target that individual companies and groups of companies may want to shoot for.

Second, InfoTest International is addressing manufacturing in context. The whole supply chain is involved from the customer back through the dealer, the manufacturer, and the suppliers. Because of that, issues like security, coordination, and standards are likely to be identified early.

Finally, though, the most exciting thing about EPR for us is that it involves real companies solving real problems with currently available technology. The challenge in manufacturing is not just using neat technology but using that technology to achieve new levels of agility, quality, and responsiveness.

QUALITY

Quality is one of those concepts that have undergone a dramatic change in the last 20 years or so. It used to be that a part of your company was called *quality control*. Its job was to inspect what you built to determine if it was "good enough" to ship. The result was what some writers have called *shipping control* rather than quality control.

Then—suddenly, it seemed—Japanese automakers started taking huge chunks of the American market by providing what auto buyers perceived to be a higher-quality product. There was no mystery to how they did this; they utilized the principles laid out by American thinkers such as Deming and Juran.

The result was a shift in thinking about quality. Quality ceased to be what we now call *conformance quality* only. Conformance quality is defined by the relative absence of defects or by matching to a minimum specification. Instead, we started thinking about quality as what Juran called "fitness for use." We also began to think about quality assurance as a process that involved everything from the specification and purchase of raw materials through satisfactory use by the customer.

While there are lots of different quality systems available for a manufacturer to consider, most of them center on various ways to share best practices. This is the kind of application that seems to be made for the Net and Web.

SHARING BEST PRACTICES

A nonprofit organization that has a great deal to do with both setting quality standards and sharing practices is the American Productivity and Quality Center. Based in Houston, APQC performs various services for industry, among them creating the guidelines for the Baldrige Award, the most coveted quality trophy in American business.

APQC has just released a study of 33 companies around the United States and their knowledge management. The core findings of the study are that sharing best practices across geographical boundaries is an excellent way to boost profits and that the Net is an excellent avenue for that sharing.

Cindy Johnson is in charge of the Office of Best Practices for Texas Instruments. It's a job she got because her boss thought it was "a dragon big enough for her to slay." It's big because best practices sharing is vitally important to TI, a company with operations in more than 30 countries around the globe.

With a geographical span that large, Johnson looked for the best technology that would get the job done. In March of 1995, TI's Office of Best Practices deployed 200 sets of Lotus Notes and began capturing best practices from around the corporation. The sharing enabled by that technology is part of an overall quality effort. The core of the program is 138 worldwide facilitators, or knowledge brokers, who devote about 10% to 50% of their time to their facilitator duties.

Texas Instruments began using Lotus Notes because it felt that, specifically, for collection and adding value to information such as best practices, Notes was a great platform. The problem with Notes was that it was not a good platform for dissemination to lots of people. For that, a browser is better, and so, in July of 1995, the best practices material was being published to the corporate intranet and was available to the 59,000 TI employees with intranet access.

At that point, people using the intranet could find out about best practices, but could not provide input to the process. With changes to the underlying Notes software, even that became possible by June of 1996. Johnson says she's committed to using the best technologies as they emerge to make the best practices sharing even more effective.

The problem, as she sees it, is "getting the Internet to pay off." What that involves, at bottom, is giving people information and knowledge that they can apply to business situations. What have the results been? According to one case, documented by the American Productivity and Quality Center, they've been spectacular.

The case involves TI's wafer fabrication plants. Improving productivity there had been identified early as the area where improvements could yield maximum cost savings. Through the best practices sharing process—leveraged by Networked sharing—Texas Instruments has been able to increase production by the equivalent of two wafer fabrication sites. That means savings of over $500 million.

The costs? A bit hard to determine but certainly far less than the savings generated. As in many companies we interviewed, the costs are strung through a variety of budgets. Also, many of the costs that tie to high-payoff activities are not intranet costs, they're the costs of training facilitators and developing the system.

The three guiding premises of the entire best practices sharing operation at Texas Instruments seem to be the following.

First, TI, like most of the other excellent and effective companies we present in this book, begins with the idea that quality is a management and leadership issue. For that reason, establishing the culture of quality and best practices sharing was the first thing that had to happen. The formal discussions of this go back to 1993 and Jerry Junkins, former CEO of Texas Instruments.

Junkins challenged the company to create a common approach to business excellence that would be enterprisewide. That approach became known as TI-BEST. Part of what came out of that was TI's Best Practices Sharing Program. And that program is based not in technology but among the facilitators of the program scattered about TI's worldwide operations. The technology becomes the way to leverage the core process and do it better.

The second linchpin of the TI strategy seems to be that, when it comes to technology, you use what works. That meant beginning with Lotus Notes and using Notes as the basis for the things it does well. It meant moving to the intranet early because of its ease of sharing information. As APQC puts it, "technology is the key enabler for global sharing."

Bill Baker, a TI best practice sharing champion for the Systems Group in Louisville, Texas, puts it this way, "We are in the middle of a Networked society. Technology has given us new ways to keep in touch with each other and share information. We have to take advantage of that technology to get better faster.

The third key point is that you keep doing it better, using new technology as it becomes available, making the process available to more people. Currently, Cindy Johnson tells us, TI is getting 50 to 100 new items every month on the intranet site devoted to best practices sharing and the number is growing monthly.

Texas Instruments is not the only manufacturer using an intranet to share best practices. Companies like Ford, Chevron, and Chrysler are making use of their intranets to share best practices, too.

The APQC makes some specific recommendations about how to do this kind of thing. It suggests beginning with an easy-to-use platform and a single technology and then connecting the people who know what you want shared. Sharing best practices could be just about that simple.

QUALITY, THY NAME IS PAPERWORK

Quality, thy name is paperwork. And thy vital functions are chronicled in ISO9000.

ISO is the International Standards Organization. ISO9000 is a global standard developed there for documenting a company's quality assurance processes and making sure that workers have access to the latest versions of those processes and supporting materials. This involves gathering and linking lots of information, updating procedures frequently, and making sure those updates are distributed to those who actually do the work. Sounds like a perfect application for Net/Web technology. David Carr and Ellis Booker of *Web Week* magazine went out looking for somebody who'd used an intranet as a medium for meeting ISO9000 standards in a real, live application.

The ISO9000 application came out of the Dowell Oil Field Services Division. Mike Gibbons, the manager of product quality has gotten nine locations certified to ISO9000, according to *Web Week*. The information system being used is an intranet with more than 4000 documents.

Key benefit number one is accessibility. With documentation for systems such as quality assurance, the big key benefit is that everybody who needs it can get to the current document quickly.

Key benefit two is updatability. This occurs on two levels. First, the review and approval process can be facilitated by the simple means of an e-mail link on the pages requiring review and approval. Then, when changes are finalized, they are made effectively and instantly. There's no waiting for stuff to be printed and returned and then sent in the most expeditious way possible out to the field. There's no collecting the old manual and issuing a new one.

Key benefit three is cost. This is the one you probably thought would be first, but here it's a by-product. There are savings in paper and postage; if some of our research in other areas is right, there are enough of those savings to pay for the cost of the system.

Those are powerful benefits from a powerful system. It's also something that's already in place. When we start considering direct process control applications using the Net/Web, though, we move to an area where the real excitement is just over the hill.

AGILITY

Agility requires a production structure that's easy to change to fit need. This is more than the custom response we talked about earlier; it's revamping information technology that supports manufacturing so that the manufacturing process itself is more effective, efficient, and flexible.

HOW INFORMATION TECHNOLOGY SUPPORTS MANUFACTURING

Under the rather magnificent title world electronics manager for Sun Microsystems, Dr. Robert Atherton's job is to help find ways that software like Java can be used to make processes more effective. Atherton says that information technology (IT) has become "an engine of production" that he considers as important as the things that "cut metal." This is a constantly evolving area of manufacturing. What he sees developing is a world in which the Internet is a connection device, the browser a universal front end, and Java a tool to link applications. That world will allow manufacturers to create a process that is more flexible and more tightly controlled than anything we've ever seen before.

There are basically three levels of IT support for a manufacturing operation. The first is the enterprise resource planning (ERP) level. Just below that are the manufacturing execution systems (MES), which deal with information and materials flows, parts, and tracking of the entire process. These set up the third level, which is process control.

What's going on in manufacturing right now is that, through a variety of means, of which the Net is one, we're driving control down to the process level. By doing that with a system such as an intranet and Java, manufacturers do not need to be as dependent on hardwired decisions that last for a long time. Instead, it becomes possible to make changes quickly and effectively. That's not all. Where, before, the changes would need to be made by information technology personnel, now, changes in the shop-floor systems can be made by manufacturing engineers.

At the process control level, that means that computers control things that paper tape or human hands had controlled before. Atherton describes this as "the world of control joining the world of computing." The systems that result are flexible enough to turn on a dime, under the control of manufacturing engineers. As a result, they're faster than previous systems, and less costly since the investment in hardware can be lower. That becomes particularly important in a world of distributed manufacturing. For one of Sun's processes, for example, nine different factories are involved. Sun, however, owns only one of the nine. In a case like this, the control of the software becomes the control of the process.

At the present stage of development, Java is not as easy to use as it will be in a few years. Many people in manufacturing are attracted to it because of its cross-platform compatibility and flexibility, but a lot of work and coordination are still to be done. That's why the developers of applications seek close ties with Sun, and why Sun is actively working with several firms to produce application programming interfaces that allow Java to work with other control programs. The idea is move control data, in electronic form, all the way to the factory floor.

VIRTUAL PROCESS CONTROL

One person who's immersed in that effort is Dave Copeland. Dave is president of Intuitive Technologies in Marlboro, Massachusetts. His firm has developed a way for technicians at remote locations to view the same process control indicators that a technician sees on the control site.

Here's how that might work. At lots of process plants, there are skilled technicians on call for special situations that the regular technicians working on the shift need help with. In most places, when there's a problem in the middle of the night, the technician on call gets paged, usually at home, and has to call in and try to solve the problem. If that doesn't work, the only alternative is for the technician to get dressed, climb in the car, and drive down to the plant. As one person who's done this for years told us, "Of course, the calls always come at the worst possible time, when you've got a sick child or there's a raging snowstorm."

With current technology, these heroics are no longer necessary. Using a common browser, through a secure connection, the technician can view the same control console readouts that the operators in the plant are looking at. Two results are likely. First, the problem will get solved more quickly, with less downtime. Second, the job of the expert technician is now more pleasant than it used to be because we've eliminated late-night trips down to the plant. This technology also deals with one of the most common problems technicians face: understanding what it is that the person they are talking to on the phone is actually seeing. With the more advanced versions of this software, animations on the browser screen mimic the actual gauges that the technician in the plant is looking at.

Now, let's extend things a bit. It's becoming common in larger manufacturing operations to try to centralize the top expertise in the company. If it's possible for people with key expertise actually to view process displays remotely, then it's possible for a process expert on one side of the world to troubleshoot a live process on the other side of the world.

That's actually happening with one company that has declined to be named. One of its newer plants is up and running in India. The company is routinely using the technology we've just described to troubleshoot and manage the process from locations on the East and West Coasts of the United States.

The benefits of this kind of process control don't end with the ability to deal with crisis. They extend further into the process to head off the crisis in the first place.

The same technology that can be used to deal with a crisis in the process can also capture the signature of that process and make it available for later review. That can help manufacturing engineers understand the root cause of the problem as well as some of the early warning signs. Then, that same signature can be played back for training purposes, just as if it were on a VCR.

Several years ago, one of our clients went through a fire that was based on a malfunction in the chemical manufacturing process. If this technology had been in place for that company, it would have captured the signature of the original problem. Our client could have sat process control technician trainees down at a browser to view the console displays that they're going to face in similar situations. Our client could then create drills that would enable the technicians to see different configurations of readouts and know which ones were likely to lead to problems.

WHERE ARE WE NOW?

For the technology we've just described, the answer is, "We're almost there." Everything described above is in place and working but not thoroughly debugged. Pieces of the total process are already working in actual applications in actual plants. But there are already some big manufacturing payoffs from using the Net/Web.

HP SAVES A BUNDLE

Hewlett Packard has had an intranet for years—they just didn't call it that. Bob Peck, technical information service manager for HP Santa Clara has been with the company for 24 years. His unit's job is to get the information from the design process out to the plants that do the manufacturing. The system he runs is called WebFire and it was developed to bring together the different databases, coordinators, and systems that used to be involved in rolling out a manufacturing application once design was finished.

What happens now at HP is that all the information that a factory will need to produce a new product is available through a secure Web site in HP's intranet. Then notice is sent to the manufacturing sites that information is available. That information includes things like bills of materials, design specifications, drawings—everything the plant needs to make the product except raw materials.

We asked Bob how he knows the system works. He laughed. "I'm sure it works," he said, "because, whenever the system goes down, I start getting calls and e-mails almost instantly."

Then we asked the big question: What's the payoff?

Another laugh. Bob pointed out that lots of the savings are hard to quantify since, essentially, what's saved is time, and people then devote that time to something else. But Bob's own operation is an example of that kind of leverage. He and his staff of four handle the information support function for 24 of HP's divisions and operations.

We pushed. What about real money? Another laugh. "I'm not a cost accountant, I'm an engineer. I know the payoff is big, big enough so that I don't have to take time out to justify it." How big? "OK, let me give you a specific example. The process of getting all this information out to the production facilities used to be about three weeks. We do it now in a day. That accelerates time to market by about 14 days for one of our divisions."

The division Bob referred to competes in a market in which it is estimated that the advantage of being first in the market is worth about $1 million per day. That means that $14 million is gained on every product launch in which HP is first to market.

The division averages four new product launches a year. That works out to $56 million if the WebFire advantage helps them get there first by 14 days on every one.

Hewlett Packard is a good example of how Net/Web technology is being used right now to make a big difference. It's also one of several companies racing to do even better in the future.

SOON WE'LL HAVE A WHOLE VIRTUAL FACTORY

Some wags have commented, "It won't be long before we have a whole virtual factory." That's exactly what one company is trying to achieve.

The company is McDonnell Douglas Aerospace, and its virtual factory has been chronicled extensively by David Upton and Andrew McAfee, both of the Harvard Graduate School of Business Administration.

McAfee and Upton begin by pointing out that virtual factories are collections of technologies that already exist. Instead of being brand-new inventions, the virtual factory, as McDonnell Douglas has put it together, is a networking or linking of things that already work.

The difference is the addition of what Upton and McAfee call an information broker. In this case, it's a spin-off firm for McDonnell Douglas called AeroTech. It's AeroTech's job to create, manage, and facilitate the Networked manufacturing community.

The sophisticated manufacturing network, such as a virtual factory, has to do several things. It must be able to accommodate a broad spectrum of information technology sophistication. At one end may be the PC in a job shop, where the fingers tapping on the keys are grease-stained from machining operations. At the other end of this spectrum is the sophisticated CAD/CAM workstation modeling parts design in three dimensions. Both of these need to be on the network, and both need to be able to work and share information.

The virtual factory has to balance both openness and security. The trick is to have enough security to keep things, well, "secure" while not having so many hurdles and steps that it gets in the way of lean, efficient manufacturing. And the network, in its operation, needs to allow the various partners in the manufacturing community to have the autonomy they need to work effectively. It's sort of distributed computing and decision making at their manic best.

That some of the partners in this community have massive computing resources that others can share is one of the things that helps drive the system. Another thing that helps make it possible is technology that has been around for a while—like EDI, groupware, and computer networks.

What makes a virtual factory possible today, though, rather than five years ago, is the technology we're talking about in this book. Internet and Web technologies can be used by a variety of computers and by operators at varying levels of sophistication.

The familiar browser and e-mail software can be used comfortably and effectively in the job shop as well as in the sophisticated design suite. And it is often already in place.

AeroTech, the McDonnell Douglas spin-off, was responsible for developing the virtual factory and for making it run. To the best of our knowledge, that role is unique to the Aerotech/McDonnell Douglas approach to the virtual factory. McDonnell Douglas sees AeroTech in the role of an information broker—the part of the system that makes the whole system work.

Like many extended extranet applications, this began as an internal operation. Prior to mid-1993, only about 50 McDonnell Douglas employees could use the system. They used it to pass data between different systems inside the company. In mid-1993, external suppliers began to be added. Then the pace started to pick up. The open systems of the Internet make the addition of external partners easy. By the end of 1994, there were over 400 users, both inside and outside McDonnell Douglas. Now there are thousands. AeroTech facilitates this by offering a lot of ways for different partners to connect to the networks. In effect, AeroTech mediates between different systems, different standards, and different levels of sophistication.

Upton and McAfee describe several examples of how this works effectively. Here is one. A partner in the network with McDonnell Douglas is UCAR Composites, a California-based manufacturer of tooling for high-performance composite components.

Prior to the virtual factory, things used to work this way. When McDonnell Douglas completed a design update, it would prepare documentation and a computer tape and express it to UCAR. The cost for that was about $400 per file for the tapes and shipping via express mail. The time was measured in days.

The virtual factory alternative is faster and cheaper. McDonnell Douglas's computer-aided design files are translated into numerically controlled machine code that works on UCAR's metal-cutting machines. McDonnell Douglas transfers the CAD file and the metal-cutting program to AeroTech.

AeroTech's system forwards them automatically to UCAR using normal phone lines. There engineers can use their own CAD/CAM systems to make last-minute checks on the program. The cost for this is about $4. The time involved is measured in minutes.

The benefits don't stop there, though. This same method of moving information that works with a sophisticated partner such as UCAR can also be used for partners with far lower levels of IT systems and experience. A combination of open systems and brokering makes that possible.

It's also AeroTech's job to coordinate all the systems that feed into manufacturing. This includes a very sophisticated though relatively simple electronic bidding system.

A McDonnell Douglas buyer using this system can send out e-mail to qualified suppliers around the world, letting them know that a job is available for bidding. They, in turn, can use the Internet to access a secure site that gives them the information they need to decide whether to bid and to prepare their bids effectively. E-mail then gets the bid back to McDonnell Douglas quickly and effectively.

As Upton and McAfee point out, McDonnell Douglas estimates that the savings from the electronic bidding alone pay the operating costs for the entire system. We're seeing it here as in other places: a dramatic increase in productivity and efficiency, coupled with a drop in cost; an increase in reach and spread that the technology makes available, coupled with an increase in the sophistication of communication.

TACTICS

Let's look at our tactics and how they are going to apply to manufacturing and quality assurance.

Think Links

Think links to everybody associated with your manufacturing operation; this can include your suppliers, distribution channels, the people in the product development department, and the customers for whom you are building and adding special customized features to your products and services. The more parts of the complex manufacturing operation you can connect using the Net, the more effective you're likely to be. Look back at the virtual factory and its explosion from around 50 internal users to thousands of users, most of them outside the corporation, within a very short time. If they're part of your manufacturing operation, or linked to it in some physical way, then they probably should be linked up on the Net as well.

Automation

Think about automating all along your various chains of information. There are two basic ways to do that. There's the "push" method, where you send things out automatically so that people get them. That's how e-mail was used in the virtual factory bidding system. It might be how best practices are shared in an e-mail discussion group.

Then there are the "pull" methods of automation. Once a push method has been used to alert potential and qualified bidders to a possible opportunity, the information they need is available only when they request it. They take the initiative to go to the secure Web site with the information they want.

We'd suggest that, for situations in which notification or time sensitivity or an interruption in a normal pattern is important, the push method of automation is probably the most effective. For other situations, consider the pull and make information available.

Customization

There are two ways to think of the tactic of customization. First, there's a method that enables you to have lots of information available in lots of different ways, so that people involved in your manufacturing operation can find precisely the information they want whenever they need it. In a global environment with manufacturing units in various areas of the world, that could mean using an intranet or Web site with discussion groups, Web pages, forums, and e-mail to share information on production.

Second, there's a special customization tactic that arises from our look at how the Net and Web technologies are being used in manufacturing: to customize to the individual partner's need by making it possible for the partner to connect in the way that's most appropriate for him or her. That might involve the bandwidth of your connection or the sophistication of the programs being used. It might just involve different comfort levels with this technology. In any event, try to make your network available to as many of your partners as you can. If our experience and interviews are any guide, once people become connected to the network, they become contributors to the network. Also, when communicating with those from very different cultures or speaking different languages, Web pictures and graphic aids can be used to enhance communications, exchange ideas, and bring them to life.

McDonnell Douglas's Long Beach, California, commercial aircraft manufacturing division, Douglas Aircraft, which builds airplanes for over 200 airlines around the world illustrates both these aspects of the customization step of the TACTICS action planning system. Douglas Aircraft is using Netscape and the World Wide Web to build a system to distribute to its customers aircraft service bulletins that can be viewed with a simple Web browser. Off the home page of their public Web site (www.mdc.com/) under Customers and Services, the division has a link to Supplier Management, which has links to the following information:

Miscellaneous Products and Services

- Intellectual Property
- Tooling Center

Product Support

- Commercial Aircraft Product Support Library

- Commercial Aircraft Services and Support Catalog
- Commercial Aircraft Spare Parts—Online

Special Programs

- Active Aeroelastic Wing (AAW)
- McDonnell Douglas Human Modeling System (MDHMS)
- Technology Development (High-Energy Systems)

Supplier Management and Procurement Information

- Commercial Aircraft EDI Implementation Guide Book
- Commercial Aircraft Process Standards Book
- Commercial Aircraft Procurement Terms and Conditions— From DAC 26-730
- Helicopter Systems Terms and Conditions
- MDC Preferred Supplier Certification
- MDC Supplier Quality Management—Approved Processor Lists
- Military Transport Aircraft Supplier & Materials Management—The Blue Book
- Space & Defense Systems—Terms & Conditions Guide
- Tactical & Training Aircraft Special Purchase Order Conditions (SPOCS)

TRANSFORM

There is probably no purer transformation tactic in existence than the sharing of best practices. Elegant in its simplicity of concept, sharing best practices moves data to information and information to knowledge by adding context, comparison, and guidance. For further clarification on this TACTIC, refer to our earlier comments on Texas Instrument's best practices sharing program.

INSIDE/OUTSIDE

Look inside/outside for applications. Inside, follow your manufacturing process from start to finish. From the outside, look at all the information that comes from suppliers and partners.

Deere integrates external and internal information, which enables it to combine corporate knowledge with resources available on the World Wide Web. According to Phyllis Michaelides, the head of the Methods, Architecture, and Data Team at John Deere's Waterloo Works Division, "There is a wealth of agricultural information on the Web, such as crop reports, weather reports, USDA information. We can integrate this information with our rich store of internal information. With Netscape, we can deliver all of this very easily through a single interface."

Deere is using its intranet to distribute information from remote test sites, where new models of tractors and heavy equipment are put through their paces. These test results take advantage of the Web's multimedia capability by allowing Deere employees to incorporate data, sound, and pictures in their testing report.

CORE FUNCTIONS/BIG PAYOFFS

To get to core functions/big payoffs in manufacturing, start by looking at documentation. Our favorite way is to wander around looking for fat three-ring binders. These usually represent information that has lots of detail and needs to be updated and distributed. You'll probably find that most of that information is already in digital form. For instance, you can use an intranet or extranet to post production schedules, bills of materials, quality statistics, and procedures. Putting it on a Net makes it searchable and easy to update. And the savings on paper and postage are almost immediate, just like the benefits of instant updating.

START NOW

Start now with something small and quick that shows off the benefits of using Net/Web technology here. Documentation, as we've pointed out is a good place to look for a starting place. That's because many manufacturing processes have been streamlined in basic operations, but documentation is still in those fat binders.

WALLY AND JEFF'S MANUFACTURING AND QUALITY ASSURANCE LESSONS LEARNED

1. Two paired lessons that leaped out at us from the manufacturing applications were how much had already been done and how much can still be done. Manufacturing operations have already made huge strides at digitizing and automating and networking their processes. There have already been massive efforts to link the various parts of the manufacturing process, including purchasing and inbound logistics, to manufacturing in such a way as to make it more effective. And those efforts have had great effect.

2. Because manufacturing is complex, involves lots of information, has lots of players, needs coordination, and is often labor-intensive, the opportunities for using Net and Web technology to improve profits here are still extensive. As an example, Fujitsu's engineers use their intranet, named JKL, application to access a shared database that covers all the information Fujitsu engineers in research, development, and manufacturing need: technical information, design standards, quality control information, cost and development know-how, CAD manuals, and general information.

3. One of the biggest concerns to be dealt with by a Webmaster and his/her team is security for proprietary information. If you just put information on the Internet, it's pretty much public domain; anyone can access it unless you do something to secure it. This is a serious challenge and there are ways to deal with it. For example, McDonnell Douglas handled this by using the Netscape Commerce Server because it provides a way to encrypt

data using RSA encryption, which is a standard. In order to view or download service bulletins, customers have to call up McDonnell Douglas's home page and choose a button labeled Access Service Bulletins. They then are required to enter their unique password. McDonnell Douglas was attracted to Netscape's security features to offer necessary information that contains proprietary information.

Deere handled security concerns by purchasing a Netscape Commerce Server with its Secure Sockets Layer (SSL). This system enables Deere to encrypt sensitive data used by authorized employees located in the field customizing and testing products.

4. Another lesson that jumps out at us from our manufacturing examples is that some of the simplest techniques pay off handsomely. Take the simple idea of information sharing, as with Best Practices, and apply it not just in manufacturing but everywhere else in your company.

5. The sophistication threshold is being driven down by new technology. It wasn't long ago that we needed to ask whether people we were interested in connecting to our network were sophisticated enough to participate. As the technology has gotten easier to use—and the open technology of the Internet and the Web have been key drivers here—it becomes possible for more and more people at more and more locations to participate. We think it's time that you move from asking the question "Are they sophisticated enough?" to the question "Who is a part of this process and needs to be connected?" Starting there should make your information sharing broader and more effective. And the odds are good that the people you want to connect are sophisticated enough to manage the tools.

6. You can use Net technology to do leaner manufacturing that is both more productive and integrated with the product development and distribution functions so that

you can easily move from one step to another in the product manufacturing process to more quickly deliver products that meet your customer demands. This lesson was effectively used by Dowell, one of the seven oil field service companies owned by Schlumberger, in their transition to be able to access up-to-date information from their Web server. They had already put their procedure and QA manuals on CD-ROMs that engineers could easily use on their computers. Then they took the next step, which was to keep this information updated and fresh by formatting the information from the CD-ROMs with HTML, embedding it with hyperlinks, and putting it up on their server.

7. It is important not to underestimate the time needed for software application design and development to be used in your Net technology system. For instance, if you are working with outside developers, you must incorporate travel expenses and the expense of the time devoted to meetings with outside developers.

8. When making the transition to using Net technology in your mutual collaboration and interaction with suppliers, strategic alliances, field engineers, employees, and potential customers be certain that they understand the value of providing information electronically and are willing and capable of participating in your Net-based operations.

9. Putting documents in digital form and making them available, along with their updates, on the Net will speed production up immensely; consider adding a search engine to obtain specific documents in your library quickly. And remember that the documentation done in the manufacturing and design stages often becomes the support documentation for customer service and technical support. You can save steps in developing that material using the Net and a habit of looking at the entire process.

Chapter 4

ADMINISTRATION

When managers get together and talk about administration, the terms are almost always derogatory. You'll hear words like *administrivia* and *paper shuffler*. What they're referring to is that great mass of tasks and functions that has to happen to make a company run. It doesn't matter if the company is big or small. It doesn't matter if the company makes goods or sells services. Administration, while it isn't the most glamorous part of the company, is certainly one of the most important. After all, this function supports all the others.

In the last few years, administration has also gotten to be one of the hardest of company functions. Rules, and regulations—governmental and regulatory scrutiny—have increased dramatically, requiring increased reporting and certification which, in turn, make it necessary for people inside the company to have a broader array of information at their fingertips.

At the same time, administrative staffs have been hit with downsizing and reengineering. The result, as usual, is that the staff has had to do more with less. In one of our client companies, for example, one full-time and two part-time staff people do the administrative and clerical tasks that six people used to do, and they deal with a growing list of things to do and requirements to meet.

CORE ADMINISTRATIVE CHALLENGES THAT ONLINE TOOLS CAN SOLVE

Today, there are really three key challenges that you can use online tools to provide Net-based solutions to overcome and enhance your administrative operations. They are:

1. To do more of the routine tasks that are necessary to support the overall operations of the company more efficiently and effectively. Both purchasing and general administration offer opportunities to be more effective at lower cost using Net/Web technology.

2. To provide and share more information that is immediately relevant and useful. Using this technology to improve information sharing in such areas as human resources, basic policies and procedures, and investor relations can have big payoffs.

3. While solving the first two key challenges, to find a way to cut costs.

The first challenge—to do more of the routine tasks that are necessary to support the overall operations of the company more efficiently and effectively while simultaneously cutting costs—simply means to do more with less, to get bigger results from smaller inputs. Use this technology to do routine things routinely. Top targets here include routine purchasing processes and routine administrative processes.

What you're after here is for people to be able to handle routine things by themselves. That might be as simple as getting the phone number for another employee or finding out what the directions are from the airport to a remote facility. It can also involve checking on benefits and any variety of routine inquiry. If you use the Net technology to handle these routinely, people become more efficient and you get the result of solving the third challenge: you do more for less money.

The second key challenge in administration is to provide and share more information that is immediately relevant and useful. That involves using a broader array of information in the decision processes, considering more sources, and evaluating more facts.

The basic objective of administrative support is to increase employee productivity throughout all the functional areas of your business by providing your employees with more information that is immediately relevant and useful for them to do their various jobs—in other words, to enable your employees to work smart and get the optimal results on their job-related activities. It also includes sharing more information with other people as administrative offices work that side of the company's information flow process.

Just as with customer service, administration gives you a way to increase the value of what you do, at the same time decreasing costs. If a salesperson can check on his or her employee benefits package or the company stock price without involving another person, things work more efficiently. If employees have a variety of things they can do easily and well, they can focus more of their attention on the business at hand and help improve your profitability.

You should also be looking for cost savings from the sheer weight of paper and postage. Brochures that you don't have to mail because people get them off the Net save you both ways. When the means to communicate and deliver this information is less expensive, you also solve the third key challenge, cutting costs.

SOLUTIONS: COST-REDUCTION BENEFITS OF USING INTERNET TECHNOLOGY

Jerry Gross, EVP and chief technology officer for Countrywide Home Loans, did a quick analysis of one cost-saving benefit. "Lets say I have a two-page document and I need to send those two pages from LA to New York. If I mail or Federal Express it overnight, it will cost me $14. Telex costs me $10. Fax costs me $4. Snail mail costs me 25¢. E-mail costs me 2¢. Web exchange costs me half a cent. So, once you go through that, you say to yourself, 'Man, this is a slam dunk.'"

Simple analysis, big result. As outlined in more detail in Chapter 7, Countrywide replaced an annual seven-figure fax bill with a five-figure e-mail bill, just on material routinely sent to the field. Those are back-of-the-envelope numbers. They don't come from rigorous cost accounting analysis, but they're big enough to herald a substantial cost saving opportunity.

In the authors' business, we have a need to send out promotional material about our speaking, consulting, training, and writing services to prospective customers. If we need to send out 50 informational packages a month and we use Federal Express it costs $700 plus administrative time and labor costs versus providing that same amount of information on a Web site for 25¢, with no additional administrative time and labor. The total cost of maintenance for the Web site is less than the direct savings in overnight packages.

On an annualized basis using the technology of the Web can save a small business like ours at least $8400 and allow us to allocate our administrative labor to more productive use of time than assembling Federal Express packages. No matter what the size of your business, if you stop and do this exercise for yourself, we know that simple mathematics will show us that you can cut costs—and thus boost your profits—by using Internet technology.

CUTTING COSTS IN BASIC ADMINISTRATION

This is the real administrivia part: filling out forms, checking boxes, filing reports, and all that. It's probably the core information sharing that goes on in any organization, and it takes up a lot of time, a lot of effort, and a lot of paper. It exists in every corporation, including the Flight Dynamics Branch at the Goddard Center for the National Aeronautics and Space Administration (NASA). Mark Cashion works there, and he finds that going paperless makes his life a lot easier.

In the world before the Internet and network automation, paper forms would be stacking up on Cashion's desk. What kind of forms? The forms you'd see in almost any kind of organization—expense reports and travel requests. Just automating the filing of those forms saves Cashion about four hours a week. That's four hours he can put to plenty of other good uses.

Lots of companies we talked to were automating information about basic guidelines. Intranets on just about every company we interviewed included the basic kind of administrative information that people need from day to day. Consider the following:

travel guidelines

mileage reimbursement guidelines

expense forms

employee handbooks

employee directories

When you put that information up on your intranet, think about where to start and how to make it more useful.

It's likely that your employee handbook and your basic policies and guidelines are already available in a digital form like a word processing file. Sure, it will help to have those available on the intranet. That's a start, but just shoveling the information onto the Net won't make it a whole lot more useful than it was before; it will only make it more accessible.

Use database technology so that people can search handbooks and policies for the things they need. Use hyperlinking technology to link the relevant parts of different policies so that people can find their own way around and arrive at their own solutions.

You might also want to pull out policies and procedures like expense reimbursement guidelines, that have to be used frequently.

At one of our client companies, the person in charge of the intranet attacked the problem this way. He developed a set of simple scripts for posting forms, checking a database, and so forth. He estimates that each script took about $200 of programming time to prepare and try out. Each then serves as a template that individuals can use to develop their own applications. His department can help users adapt the templates if they need it, but then there's an internal accounting charge.

SNAPSHOTS OF ADMINISTRATIVE OPERATIONS ONLINE

Consider, also, segregating policies that aren't needed every day but are used frequently. At Westinghouse, for example, the company policy for hiring part-time employees is posted on the intranet. What makes that especially helpful is that most people don't hire part-time employees often. When they do, they'll need to look up the guidelines and figure out what steps to take.

Don't stop with the routine administrative stuff. Look for anything that might be of interest to people or that might be helpful. Fletcher Challenge is a Canadian pulp & paper company based in Vancouver. Its intranet includes all the things we've talked about, along with company financial data, employee newsletters, internal surveys, and lots of other things, including an up-to-date schedule of the availability of the company's fleet of helicopters.

At Home Box Office, the intranet lets employees access information like organization charts, human resource handbooks, the company newsletter, and menu items from the cafeteria. It also allows the employees to tap into the corporate database to access information about movies. Employees can get such information as listings of film stars, producers, and distributors, along with revenues and movie distribution rights, and can link into the Neilsen database for tracking movie viewership information that allows them to sell, plan research statistics, and predict programming trends more productively and efficiently.

At IBM, the intranet includes information about different IBM locations. An IBMer traveling to a place he or she doesn't know can find out the best way to get there from the airport and get a map of the site and, sometimes, of the particular building. In some cases, it's also possible to check out the personal page of the person who's going to be visited to find out a bit about what that person's interests are and even to get an idea of what the person looks like.

Now, how does all this help? There are two obvious savings: the cost of publishing all this information on paper and the postage or internal mail work involved in sending it.

Because Net technology uses seamless interoperability, many companies, such as AT&T, have the building blocks already in place to take advantage of the cost savings of Web technology to consolidate their various preexisting individual networks. All a company needs is a computer for its employees and a server to handle the traffic. Just about any type of computer—from an old 386 to a MAC to a high-end workstation—can access the company's intranet. AT&T estimates it saves $30 million a year because this feature of Net technology enables them to greatly reduce the duplication of people, equipment, individual network systems setup and tariff costs by consolidating its many individual networks into a global unified network.

There are also some clear gains in efficiency. People don't have to wait for the information they need. They can search through information to get exactly what they need or put together the bits that are most important to what they want to achieve. And they usually can do all this without involving the time or effort of someone else.

There's also the advantage of immediate updating. Steve Telleen, who developed Amdahl's intranet and is now with Silicon Valley Intranet Partners, refers to this as a movement from date-based publishing to need-based publishing.

In the old paper world, a company like Lockheed might publish its internal telephone directory once a year, in July, taking all the updates it had then and producing a paper document, which it then printed and shipped out. The directory was out of date by the time people got it. With an intranet-based directory, not only can the changes be made immediately but they can be made by the individual whose number is being changed, without creating work for anyone else. Result: a more accurate document and cost savings.

CUTTING EMPLOYEE BENEFIT COSTS USING THE WEB

One of the most fruitful places to look at the cost reduction with Net technology is in the area of employee benefits. As Chris John of Resource Financial Group puts it, "… a lot of employees really don't understand their employee benefits; they just take that stuff for granted. It's an entitlement to them." And that's in an area that may be one of the largest single cost factors for a business. The U.S. Chamber of Commerce, for example, estimates that, on average, U.S. companies spend an amount equal to 40% of payroll on employee benefits. And employees don't understand them and don't use them effectively.

By putting employee benefits information on an intranet, you make it possible for employees to check out information about their

specific needs, when they have the need. If they want to find out
about their 401(k) plan and how it's doing, they can do that. If
they'd like to check into the details of the vacation policy, they can
do that. If they wonder what sorts of things are covered by the medical plan, they can find that out.

The benefits here are enormous because people become more effective users of benefits that are already being paid for and find out
about them and often utilize them without generating any additional costs.

One problem, though, that seems to crop up in several areas relates to privacy concerns. You can expect conflicts between information-sharing and privacy concerns to be commonplace. To take
an obvious example, let's consider the case of an employee who's
interested in finding out if the employee assistance plan covers al-
cohol counseling for his or her spouse. Having that information
available on the intranet probably makes it more likely that the employee would actually check out such a sensitive item, particularly
because it's not necessary to make any phone calls or talk to anybody. But the employee has to be sure that there's not some kind of
tracking of individual usage going on. The trick is to make as much
information available as possible, at the same time holding the reporting down to those things that are necessary and legal to gather,
as well as avoiding stepping on any individual's privacy rights.

Net technology has helped accelerate the trend toward out-
sourcing certain areas of employee benefits management. Chris
John is president of a mid-sized company called Resource Financial
Group. He described the changes this way.

> We are an employee benefits brokerage and consulting firm.
> We believe that there is a paradigm shift taking place in that in-
> dustry. In the past, employers, say, for their group insurance,
> would go to their friendly neighborhood insurance agent and
> buy a medical insurance plan. That insurance agent might also
> sell life insurance, stocks and bonds, or maybe disability in-
> surance. In other words, he wasn't really a specialist; (medical
> coverage) was just one of the different articles he had to sell.

> Now employers are no longer going out and buying just a

group insurance plan. Rather, what they're doing is they are trying to figure out how to outsource all of this stuff. So they'll go to a firm like our firm, Resource Financial Group and they will say to us, "We want to set you up as our virtual employee benefits department." That's what we become.

So we've created on the World Wide Web a system called the employee benefits center system. ... for instance, when employees need to look up their medical insurance program, they can go to the World Wide Web and look up the deductible whether their doctor is on the list, all that kind of stuff. If they want to look at the 401(k) plan, they can do it—how did it do last month? What are the plan specifications? That sort of thing. If they want to look at their dental insurance they look up their dental insurance. If they want to look up life insurance, they look up their life insurance. Essentially, what we've done is we've taken all that stuff and we have published it on the World Wide Web for the employees of our client employers and we've made it very simple and friendly for them to get information.

Susan Wood, marketing manager of the Business Edge Group of Financial Services Corporation, says Chris is one of their field affiliates and was very instrumental in nudging the company to consider Web technology before it set up its extranet. According to Susan, a couple of years back, Chris's wife, Tina, decided that she wanted to take an around-the-world tour. Chris wanted to go, but he had a business to run. Resource Financial Group wasn't going to run itself in his absence. And that raised the question of whether the company could be run over the Net via e-mail and the Web.

Apparently, Chris does travel a lot because, when we e-mailed him about an interview him for this book, he and his wife were in Katmandu presenting their application to adopt a child to the national orphanage. He e-mailed us back and had this to say, "Susan Wood spoke the truth. We did backpack around the world for six months, and now, as you can see, we have decided to return to Nepal. We will be back in the U.S. (with our new baby daughter whom we are adopting here in Nepal) late this year. ... Frankly, the secret to our success is not just a heavy reliance on technology but a fantastic team (which includes FSC). Technology merely magnifies the good and bad characteristics of an organization."

Chris's company sits right in the middle of one of these webs of relationships and information we're talking about. As an associate of Financial Services Company, Chris is a buyer of financial services and a user of the information that FSC provides. On the other side, Chris's clients have an experienced benefits manager not only running their program but giving their people access to it on the Net. It's a win for all concerned.

The Resource Financial Group situation underlines one of the key aspects of doing business in the new Net world. Information flows in rich relationships, and those relationships extend beyond the traditional organizational boundaries. One place where we see that extensively is in the area of investor relations.

NET TECHNOLOGY FOR INVESTOR RELATIONS

Publicly traded companies have a vast array of information that they are required to make available to their investors. Historically, this has been done through the annual report and some printed updates. Annual reports have usually been extensive printed documents with lots of pictures and color photography, each one bearing significant costs both to produce and to mail to investors. Even at that, the information sharing was, in most cases, somewhat pro forma. One annual report a year just doesn't have enough information to be of much use.

Companies around the world are seizing the opportunities offered by the Net to improve the quality of their information sharing while reducing its cost.

Schlumberger is known as one of the best-managed companies in the world. It's one of many that have moved a large chunk of their investor relations to the Net. You can get to the Schlumberger Investor Relations page from a prominent link on the main Schlumberger page. The site is www.slb.com. One thing you notice about the site is that there's a lot of information available in a lot of forms. There are annual reports for more than one year. Current financials are available, as are current 10Q and 10K forms, which all publicly traded companies must file.

There's a link to News and Publications that offers the investor (or interested visitor) a variety of information. There are Schlumberger news releases going back a couple of years. There's also a list of other publications from and about the company. Articles that are available on the Web are appropriately linked.

Even though you're on the News and Publications page, you won't forget that this is investor relations. The banner at the top tells you. And the links to financial information remain in place.

Another link takes you to an area of investor relations that's called Recent Presentations. On the day that I checked it, there was a presentation titled "Harnessing Technology to Manage Change." This was a strategy paper by Ian Strecker, executive vice president of technology and communications. Schlumberger made the paper available in several different downloadable formats so that people could choose what was best for them.

Back on the main Investor Relations page, you find stock price history (neatly graphed) and links to services providing stock quotes on the Web. The information for an investor is comprehensive, current, and easily available. We don't know yet if all this will affect share price, but making it available costs Schlumberger a lot less that it would to regularly mail even a small fraction of the material.

The Net can be helpful in other investor-related information sharing as well. Two of the most interesting takeover/buyout situations in the last few years have been the coming together of IBM and Lotus Development and the acquisition of McDonnell Douglas by the Boeing Corporation. In each case, the acquiring company followed the same basic Net strategy.

When the companies announced their offers to acquire, both Boeing and IBM set up Web sites with information about the proposed deal and the consequences for all concerned. That immediately gave people with an interest in the deal a place to go to get more information about it. The first people to show up on IBM's Web site about the Lotus purchase were Lotus employees. They were followed closely by members of the investment community.

The result of all this was something that had not been available before. It was an opportunity for the employees of all the involved companies, as well as the investment community, to find out what the key issues were and to evaluate them from their own perspectives.

CUTTING PURCHASING COSTS ONLINE

The purchasing function is another administrative function that has seen dramatic cost reduction and efficiency gains along with more information sharing. One good, simple example is the Liberty Mutual Insurance Company. According to Michelle Flynn, vice president of information systems, one of Liberty Mutual's key successes has been to move toward allowing the firm's line managers to purchase office supplies on their own. This is a kind of supply known to many purchasing people as MRO for maintenance, repair, and operations supplies.

Two issues are at stake in this kind of purchasing. The first is that many purchasing systems require that all purchases, even routine purchases for MRO items, get routed through the purchasing department. That means that someone has to deal with them, decide on them, and process them. That someone needs to be paid and supported, therefore generating costs. That process also takes time.

In many corporations in many situations, line managers find that they need those routine supplies faster than they're going to get them routing a standard purchase order through the purchasing department. So what do they do? As anyone who's ever worked in a corporation knows, they go out and buy them on their own and then seek reimbursement or persuade the vendor to bill the company and then try to generate a purchase order afterward. The result is that, for the same amount of administrative work as in the routine process, a purchase is made that's often not from the preferred supplier, and often at a higher price. This is a lose/lose par excellence.

What Liberty Mutual did was elegantly simple. First, the company selected specific products that employees could purchase. Obviously, the range had to be broad enough to make it worth the managers' efforts to look at the internal system first.

Next, Liberty Mutual paid attention to making the process easy. The philosophy here is that, if you make it easy for people to do something, they're more likely to do it. In this case, making the easiest option ordering from the preferred supplier increased the likelihood that orders would indeed go there. This was coupled with a negotiation with suppliers to provide delivery within 48 hours using the automated system.

What are the results? Result number one is that 2200 administrators of Liberty Mutual can now purchase their own supplies and get them within 48 hours. Result number two is that the company has reduced the number of its purchase orders from more than 17,000 a year to less than 8000 a year. And that generates savings.

How big are the savings? The National Association of Purchasing Management estimates that the average cost to generate a purchase order for requisition through the final order itself is $150. That counts all the costs on the purchasing side, but it doesn't count the efficiency gains that the line managers can achieve by getting their stuff when they need it. If we multiply the reduction in purchase orders (over 9000) by the average cost to generate a purchase order ($150) the estimated annual cost reduction is $1,350,000!

The Liberty Mutual example is a fairly simple one, but we can see the power of using the Net in purchasing if we look at an example that is larger and more advanced in its development and application. And one of the best we found is GE's Trading Process Network (TPN).

HOW TO ACCESS $1 BILLION IN TRADE WITHOUT LEAVING YOUR DESK

A company like General Electric that makes a lot of things also buys a lot of things. And so the benefits of automating and streamlining the purchasing function are particularly powerful. The problem is that, while purchasing is important, it's also fairly complex in a corporation the size of General Electric. It involves going out for bids on a variety of products at a variety of times with a series of different timelines.

General Electric had already been working on this problem for a number of years. It already had a preferred supplier system in place that was primarily EDI (Electronic Data Interchange)-based. Moving to the Net lets GE offer a system that is easier to use and open to more trading partners.

When we spoke to Bruce Chovnick, vice president of GE's Internet and Consulting Services, he said, "We started a joint venture with Netscape, Atra Business Systems, to develop business-to-business electronic commerce software that hopefully would set standards for the way business-to-business electronic commerce will occur in the industry, and that has been very successful. We also started a systems integration business, which I refer to as "Building more custom-type solutions around open technologies." This, along with other efforts by GE, has resulted in developing a valuable Internet tool called Trading Process Network.

So, what is General Electric's Trading Process Network? Harvey Seegers, GE's CEO, says, in simple terms, it is a productivity tool for business. It uses the latest in Internet technologies to allow buyers and sellers to meet one another, exchange RFQs, order products and services, and conduct business transactions with less cost and greater efficiency. Trading Process Network (TPN) is aimed at small and large businesses in industrial manufacturing, automotive, and aerospace industries.

From the supplier's standpoint, things work pretty much this way. Suppliers can go to the GE Web site and check out what kinds of products General Electric buys from different kinds of businesses. If they want to be considered for the preferred bidders' list, the next step is to work through the qualification process. That can start right on the Web site and be handled with electronic transmissions.

Once a supplier is approved, it is then on the list to bid for products for which it is qualified. The bidding process, using the same open architecture, is fast and secure.

General Electric sees TPN accomplishing these three major goals for businesses both large and small:

1. Increasing productivity in the purchasing arena for buyers because most of the process is virtually automatic.

2. Establishing a global reach in marketing for both buyers and sellers. GE will get proposals from more potential suppliers from around the world. The suppliers can use TPN to extend their reach.

3. Decreasing costs and cycle times in sales efforts for suppliers as the costs and time delays associated with mail or express delivery are eliminated.

General Electric is not the only company that's done this. Another example is McDonnell Douglas. Using its virtual factory electronic bidding system, a McDonnell buyer can now e-mail qualified suppliers throughout the world to tell them that a job is available for bidding. Suppliers can access information about the job, parts specifications, and bidding requirements via the McDonnell Douglas extranet.

Once the potential suppliers have prepared their bids, they can use the Net to forward the bid to St. Louis for consideration. In McDonnell Douglas's case, the system can even do an automatic ranking of the bids on the basis of cost.

Here linking, automating, and customization are all at work. The results are some huge cost savings. For McDonnell Douglas, sources inside the company estimate that the savings from electronic bidding alone pay for all the costs of operating the entire intranet system.

And, in addition to companies setting up their own specialized intranet/extranet bidding systems, there are also several proprietary systems out there that both buyers and sellers can participate in. Perhaps the best known of these is Industry.Net. This service of Nets, Inc., is headed up by Jim Manzi, former head of Lotus Development.

Industry.Net was one of the very first companies to consider bringing together buyers and sellers of industrial goods. The company was founded in 1990 by Don Jones, whose idea was to streamline industrial purchasing by making use of the Net's ability to put buyers and sellers together. The core of Industry.Net is its Web site and the people who show up there.

One group is called Buying Members. These 200,000-plus people are mostly purchasing and specifying professionals. They represent 36,000 corporations, according to Nets, Inc., Industry.Net's parent. They show up for product information, news, and discussions.

The other key group is called Selling Clients. These are a variety of types and sizes of businesses with interest in selling to the Buying Members. They provide the things that draw the Buying Members to the site.

What kind of things? A purchasing agent or other buyer will find catalogs, corporate profiles, product and service descriptions, drawings, specifications, and more provided by the sellers. News and other information are provided by Industry.Net.

Industry.Net is not alone in providing this intermediary function. The famous Thomas Register, the book that sits on the desk of just about every purchasing agent in the world, has put up its site as well. Its Web site at www.thomasregister.com bills itself as the largest industrial Internet site. It contains the entire database of the print and CD-ROM editions of the Thomas Register.

Here's what that means. The site gives users access to more than 2300 online catalogs and 40,000 distinct screens of detailed product information. The database online consists of 155,000 companies and uses a proprietary search engine. There are 55,000 standard product and service classifications.

Thomas says that the site has had an average of 15,550 new registrants signing on each month since May of 1996. The Thomas Register claims that more than 85% of all its online catalogs on the site are viewed monthly, with more frequent and longer access periods recorded for catalogs that have remained on the site longer than three months.

Both these services aim at providing more than just information. They want to extend their traditional print franchise to the creation of a true marketplace, where buyers and sellers come together to do business.

There are also industry-specific sites to help aid the purchasing function. Buyers of electronic components can find what they're looking for on a site on the World Wide Web at centralres.com. And buyers and sellers from over 26,000 companies in the apparel and textile industry can get together at www.apparelex.com. Other sites and services are being developed by trade associations, and more are springing up all the time.

In the case of General Electric, the purchasing function is seen as the front end of the entire supply chain. The buzzwords *supply chain management* resonate through discussions of intranets and extranets and the use of the public Internet. The supply chain is seen as the channel running from original suppliers to ultimate users. And one of the key principles is to automate the path along that supply chain as much as possible. That just makes good sense. Most movement of goods and services through the supply chain involves repetitive activity, operations that are done again and again in the same way. They also involve information that ideally should be entered only once at the earliest possible point in the chain and then passed from digital hand to digital hand, saving on labor costs and cutting down on errors.

That brings us back to about where we started, looking at the overall administrative functions and how intranets, extranets, and the Internet are helping to perform those functions more effectively. The companies that we considered looked consistently for ways to enrich the quality of information links along their various administrative paths. They automated as many functions and data entry points as they could. Handling routine matters routinely was also a dominant theme. That way, highly skilled human judgment, like that of an expert purchasing agent, could be used effectively in the places where it had the most effect.

We also saw an increased sense of the need not only for sharing information but for sharing it effectively. We saw companies utilizing databases, indexes, links, as well as availability, to make information available to a much wider array of people than was ever possible and in a much more effective form than was ever the case before.

TACTICS

As you review the ideas in this chapter, think about these key ways to use tactics to be more effective.

THINK LINKS

Think about the links that already exist for information sharing. In most organizations, there are already clear information paths. Start with those and look for ways to use them more effectively. Use this technology to do routine things routinely. Look for places to take "the other person" out of the loop. The "other person" is the one reading from a manual or a computer screen. Let the computer do that part.

You can use Net technology to put policy and procedure manuals in digital form so that they are updated regularly and are easily accessed via the Net by all employees. We have seen companies use intranets and the Web technology to cut costs and enhance operations for the following administrative applications:

- Benefit selection tool—New hires can make benefit selections by using the new benefit enrollment system. Current employees can use it to change their selections. Read benefit summaries.
- Internal job opportunities listings.
- Browse internal class schedules and enroll in courses right from a desktop Web browser.
- Employee news.
- Employee connection newsgroup or discussion group.
- Health advisory.
- Having employees update their own information in personnel files and directories.
- Personal home pages.
- Hypertext hotlinks to frequently used forms, which might include a searchable employee directory, a suggestion box to submit ideas for how to improve the business, a project time tracking system, vendor information forms, employee expense reports, a purchasing needs section for suppliers like General Electric Information Services (GEIS) trading partner process.

And look for other places where information could be shared or for other people who could use it. Ask, "Who do we need to share information with?" Even though reengineering and business process reorganization have attempted to get rid of the old functional silos, they still exist. Look for ways to set up links across what used to be organizational chasms. Sometimes, this means setting up interactive e-mail discussion groups or newsgroup forums on everything from product development issues to soliciting employee feedback on proposed benefit plans. Other times, it might mean that administration helps put information in easily accessible Web pages.

Southern California Gas's administration supports its customers and account executives by using its intranet to keep them up-to-date on regulatory issues. Before Netscape technology, it had to maintain a full set of "current and effective" tariffs stored in 4-inch binders at 60 different locations within the company's offices, as well as at its regional offices. When a business unit planned to offer a new service or product, the utility contacted the tariff group, who then drew up the tariff and submitted it to the Public Utility Commission for approval. Because the tariff binders were updated whenever a new tariff was printed and there was no administrative assurance that all the updates reached all the binders, executives were not always certain that the tariff they were reading was the current version.

When SCG's customers or other interested parties needed a copy of a tariff, they contacted a member of the tariff group by telephone, who located the appropriate tariff, made a copy of it, and mailed or faxed it.

Now, after Netscape technology, whenever a new tariff is approved, it becomes part of the "current and effective" file in a Paradox database. Each night, a batch process prints all changes made that day in the current tariff database to a GIF file and a PDF file, which are then automatically "pushed" to the external Web server's tariff book Web page. The only tariffs available on the Web page are those that are current and effective.

Southern California Gas's administration has found a way to support and share need-to-know information on tariffs. Now, account executives and external parties with Web access can access and view any tariff of interest by pointing their browser to the tariff page, sorting through the tariffs using a table of contents, and double-clicking on the appropriate link.

AUTOMATE

Consider automating at least one side of information sharing. To do that, hunt out situations in which two people are involved in the process. If you've got one person reading to another person from a manual or computer screen, that's probably a good place to automate at least half the process. If you've got situations in which a sin-

gle individual in an office sends out the same information again and
again to lots of places, consider ways to post that on an intranet or
extranet, so that people can get access to it.

If you do that in the administrative processes, you'll almost automatically set up ways for people to customize the information to
their own needs. But don't stop there. Instead, look for ways in
which people can customize what they want with searchable databases, intelligent agents, and other technology. Look for ways in
which people can manage independently and immediately things
that they have to get help with, such as their benefit plans.

TRANSFORM

Look for ways to turn information into knowledge by tapping those
knowledge resources that exist within your organization and within
your partners. Find ways to collect that knowledge and to make it
available to others. Corporate legacy knowledge and "top-down"
knowledge can be very valuable and a welcome communication by
employees from senior management.

Consider doing what Amdahl did to facilitate this process. It created the WOW Club. Its purpose was to sit down on a one-on-one basis with senior management and their secretaries to teach the value
of the intranet and create personal Web pages for these senior employees. Though time-consuming, this method assured support for
the intranet initiative at the highest levels within Amdahl.

And the same kinds of best practices sharing that we outlined in
Chapter 3 for manufacturing can be applied in administration as
well.

INSIDE/OUTSIDE

Look inside and outside the company for places to share information. Are there vendors or others with whom you have lots of routine information-sharing contact? Are there places inside the
organization where there's frequent data or information transmission that's now paper-based?

Consider using the Net to allow your vendors to start the qualification process. Use your Web site as a place where investors can

contact you. When you do those, make sure you've put the systems in place so that you can respond to their requests.

CORE FUNCTIONS/BIG PAYOFFS

The big payoff from the Core Functions/Big Payoffs TACTIC in administration are likely to come from those two-sided information-sharing situations we've already described. Also, try having your people rank the forms they send internally by frequency. You'll usually see a few of the same forms at the top of lots of lists. Those are the ones to put on the Net first.

Another big payoff often comes from using e-mail to replace fax because of the elimination of telephone costs.

START NOW

Start now. Lots of the companies we talked to started with information in the human resources area. That information is usually already in digital form. It has broad application across the entire organization. And it often yields big savings.

WALLY AND JEFF'S ADMINISTRATION LESSONS LEARNED

1. Basic human resources information is a great place to start with an intranet. One reason for that is that most of the material is already in finished print form. Another reason is the major benefits that come from putting this information on the Net. People seem to feel that having this information where they can find it quickly and privately is a big advantage. Key human resources personnel are freed up to do things that make better use of their training and experience than reading from a manual.

2. Consider things like travel guidelines, mileage reimbursement guidelines, expense forms, employee handbooks, employee directories, and so forth, as a place to start with your intranet.

3. Don't just assume that, because you have it in digital
    form, it's appropriate for the Net. Modify the way your
    information is structured to take advantage of links—
    the power of the Net. Add graphics that help get the
    message across.

4. Evaluate whether the vast amount of information on
    your intranet necessitates a strong search engine and, if
    needed, don't wait too long to implement this key piece
    of technology. A search engine should be among the
    early technologies used.

5. Be ready for the social phenomena we refer to as the
    "Webmaster is God syndrome." What we mean is that,
    soon after a company establishes and releases a Web-
    master's e-mail address, the recipient of that e-mail can
    expect to be bombarded with a flood of inquiries about
    everything from finding individual e-mail addresses to
    highly specific product inquiries. It is important that
    you position your company to handle these requests ap-
    propriately within your budgetary guidelines. Many
    companies, such as Columbia/HCA Healthcare Corpora-
    tion and Amdahl, have resolved this problem by creat-
    ing a cross-functional Webmaster council to put
    structure and policies around the intranet/Internet
    process.

    The cross-organizational and cross-functional collabo-
    rative nature of the council fostered and promoted best
    practices while avoiding internal structural or bureau-
    cratic hurdles. For example, Amdahl underestimated
    the amount of time required to do the Webmaster's job,
    as well as the scope of the job. Initially, the plan was to
    create a single Webmaster position. Once the company
    realized the range of requirements, from the technical
    aspects to programming, project management, public
    relations, and evangelizing, Amdahl recognized that as
    many as four people were needed to handle the Web-
    master's duties.

Other companies avoid overburdening the Webmaster by having different e-mail response addresses on different pages, depending on the material covered. One client of ours has even gone so far as to remove all automatic e-mail response devices from its public Web page. The e-mail addresses are still listed, but it's not as easy to send a message.

6. Look at the processes and paper flows you currently have. Then, convert them into information flows. You'll find that the Net allows you many ways to share information quickly that paper does not. Analyze how the administrative support information flows in your business (filling out forms, checking boxes, filing reports, etc., which constitute the core information sharing that goes on in any organization), and consider how to automate the process using Net technology. Your cost reduction based on paper weight alone will justify the expense of the system.

7. Sometimes, time is better spent creating content and links to important information than incorporating the latest Java or Shockwave software program.

8. Lots of companies we talked to were putting information up on their intranets about basic guidelines. Intranets on just about every company we interviewed included the basic kind of administrative information that people need from day to day.

9. Use database technology so that people can search handbooks and policies for the things they need. Use hyperlinking technology to link the relevant parts of different policies so that people can find their own way around and come to their own solutions.

10. Don't stop with the routine administrative stuff. Look for anything that might be of interest or helpful. Fletcher Challenge is a Canadian pulp and paper company based in Vancouver. Its Intranet includes all the things we've talked about but also company financial data, employee newsletters, internal surveys, and lots of other things.

11. With an intranet-based directory, not only can the changes be made immediately but they can be made by the affected individuals themselves, without having to involve other people. The result is a more accurate document and cost savings. Look for ways to have employees update their own information.

12. The initial challenge of populating your Web server with your company's information can seem overwhelming. Lockheed Martin confronted a number of these challenges as a result of the Lockheed–Martin Marietta merger when it had to put standardized policies and procedures on its intranet. What was the solution?

    International Data Corporation (IDC) reported, "Throughout Lockheed Martin, the standard became this: if an organization has policies and procedures, they must be on the network. To do this, hundreds of thousands of lines of information on the mainframe were run through a filter and converted to HTML. Information that was contained in hard copy manuals was optically scanned and also converted to HTML. Corporate and companywide policies and procedures were now accessible to employees with connectivity to the intranet." What were the results?

    Bill Buonanni, Lockheed Martin's director of World Wide Web Initiatives, said "Our Netscape-based intranet is really paying off. We've already isolated direct cost benefits attributed to our policies and procedures intranet application."

13. Investor relations is a great place to move information sharing to the Net. Investors like it because they can get comprehensive information quickly. And you'll save on publication and mailing costs; and the savings often are extensive since publications in this area tend to be elaborate, expensive, and heavy.

14. Use the Net to automate and streamline the purchasing function—the purchasing function can be seen as the front end of the entire supply chain. But don't forget to

tie your efforts here to your management efforts or process redesign efforts. Look back at the Liberty Mutual example, which starts by giving line managers authority to order and then uses this technology and partnering to find ways to make ordering easy and efficient.

15. Look at all the different ways to make connections with key vendors or qualified bidders. There are lots of tools here, including e-mail, extranets, and private networks like Industry.Net. Consider them all and choose the best mix.

16. Many companies recognize that the vast amount of information on their intranets necessitates a strong search engine. Don't wait too long to implement this key piece of technology and put it on the early list of technologies to include.

CHAPTER 5

RECRUITING AND TRAINING

You've heard the business slogan, "People are our primary asset." Cliché or not, that's true for most companies. Great companies start with great people, and that starts with recruiting and follows up with training.

As times have gotten more competitive, and staffs have gotten leaner, the importance of having the right people in the right positions and properly trained has become even more important for businesses around the world.

CRITICAL CHALLENGES OF RECRUITING AND TRAINING

Finding the right people and providing them with the skills they need has never been easy. In today's world, the challenges have intensified. Some of the following challenges we've always faced and some are new:

- Finding more and better applicants at a reasonable price.

- Providing consistent and high-quality training across the enterprise.

- Providing consistent and high-quality training across a range of jobs.

- Developing effective training for today's environment and relationships.

- Using training as part of competitive strategy.

Finding more and better applicants at a reasonable price has always been the challenge of recruiting. The competition for top candidates is especially intense for highly skilled positions, such as physicians or programmers, and in high-value business areas. It's also intense for businesspeople with highly desirable qualifications like computer expertise or science backgrounds.

Providing consistent, high-quality training across the enterprise and across a range of jobs is a challenge that's especially intense if your company has multiple locations or lots of jobs at varying skill levels.

When we say developing effective training for today's environment and relationships, the environment we're talking about is the highly competitive business environment, but it's also the technical environment. The Net and Web provide great reach across geography and time, but there are special challenges in designing training there.

Training can also be a way of strengthening relationships both inside and outside your organization. As you reach outside, you also can begin to use training as a competitive advantage.

SOLUTIONS

Now let's look at some solutions being achieved by businesses using Net technology.

COLUMBIA/HCA HEALTHCARE CORPORATION MEETS A HUGE RECRUITING CHALLENGE

Founded in 1987, Columbia/HCA Healthcare Corporation is one of the largest employers on the planet—the 22nd-largest, in fact—and the largest health care provider, with 347 hospitals, 180 home health agencies, 125 outpatient surgery centers, and 75,000 affiliated physicians. To achieve its mission—serving its communities with the highest-quality health care—Columbia/HCA is always looking for more effective ways of doing business.

Tod Fetherling, director of interactive marketing for Columbia/HCA, tells how the company started using Net and Web technology, "The original idea came from Rick Scott, our CEO and chairman. He's very much of a visionary, and pretty much said this is going to be a major trend in our lives, and we need to get Columbia/HCA in position to take advantage of it."

Like lots of companies, Columbia/HCA began with a public Web site in April of 1995. The first site was "just a corporate advertisement site." There wasn't a lot of activity. Then, Fetherling says, " ... we changed that focus to be more of an information resource. And that's when things really turned around for us."

Now one of the most popular medical Web sites, with more than 600,000 hits per month, Columbia/HCA's Internet site provides visitors with:

- articles about health issues

- downloadable healthy recipes

- a directory of Columbia/HCA facilities

- online magazines

- a schedule of online physician chats

If the World Wide Web hadn't come along, there might have been no way for Columbia/HCA Healthcare Corporation, which had only four hospitals five years ago, to grow into the 347-hospital network it has become since then. The Net/Web became a way to integrate all the new people and facilities. Tod Fetherling says, "We just want to strengthen our relationship with our vendors and allow the clinicians who are actually in the day-to-day patient care to have access to the best information about the tools that they're using to deliver quality patient care. That's the number one goal."

A COMPANYWIDE INFORMATION AND EDUCATION SYSTEM

Columbia/HCA's intranet, KOALA, supports the overall education and growth of its employees. Tod Fetherling says, "We now have 275,000 employees: we needed a more timely and cost-effective method. Paper uses money that would otherwise be spent on improving health care service delivery."

KOALA houses an up-to-date corporate directory, provides reports, posts résumés collected from the Internet site, and trains employees on procedures. Using Netscape News Server software, Columbia/HCA offers threaded newsgroups where employees can exchange information that covers a broad range of personal and business topics.

Online report distribution has significantly decreased costs. "We believe that anything worth doing is worth measuring, so we produce weekly tracking reports," says Fetherling. "By distributing the reports online, we're beginning to save trees. We'll document costs as we move forward, but the potential for our $20 billion corporation is astronomical."

Part of the original impetus for this massive company's move into Net and Web technology was to improve its recruiting function. With hundreds of locations and thousands of jobs scattered around the United States, that is an enormous function.

RECRUITING QUALIFIED PHYSICIANS ONLINE

To make things even more complex, the jobs for which Columbia/HCA needs to recruit run the entire gamut of specialization. At one end of the complexity spectrum are the high-turnover jobs, such as intake clerks, as well as a variety of other clerical and routine positions. At the far end of the complexity spectrum is the daunting challenge of recruiting physicians for Columbia/HCA's many facilities.

One of the best ways to start on a complex task such as this is to go to the experts, and that, in fact, is what Columbia/HCA did. Rather than immediately develop both the recruiting and the Web capability in-house, they outsourced the task. The first Web site was handled by Netcom at its site in Palo Alto, California, and the development of the recruiting function there was handled by Bernard Hodes Advertising. That last was a particularly stellar choice.

Bernard Hodes Advertising is the world's largest recruitment advertisement company, doing more than $200 million per year. It has experience in helping companies of all sizes improve their recruiting for all kinds of positions. That made it a great choice from the recruiting side.

The agency was also an excellent choice on the Web side. Bernard Hodes Advertising is the developer of CareerMosaic, which was the first big recruiting site on the Web. Today, CareerMosaic has ads from more than 200 employers, paying $40–$150 for each of their job postings. The service draws hundreds of thousands of job seekers every month.

When all this started, though, it was CareerMosaic's unique experience that made it a great match for Columbia/HCA was able to improve the quality of Columbia/HCA's physician recruiting. Now, as applications and résumés come in on this highly professional area, those can be maintained on the company intranet. Having them on the intranet makes them available to people who will actually face recruiting challenges at any of Columbia/HCA's sites.

Practice opportunities are posted on the Internet site. Résumés submitted online are posted on the intranet. Hospitals can then approach the health care providers whose qualifications and location match their individual requirements.

Columbia/HCA isn't the only major company to employ this kind of recruiting. Lockheed Martin has also gone in for Web-based recruiting in a big way.

RECRUITING WEB SITE AT LOCKHEED MARTIN

Lockheed Martin began by putting its recruiting function on its Web site, about one layer down from its home page and linked under its Corporate Overview section in the Operating Units and Subsidiaries Library. Bill Buonanni, director of World Wide Web initiatives for Lockheed Martin, said "That has become so successful that the corporation is now considering moving the recruiting function to the main Lockheed Martin home page to increase the size of the exposure of its recruiting offerings."

Things don't stop there for either Lockheed Martin or Columbia/HCA or for other companies we talked to who use the Net to improve their recruiting. Many of the functions are not limited to the public Web site but also move inside.

At Lockheed Martin, for example, job opportunities are posted on the intranet. Lockheed Martin employees are able to search for a job that they might want to fill and can even apply online. Once their application has been filed, they can check on the status of the application using the intranet.

So, what's the current status of using the Net for recruiting? Well, as you might expect, the very first jobs to have effective Net recruiting were technical jobs in the computer area. As time goes on though, increasingly, other, even nontechnical jobs, are having a Web site and internal posting as part of their process.

For companies with an intranet, posting job opportunities on the company Net, perhaps on a human resources page, is an effective way to make opportunities available throughout the firm. Posting all available openings and opportunities this way also meets established fair practice standards for making the job notices available to all.

At the same time, allowing people to apply online and to use the Net as a way to check on their applications automates a process that would otherwise require a great deal of human intervention.

ONLINE RECRUITING—A GROWING PHENOMENON

Companies are starting to look at online recruiting as a key part of how to find top people. Sure, recruiting for high-tech jobs is the biggest part of the effort now, but that's changing. United Parcel Service, for example, has a job opportunities page on its public Web site. The majority of the jobs posted there are for UPS's package-handling operations.

The William Olsten Center for Workforce Strategies conducted research at the end of 1996 that offers a good view of current usage and trends. Its research shows that about 35% of companies with more than 10,000 employees use the Web as part of their recruiting efforts, but that only 7% of smaller companies (100 employees or less) do so.

That's not the whole story, though. Of the companies polled, 85% felt that the Web would have a growing role in their recruiting operations. That's likely to happen more frequently as software companies develop ways to link Web recruiting sites to the résumé-reading software that's already in use by many larger companies.

FROM THE JOB SEEKER'S SIDE

From the job seeker's side, both within the company and outside, there are major benefits to this kind of recruiting as well. The first of these is that there are a lot more opportunities available on the Web than might pop up in the local paper.

To check this out, we took a look at the *San Jose Mercury News* Sunday Edition and the Web sites of some of the companies that advertise there. The *San Jose Mercury News* is in the heart of Silicon Valley, and we figured that firms advertising there would also be very likely to have active Web sites and to have integrated their processes into those sites. What we found was interesting.

For most of the firms we looked at, there were between five and ten help wanted ads. To find them, you had to know exactly what category they had been posted in. The ads themselves were, for the most part, fairly short and cryptic.

The Web sites were another story altogether. There were between five and ten times as many opportunities posted. True, not all of them were for the same geographical area covered by the *Mercury News* edition, but that's a pretty large multiple. In addition, many of the Web sites, including those of CareerMosaic and other service sites had search functions that enabled a job seeker to find precisely the kinds of opportunities he or she was seeking.

The benefits to the job seeker don't end there. If the job seeker finds an opportunity, for example, on the Lockheed Martin site, then he or she also has the ability to find out a good deal about Lockheed Martin on that same site. The result is that applications are more likely to be focused on best possibility and highest interest areas.

In large companies, a portion of the screening process is even automated with résumé screening software. If applications are already being filed electronically, they can flow right into this process without the need for any document scanning.

What all this does for both sides of the recruiting issue is make it possible to search a wider array of possibilities and then concentrate on the ones that are most likely to be successful. In addition, by automating several of the steps and saving both time and individual effort, the companies doing the recruiting are able to spend their time on the best prospects and the most significant recruiting challenges, thereby using human resources where they have the highest payoff.

The objective here is to get qualified people to jobs quickly and effectively. Recruiting is just the beginning. Once those people are onboard, it's time to train them.

USING THE NET FOR TRAINING

We can start looking at the benefits from training by looking again at Columbia/HCA. When we asked Tod Fetherling what Columbia/HCA was doing in the area of training, he said,

> We have some of the leading experts in the entire country in that area. But right now we do online training courses, and there are two courses that we have offered right now. One of them deals with transitioning into an integrated delivery system. And then we have another one that deals with physician alliances and partnerships. And these are for executives within Columbia/HCA so that they can begin to understand what are the economics that are driving the health care system. We're very much of a learning organization, I mean, we're constantly learning from ourselves and from others about how to do a better job for our patients and vendors and employees alike.

CUTTING TRAVEL EXPENSES FOR CONFERENCES

Let's consider the training and professional development requirements of a physician. In the world before the Net, a Columbia/HCA physician who wanted to keep up his or her skills in a particular specialty area needed to go to a conference. What does that entail?

First, it implies time away from the office, even if the major reason for going to the conference is only one or two one-hour workshops. Travel time is about a day to a day and a half. Then, there's the day or more at the conference itself. And there are registration fees, travel and hotel expenses, food, and the costs of lost productivity. All in all, Columbia/HCA figures that it adds up to about $6000 for a physician who attends one conference. Another way to look at that is that each time you can achieve the training objective without a conference, the saving is $6000.

That's why Columbia/HCA has its own professional training subsidiary. Columbia/HCA purchased Quantum, a firm that designs and delivers training and that, through a series of metamorphoses, became Columbia/HCA Quantum Innovations. The company is headed by Ann Yakimovicz, the director of interactive distance learning. Yakimovicz came to Quantum in October of 1995 with a Ph.D. in educational human resource development and a specialization in continuing professional education and distance learning. She's also done research in computer-mediated communications. So, she's just about the perfect person to head up this kind of effort.

Ann Yakimovicz believes that Web-based technology lends itself well to reinforcing performance improvement and filling the ongoing need for exchanging knowledge between employees. She said, "What we see is an overall strategy for performance improvement, performance management, change management within the organization ... there are a lot of different ways to use education and training media to achieve those kinds of strategic goals, and obviously one of those is the corporate intranet."

The health care environment itself presents a challenge. Says Yakimovicz,

> ... The whole field of healthcare is undergoing substantial change in the way we deliver healthcare services. We're looking at managed care, HMO's, PPO's, the different kinds of structures that are now beginning to look at delivering quality services in a very cost effective kind of way. And that requires substantial change in thinking about how we work together. So

we see the intranet as a way to begin doing some of that. We can look at targeting audiences across the enterprise. We can look at senior-level executives and deliver training to them on thinking very differently about healthcare, thinking about being risk managers and some of the different positions and roles they now have to play in a healthcare environment.

EXECUTIVE TRAINING AT COLUMBIA/HCA

The challenge comes in a variety of forms. At one level, there's the need to train top-level executives in the economics and mechanics of the changing health care industry. That results in a course called Leading the Transition to Integrative Healthcare Delivery.

That's a course designed for executives who can take it on the intranet. And, by the way, this isn't just a bunch of dry textbooks or lecture notes dumped out on the Net. What Yakimovicz has done is to apply high-quality, instructional design to the courses that Columbia/HCA delivers to its people.

ADMITTING CLERKS AND HOUSEKEEPERS NEED TRAINING, TOO

Executives aren't the only people who need training, nor are physicians. There are also specialists in various technical areas, as well as clerical staff.

One of Columbia/HCA's courses is for admitting clerks. This is a high-turnover position. Each admitting clerk needs to take the time to do certain things right, but that's not enough. The clerk also needs to understand why things are done in a particular way. Yakimovicz and her team have designed training that helps explain not only a process but also its underlying principles.

This is the same kind of challenge that faces other industries. Think about the hotel business, for example. Reservation clerks, desk clerks, and even housekeeping staff all require basic training in the core jobs they do. But there's more to it than that. Housekeeping staff, for example, need to understand what to do in certain critical customer contact situations. These are the things that Ian Carlson, years ago, called "moments of truth" in his book of the same name. That's why Sheraton has designed a training program to meet its specific need. The materials are geared to the educational level and understanding of the people being trained. Graphics, feedback loops, and other mechanisms make the training interesting and interactive as well as effective.

COMPUTER-BASED COURSES ONLINE

Bill Buonanni, director of World Wide Web initiatives for Lockheed Martin, said, "We have a series of computer-based education and training, courses available online that we provide to any Lockheed employee who wants to get to it." These programs are designed to bring everyone up to speed in understanding how to use the Internet technology. Lockheed Martin is committed to apply Internet technology to all its business functions and activities. There is no wonder why when you consider that, according to an International Data Corporation ROI study of Netscape intranets, Lockheed Martin had an ROI of 1505%, with qualitative yearly savings benefits of $1,807,838 direct reduction in staff time, $3,699,114 in productivity gains, $9000 savings in communication and $966,000 in mainframe upgrade savings.

There are also good operational reasons for moving the training to the Web. The accounting firm of Ernst and Young, for example, is making the effort to move all its training previously available on CD-ROMs to an intranet. That's because training available on its intranet is much easier to update. In Ernst and Young's situation, updates on tax code and regulatory requirements are particularly important. Training on the Net can be updated almost immediately.

That brings us to another important feature of the Net that other training mechanisms often do not have. Training on the Net is available whenever it's needed. In a traditional sense, that blurs the line somewhat between training and job aids, but it's actually a big advantage. It means that training materials can also be a form of reference material that provides information about how to do the job right at just the moment that it's needed.

CONTINUING-EDUCATION COURSES ONLINE

The Boeing Corporation has one of the most extensive intranets in the world. One of the administrative-like tasks that executives and managers at Boeing can do on their intranet is check out courses that might interest them. Using the Net whenever they want to, they can find out what courses are available that fit their interests and needs.

OK, that's not such a big deal. They could probably do that with a course catalog. Sure, there is an advantage to having the catalog updated frequently, but that doesn't seem like much. But wait.

A Boeing executive can search for a course and then can check out details of the course, sample some of the materials, and find out the reactions of others at Boeing who have taken it. That makes for a much better decision about whether a particular course is worth the effort of registration. If it is, online registration is fast, effective, and cost-saving.

MAKE OR BUY? AND HOW?

So far, we've talked about training that's already designed and in place. But another major challenge for companies today is making sure that training is well designed and does what it's supposed to do. For traditional training, that can involve buying training off the shelf, having someone else provide it, or developing the course materials in-house. All those options are also available when training moves to the Net.

COLUMBIA/HCA DEVELOPS TRAINING

At Columbia/HCA's wholly owned training subsidiary, Columbia Quality Innovations, the challenges go beyond just delivering top-quality training. There's also the challenge to make sure that training helps to establish a common style and culture for a group of people and organizations that weren't part of the same team just a couple of years back. That means that control of the training design is very important. According to Ann Yakimovicz at Columbia/HCA, you have to develop a process and structure for getting it done right. And that takes adjustment on two sides.

Independent programmers and other consultants brought in from outside are used to a regular software development process and standards. That meant that Columbia/HCA had to develop clear guidelines about how the code was to be written and documented and follow a standard, sequential development process. As Yakimovicz says, "HTML and Web pages are so simple to create that we hadn't been using standards. As projects became more complex and fast-tracked, we recognized that we have to be able to manage the development process to assure consistency and maintain the product."

There's also constant tension between doing something exactly customized for a particular training challenge (probably a better training solution but slower and more costly) versus using materials already developed. The Columbia/HCA solution is to try to develop materials as they go along that can be used in later programs. There are also some presentation standards such as, no more than two frames per page, white page backgrounds, and logo on every page.

Here are some questions Ann Yakimovicz suggests you answer if you're considering developing your own Web-based training.

> Is the Web the appropriate medium? Lots of audio and video, for example, might mean that CD-ROM or a CD-Web hybrid would be more effective. Also, make sure the people you want to train have the access and skills they need.

> Do you have clear training specifications? These are often difficult to develop up front, and you'll probably need several tries to get it right. Build those into your process.

> How much material that you already have will work? This is a new medium, so just "throwing stuff over the wall" from classroom or computer-based courses will not work well. Look at what needs to be adapted and what must be redone.

Remember, Yakimovicz cautions, that it's not just the browser that you must consider. There's also all the background software, databases, Java applets, and so forth that have to work together.

She adds one more caution.

This *has* to be a team effort. There is no way that the level of expertise required to do this stuff can be put together by one person. Too much understanding [is required] of networked delivery systems, browser operations, programming, HTML markup, graphics, screen design, user interface design, content, and instructional design, not to mention management of that entire crazy group of people from various disciplines, various ways of thinking and working, and not understanding each other's viewpoints!

Now we'll add a caution of our own. This is possible for Columbia/HCA because it has an expert, Ann Yakimovicz, onboard. You need to have or bring in people familiar with training design, the unique aspects of the Web, and project management. That may be a team instead of a single person.

Sometimes, the solution is to look outside your company.

TRAINING PARTNERSHIPS

We're beginning to see outside vendors develop businesses around delivering training to highly specific groups. One of the most interesting comes from Princeton Learning Systems.

The business idea is based on the fact that almost every licensed profession has government requirements for continuing education as a condition of maintaining a license or certification. In addition to loss of license, there are also penalties for practicing the profession without a license. And, just to make things more interesting, the employer is often liable for penalties along with the employee. That presents two business needs: tracking continuing education compliance and providing the training to meet certification or licensing requirements.

That's exactly what Princeton Learning Systems' Financial Services University says it will do. The Internet-based service will work this way.

First, FSU will monitor continuing education requirements for each licensed employee. When the employee is near deadline, FSU will issue a warning to both the employee and his or her employer.

That's only part of the story since, up to this point, we've got a warning but nothing more. Financial Services University will go further by delivering, online, courses and approved tests necessary to meet the requirements. The courseware and testing materials come from content publishers.

The service is intended to be sold, at least in the beginning, only to companies. According to Steven Haase, PLS's vice president of planning, subscribing firms will be able to customize the program to their own special needs. They can even incorporate their own training programs if they want.

The first versions of FSU are aimed at the securities industry, but Princeton Learning plans others to follow for industries such as banking and insurance.

There are other training partnerships being forged as well. Drexel University, for example, provides courses in conjunction with several corporate partners. And many firms that have provided training for years are developing packages for use on corporate intranets, often on a site-license basis.

WHEN TRAINING ISN'T TRAINING AT ALL

Dianne Woods, vice president of global strategies and organizational development at Levi Strauss, has said, "In a learning organization, employees capture their knowledge and learning and make it widely accessible."

An intranet enables employees to work smarter and learn from one another. It enables them to collaborate in the exchange of knowledge, reinforcing and adding to what they learned in their earlier training so that they can respond more productively to their environment and do their jobs with increased effectiveness and efficiency.

Sometimes that informal learning is designed into the system, such as with Booz-Allen & Hamilton's Knowledge On-Line. At other times it grows out of idea-sharing processes in which sales representatives, for example, get together for virtual chats. And, sometimes, it develops out of formal idea-sharing programs, like Best Practices sharing.

Training as a Competitive Strategy

It's turning out that training that you deliver for your people may have another use. The Net/Web lets you extend your training outward to others in your value chain.

EXTRON ELECTRONICS

Not all networks are computer networks. There's the human kind as well. That's how Gary Kayye and Extron Electronics got into training on the net. Extron Electronics, where Kayye is vice president of Sales and Marketing, makes computer video presentation products.

Gary went to the University of North Carolina, where he was in a fraternity. One of the other members of that fraternity was Rich Gleeson. The two met at a Christmas party, began talking about UNC and about computers and the then-new World Wide Web. Gary hired Rich to head the MIS Department, and they kept talking.

They checked out the Web together, starting with the UNC page. And they talked about what you could do and what other people were doing and how they were doing it. Gary Kayye describes himself as a "semi-computer geek" who didn't know nearly as much as Rich. And Rich has a gift. He can explain things.

The two started playing with putting together a Web page for Extron. They'd sit up at night using programs like Internet Assistant to put the page together, sending revisions and thoughts back and forth by e-mail and chatting on the phone.

If this sounds a bit crude by today's standards, it was, but it worked. Extron rolled out a Web page, the first English page in the industry, at the Info Com, the industry trade show. It really was a first. Big players in the business like Sony didn't have a presence at all at that time. Mitsubishi had a page but it was in Japanese.

Through a deal with Netcom, Extron began distributing disks that helped dealers, distributors, and other manufacturers get on the Web. The default page on the Web Cruiser browser on the disk was Extron's. Everyone who signed on got to see that page.

Extron was putting product information and monthly specials and other information on its site but, within a year, everyone was doing the same thing. The competitive advantage, Gary thought, could lie in training.

Dealers and even end users will be able to schedule themselves for video training on the Net, using new technology that allows the participant to get the training at whatever speed of connection they have. For example, a user with a slow modem connection would get a slide show presentation, whereas a person with a T1 line would get streaming video. The content grows out of training Extron already does in such things as how to set up video projectors, but it will be available on the Net.

What's the benefit here? The training materials are already together, and so development costs are low. The strategy is an extension of what Extron's already been doing, and it's based on information sharing that pulls products through the supply chain.

That's one way to start, by training those outside. Sometimes the development moves in the opposite direction, as it did at Marshall Industries.

MARSHALL INDUSTRIES

Marshall Industries, from El Monte, California, uses the Net to train its own people but also to train people from its partner companies. The development sequence was a bit different than Extron's. Originally, Marshall put the training online for its own people. This training was in a variety of areas. Some of it was technical. But some was in basic administrative or person-to-person skills. It was good enough that Marshall's partners wanted in on the action.

Marshall now uses its extranet to provide training programs for people outside its own company, who participate just as if they were Marshall employees. What's the benefit? Cementing an already strong business alliance and building value in the relationship between customers or suppliers and Marshall.

TACTICS

Here's how to apply our TACTICS system when reviewing the recruiting and training area in your business and this chapter.

THINK LINKS

When you're thinking about links in this area, look for ways to extend more links and to enrich the links you have. Look for the ability to cast a wider net in recruiting. Look for the ability to extend training to more people within the organization or even to people outside it. When you think links, consider setting up hyperlinks to:

- An online library of the corporate curriculum that contains details of all development activities for each skill or behavior required by the corporate framework, possibly with hyperlinks and a search system for related current and legacy information on what is needed.

- Frequently asked questions (FAQ) documents available on all jobs, designed to be a self-educating reference and reinforcement tool by answering the typical questions of new hires.

- An internal job-posting system that allows employees to search for, apply for, and request job opportunities throughout the business.

AUTOMATE

Automate your recruiting by finding ways for the system to handle some of the routine screening tasks and ways to design your processes for self-screening. For example, when we asked Lorraine Darrell, the marketing director of the Arkansas Federal Credit Union, about her credit union's use of recruitment on its Web site, she said,

> Whenever we advertise for positions in the newspaper, we say, "To apply for this job, visit any branch office or fax your résumé to this number." Now we've added, "Visit our Web site" with its address. We recently advertised for the position of purchasing manager. We received 14 applications via the Web site. And the individual who got the job was one of those applicants who used the Web site. You can imagine that we, as a credit union that is deep into technology, would require our employees to understand how to use a computer and the Win-

dows environment. If someone has gone to our Web site to apply for a job, we feel pretty safe that they know how to turn a computer on and can navigate.

Automate the training task by delivering appropriate training in an automated form. Make it possible for people to get the training, participate in it, and receive feedback without necessarily having to involve another person unless it's necessary for the training function.

CUSTOMIZE

Customize your recruiting and training functions by giving people both the technological options and the wealth of information that let them develop a solution that's right for them.

In the case of training, the kind of Net technology applications you use to conduct training over the intranet/extranet/Internet is heavily dependent on two issues: (1) the bandwidth at which your end user (trainee) will access the Net and (2) how wide an array of dissimilar levels of technology you and your end user have available to you.

It is important to customize how you deliver training based on both the speed of your targeted training group connection to the Net and the varying levels of technological equipment they are using. You can conduct a formal or informal survey to determine what your situation is and what your approach is to delivering training over the Net.

For example, Marshall Industries conducted a survey and discovered that people showing up on their Web site had the capability of connecting at higher bandwidth than they thought (56 kps on average), which enabled them to take advantage of Net technology applications like streaming video. Columbia/HCA had the challenge of conducting training in a wide array of technology of varying levels and, thus, in most cases, lower bandwidth, so that they had to meet and adapt to this challenge by using basic text Web hyperlinking and e-mail discussion groups. Extron implemented a system that allowed the end user to receive the training content and presentation adapted in three different formats based on three different levels of bandwidth connection on which the end user was accessing the Net.

TRANSFORM

Transform data into information and information into knowledge by looking at ways to share resources that are already available in your organization and in your business partners. You can achieve this transformation by giving people opportunities to use interactive push and pull Net applications such as:

- Real audio with streaming audio and video presentations.

- Webcasting systems, such as Pointcast, designed to deliver customized information to the employee.

- Real-time chat, forums, e-mail discussion groups, and news-groups focused on various special-interest topics or around discussing course topics.

INSIDE/OUTSIDE

Go inside/outside. Take information from your recruiting efforts outside, including those you gather on the Net, and make them available inside and organizationwide. The Credit Union Executives Society supports its member credit unions with a link off its public Web site home page to an area entitled Job Postings. There you can find two primary links. One link is to Positions Available, where credit unions from all across the country list job openings they have, and the other link is to Positions Wanted, where anyone can submit a request for a particular type of job by describing what they are looking for and including a brief résumé. Lockheed Martin has a searchable positions available on its Web site and a virtual place on its Web site, where employees can enter detailed descriptions of the kind of jobs they are looking for.

Look at training as something that's often not limited by the firewall. Extron Electronics is setting up its training application off its public Web site to service its dealer network. Gary Kayye, Extron's vice president of marketing and sales, said, "We are known to do videoconferencing training on our World Wide Web page. So, what we're going to do is we're going to train our industry through the

World Wide Web. We're going to set up a training schedule that you'll be able to download, and you'll be able to schedule yourself for either a full video bandwidth conference, a full download video-conference, a partial download videoconference, or an Internet conference."

CORE FUNCTIONS/BIG PAYOFFS

The big payoff in hard dollars for both recruiting and training is probably the reduction in travel costs. Other big advantages in efficiency result from better choices and information being available all over the company.

A big training payoff that no one's found a way to measure yet is the benefit that comes from people having training information available when they need it. There's a clear saving if a person with a question about a procedure can get the answer when it's needed without bringing in someone else. Staffing costs drop. And the operation itself will be smoother with less "learning downtime."

START NOW

Start now to consider two big payoff possibilities: travel reduction and quick access to information that answers basic how-to questions. Then, get beyond that to more sophisticated and partner applications. Be sure to check out the off-the-shelf training development and training materials, as well as turnkey training solutions.

Always keep in mind that, for best results, it is critical that you see early on that this technology is too complex for one person to do it all. You really can't go to the training department and say, "Here, buy some software. You all can start doing Web-based training." Because, in order to put this together, you really need people who have a computer programming background, a graphical user interface background, an instructional design background, and a graphics multimedia kind of background. It's just too complex for one person, or even a couple of people, to know. And it has to be very carefully designed in order to get really effective training out of it.

You're no longer in a situation where a trainer standing up in front of a group of people can recognize that people aren't getting it. You can add additional examples or get some discussion going. The interaction is primarily between the learner and the content and, to a smaller extent, between learners in chat rooms, for instance, so that you have both real-time and asynchronous chat—and possibly with a conference moderator. But, because you really don't have the traditional kind of communication going on, the material has to be very carefully orchestrated.

That means that you have a larger team, a multidisciplinary team, and you have to manage your team's activities rigorously. You have to know everything that's going on as you generate new files, you have to track the versions, you have to make sure that your files transfer back and forth correctly, and you have to look at applications that can tie into each other.

WALLY AND JEFF'S RECRUITING AND TRAINING LESSONS LEARNED

1. A lot of recruiting happens in the public arena. Use your public Web presence to tell prospective employees who you are, what you do, and what you value. Also, look at ways to tie your recruiting efforts to other public relations efforts that are based on your Web site.

2. Companies we looked at that did recruiting on the Net didn't neglect internal recruiting. Don't miss the opportunity your intranet offers to make people already on-board aware of job openings. They might be interested but, even if they're not, they're in a position to refer people.

3. The Net offers you many great training opportunities, but remember that training on the Net is different from classroom training. Make sure you've got good design, delivery, and support for your Net training efforts.

4. We saw companies taking advantage of the intranet to deliver training exactly when people needed it. The ter-

minology varied. Some people didn't call it training, they called it job aids or reference material, but it had the same effect. People who needed information about how to do their jobs more effectively got it from the Web.

5. Training on the Net can cut travel and expense costs dramatically. But even the most ardent Net trainers aren't replacing all classroom or conference training with Net-based training. There's still a need for people to get the social benefits that go with conference attendance.

6. We saw several instances of companies using the intranet to tell people about internal training offerings and to handle the registration process. Don't forget that the intranet can offer you the opportunity to get feedback from people who've taken training. Then you can use that feedback to improve the courses as well as to tell others about the benefits.

7. Don't miss opportunities to develop training on your intranet. Roll out a prototype. Get some feedback. Modify the program.

8. Deere, Financial Services Corporation, Booz-Allen & Hamilton, Columbia/HCA, and Cadence Design Systems all reported varying degrees of difficulty in educating people about what their Net-based system could do. Many employees who lack computer skills will need trainer-driven seminars and hands-on coaching to develop their comfort level with your Net-based system and make maximum productive use of it. Training on how to use your Net-based technology system productively will need to be high on your priority list and should be incorporated into your budget early.

9. This technology lets you do more rapid prototyping training, which is a real advantage. You can put prototyped training programs out on the Web and get immediate feedback via e-mail. This allows you to do much more testing and refining of your training activities.

CHAPTER 6

ENHANCING SALES EFFECTIVENESS

"Nothing happens until someone sells something."

It's true. Without sales, there is no business. That's why, over the years, the selling function has become separate and specialized in many companies. Even in a small company like a one-person consulting firm or design firm, you don't last long if you can't find a way to get the sales done.

So it's not that selling is more important today than it was years ago. It's just that it's gotten harder.

We're not talking about selling things on the Web. There are people doing that, but what we're going to deal with here is how you use Net technology to enhance the effectiveness of your sales force.

CRITICAL CHALLENGES OF ENHANCING SALES EFFECTIVENESS

Today's businesses must enhance the effectiveness of their sales force in a hypercompetitive, worldwide, and speeded-up economy. What are the key challenges? There are four primary challenges you can use Internet technology to solve. These are to:

1. Manage, coach, train, and inform a sales force that only makes your company look good when it's selling, often in the field away from your office

2. Disseminate timely, updated product and service information, often over wide, even global, geographical territories

3. Deal with special selling challenges, like major joint calls, and trade shows, and with the special problems of retail sales.

One of the critical challenges in sales today is that so much of it happens outside the office, on the road. One estimate is that 40% of the U.S. workforce is on the road at any given time and a large proportion of that force turns out to be salespeople. That poses a dilemma for management. If you bring those salespeople into the office, you can share information with them fairly easily and effectively. While that's going on, though, no one is selling anything.

Whether you're the new person on the team or the experienced pro, having timely, updated product and service information can make or break a deal. The second critical challenge that's out there today in sales is that, increasingly, customers expect salespeople to know their stuff when they show up.

There was a time when it wasn't that way for new young salespeople. They could show up carrying a kit and speak to the person handling purchases for a customer and tell them that they were new and learning the ropes and maybe even get some help. But the word from the front lines is that this is true in fewer and fewer cases. Purchasing agents have gotten more sophisticated, sales have gotten more complex, and salespeople have to know their stuff earlier.

With downsizing, reengineering, and all those other buzzwords, there are also fewer salespeople handling more accounts these days. In order to be more effective, they need information. That's especially important as the cost of a face-to-face sales call soars.

Salespeople often need to be briefed on the client situation as well as on their own material before going in to make a sale. And, the more complex the sale, the more important that briefing process is. All this adds up to the importance of both the experienced pro and the new person having timely, updated information that can be tailored immediately to the prospective customers' needs.

The third area of challenge is what fast-growing sales organization have always faced—meeting quotas, generating leads, training new salespeople about how to sell the right product to the right customer at the right time, and adding 20 to 50 new representatives every year.

The fourth critical challenge facing companies today is to reduce the costs of their selling efforts. With the average face-to-face sales call now costing $400 or more in many industries, businesses have to find ways to cut costs. That means that you want those expensive calls to be as productive as possible. In the heat of a competitive sales situation, you want your salespeople to have the knowledge, skills, and tools that will optimize their ability to help a potential customer make a decision in your company's favor. And all this needs to be done in the least expensive way possible without sacrificing the quality of your salesforce's efforts.

As always, there are special selling challenges. For industrial companies, that can be coordinating efforts for a major call or a trade show. Retail stores need to drive quality traffic to their locations. Professional services organizations need to make their processes more efficient and build referral networks.

SOLUTIONS

Let's see how some of the organizations we talked to when we were doing our research for this book are supporting their sales using Net technology.

STARTING FROM A GREEN SCREEN

For Financial Services Corporation, the whole Net and Web adventure began with an attempt to upgrade the system. According to Marketing Manager Susan Wood, FSC was considering moving from an older, command-line interface, green-screen kind of system to a graphical user interface or Windows type of system.

It was at that point that Helen Prater, head of information services, came to Susan and said, "I think there's something you ought to look at." At about that time they also heard from Chris Johns, who is one of FSC's field associates, that Web-based technology might be something FSC would want in order to accomplish its objectives.

Susan Wood said, "So we actually went onto the Web. And, at that point—this was probably the beginning of March—I had never been out on the Web. I had never been out on the Internet. I'm a marketing person. I don't do technical stuff. We did go out and we looked at some existing sites. ... we went in and looked at what the application was. I said our problems are solved, I think this will do what we need and will give us what we want."

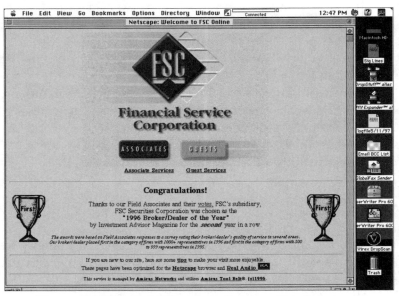

Figure 6.1 Financial Services Corporation home page.

The something that Helen Prater had spoken about was the World Wide Web, which turned out to be the answer for where FSC was going to go to help support its corporate objectives and sales efforts. The company has set up an intranet, with an extranet that is accessible from the Web by its field affiliates and business partners using a Web browser and inputting the appropriate password and user ID.

When we asked Susan Wood about how FSC planned to offset the costs of setting up an extranet/intranet system, she began talking about goals: "... for example, one of the goals that marketing has is retention. How do you retain your customers? ... Our field associates are our best source for providing services to increase our customer retention. ... We try to give them the very best service that they can get."

She went on to discuss what that means from a field person's perspective: "If I'm a salesperson, I need to work when I need to work. That means having information available when I need it, and that means having information in a format that's easy for me to understand."

The information that's available on the Web is always the most current information. That's especially important in a business that's highly regulated. There are cost savings as well. "We're not going to be sending out all this paper. And if we're not sending out all this paper, that's going to be an expense we don't have. Now, are we going to make money from that? No, we're going to offset the cost of implementing the technology."

Financial Services Corporation has 60 business partners and serves over 1400 independent business consultants with financial products. They're part of what Dennis Passovoy, president and CEO of Amicus Networks, calls the food chain in financial services. Amicus is the company that helped FSC set up its system.

When we talked to Dennis Passovoy about this, he said,

If you think of the food chain within the securities industry—and it's really the same in the insurance industry—it is represented by a typical three-tier distribution model. You have a manufacturer, a distributor, and a retailer. If you look at the securities market where FSC operates, the manufacturer or wholesaler would be Kemper, Putnam, Fidelity, any of those companies that create mutual fund or annuity products. You come down one level to the distributor and that's where you find the broker/dealer—that's FSC. They distribute downstream to financial planners or independent representatives,

who then in turn, sell securities products to protect our retire-
ment or our children's college education.

The job of FSC, then, is to support the people down the chain that
actually sell the products. That sounds like a pretty simple and
straightforward task but, like many in business, it's simple but it's
not easy.

As Susan Wood says, FSC began with a couple of assumptions.
The first of those was that some employees and field associates
were not going to get onboard early. The second assumption was
that the top producers would be the people most likely to seize on
anything that would give them any kind of competitive advantage.

MOTIVATING AFFILIATES TO USE THE EXTRANET

When we asked Susan what kind of adoption rate FSC had going currently she said, "Based on the kind of information that we have, I'm
saying FSC's adoption rate is approximately 10 percent of our customers and approximately 60 percent of our production. Remember
the old 80/20 rule, what we're finding is that the 20 percent of the
field associates that makes 80 percent of the money is adopting the
extranet system."

That's true not just in the securities business. We did some research for a wholesale distributor in the construction trades. That
distributor sells directly to contractors and the question that the
distributor was interested in was how many of the contractors had
the capability of, and interest in, using a Web site. We found that
less than half of the contractors who were already customers of the
distributor fell into that category. But that wasn't the significant
finding. We also found that more than three-quarters of the top 20%
of contractors (as measured by their sales and profitability) had
Web capability and interest.

So FSC set about to bring people onboard. Sometimes, the methods are fairly subtle. Information on some performance measures is
sent to everyone, but it's available first through the secure Web site.
That means that the people with Web access get the information
ahead of those who don't. That's an incentive to sign on.

Financial Services also decided that it was best to make the information available on the Web site in ways similar to the way it had been made available on paper. What that meant was that the initial versions of the FSC Web site were actually laid out in a pretty linear form. The information was there, but people would have to drill down several levels to get it.

As the site develops, it will become less linear. It will become easier for visitors to jump from one place to another without going though a series of menus. Keyword searching across various areas of the site is likely to become possible.

FSC has also dealt with the issue of updating. The answer here has been to update sensitive and important parts of the site more frequently than others. That means that, while most updates on the site are handled three to four times a week or so, updates to the trading desk portion of the site happen three to five times per business day.

AN INSIDE VIEW OF FSC'S EXTRANET SITE MAP

Susan Wood describes the kind of sales support information FSC posts on its extranet site to enhance the effectiveness of its sales force.

> We put out what I would call sales support information. I can check mutual fund news. I can see if any of our preferred business partners have happened to have changes in their mutual funds. Maybe a manager left or somebody new came onboard or there's something new happening at that company ... or information on some of the mutual fund variable annuity, etc., products. That kind of information I would call sales support information. We also provide them with some marketing information ... some things you could do if you wanted to sell more. And we also give them a pretty significant area to network with each other, to learn a little bit about each other's practices, find out sort of what the successful people do, etc.

That was in the beginning, but FSC's site is evolving (Figure 6.2 and 6.3). Now FSC is adding significant chunks of what it calls sales support material, that is, operational information that FSC needs to do the day-to-day field office administration and information required by the regulatory agencies.

Figure 6.2 FSC extranet entrance.

Figure 6.3 FSC extranet site map.

Financial Services Corporation's goal is to provide information and links, along with other support, that help the individual affiliates sell more financial products. It's just about that simple. Here's how it works.

The site provides the ability for field networking, ways for individual affiliates to contact each other. That gives them the ability to ask questions, share information, and pick up tips. Those tips can be of several different kinds. One kind might be in-depth information about how a particular product can be tailored to a particular customer's needs. But it might also include insight from another affiliate about how the presentation of that product can be made in order to make it more likely to result in a sale.

Part of this happens in the virtual conference rooms that are available to affiliates, as well as several of what FSC calls Q&A sections, where the affiliates and partners can go to find information about things they're interested in, such as commissions. But it's also where information about products and in-depth information about techniques and other things are available as well. There's also the ability for individual affiliates to order support literature and to pick up information about new compliance requirements.

The end result is that the site supports the building of knowledgeable affiliates and partners. And knowledgeable as a term that is chosen carefully because it refers to the knowledge that's sharable because, very often, the people who have knowledge are not in competition with the people who need it. They're selling in a particular geographical area or a particular niche market and can easily share what they know. While that's not true for every company, it's a powerful benefit in situations like FSC.

By using the conference rooms and field networking possibilities, FSC builds the ability of an individual affiliate to gather knowledge that's inherent in the heads of other affiliates and put it to use. This kind of information could almost come under the heading of training. What you call it isn't important, but the sharing and individual salesperson development is.

That's what we saw all our sales support people trying to do, leverage knowledge in their sales force so that it was easier to pass around and increase collaboration between affiliates so as to make sales more effective.

All the systems that we're talking about here that allow for individual participation let individual salespeople share information about what works and what doesn't—that stuff about how to close hard sales or deal with difficult clients, how to use the individual services or products that their company makes available, how to present those products and services in a way that's most effective, and even how to use the compensation system most effectively.

Susan Wood was very candid about her thoughts regarding the return on investment FSC was receiving from its investment in their extranet. She said FSC used to send regular product and compliance information to the affiliates, who were supposed to put it in a reference binder, but they didn't. What usually happened was that, when they needed to consult the binder, the envelope was often still untouched on the shelf, and all they had was outdated information. Sometimes, they would have to take time while a customer was waiting to hunt for the envelope or play telephone tag to get it from headquarters.

Now that FSC has an extranet, product and compliance updates are incorporated electronically into the existing documents, so that current information—and only current information—is readily available to all affiliates at all locations. FSC reduces its liability costs for things like bad commission information that goes out, bad information on products that goes out, information from a compliance or regulatory standpoint that just simply gets old in the field associates offices.

GETTING ACCOUNT INFORMATION WHERE AND WHEN IT'S USABLE

One sales manager at IBM has his people collect what he calls "fun facts." A fun fact is something about a particular client or application that the salesperson finds interesting. Collecting it, in this case, means putting it on the corporate information system tied to the application or to the client. That means that the information is available the next time that salesperson goes out on a call on the same client. It's also available if someone else has to make the call. It's also available to inside salespeople when the customer calls in with a question or comment.

A salesperson might make note, for example, that a particular customer is interested in a specific feature set. If that information is available to the inside salespeople the next time the customer calls, they know which features to stress from the array of features available and which benefits matter most to the customer.

That's knowledge, how to apply information in an effective way. Cadence Design Systems was another company that needed to find ways to apply knowledge in diverse sales situations. Cadence is a leading supplier of electronic design automation software. Right now, you may be thinking, "Oh yeah, software—that's not what I do." But wait for a second. The problem facing Cadence Design was similar to almost every industrial sales company we've encountered.

Cadence's move to using the intranet for information began with the understanding that its clients increasingly expected a consultative selling process. As with other companies, the customers were expecting the salesperson to show up and act as a consultant. They were expecting this salesperson to understand the product line in depth, understand their particular needs, and understand the process of putting the two together without using a hard sell. They were looking for sales processes based on consultation and relationships, like those long advocated by sales trainers like Mack Hanan, Jim Cathcart, and others, as well as the authors of this book.

At the same time, the learning time that could be allowed for a salesperson to be productive was shortening dramatically. Cadence's representatives needed an in-depth understanding of a broad product line (over 1000 products and services), and they needed it pretty much from the first call.

Now, support had been available to the sales force before the intranet. There had always been sales managers. There had always been experienced salespeople who could share their information and knowledge. The difference, according to Tim Herbert, director of worldwide sales operations, was that "people supported the sales reps on a point-to-point basis that relied on individual personal relationships that took time to build."

That simply wouldn't work anymore, especially with Cadence adding over 40 new sales representatives every year. What Cadence needed was consistent, valuable, and focused information available to a sales force that might not yet have developed the personal contacts to get it for themselves.

As Barry Demak, manager of sales operations, said, "The challenge was to build an infrastructure where any sales rep can access the collective knowledge of the organization." Cadence went after a Web-based single point of information that supported the sales organization.

Working with a company called Sage Solutions, Cadence developed OnTrack, a system that uses a home page with links to other pages, information sources, and applications to help a sales representative at any point in the sales process.

What's available? All kinds of things, from customer presentations, sample letters, and internal forms through advice from other sales representatives and people in management. The people that provide the information are responsible for keeping it current and accurate in the OnTrack system.

The big advantage to OnTrack of using Web technology was that it was a known and usable system. That enabled Cadence to focus on the sales process and bring about a reengineering of the sales process without having to worry about whether the technology being used to support it was learnable and usable by its sales force.

Cadence also made a decision early on to design a process and infrastructure that could deal with 80% of the possible sales situations rather than 100%. That scaled the project down to the doable and made it possible to move right out on implementation.

Overall, Cadence's Netscape-based system:

- Maps out each step of the sales cycle with links to sales support resources.

- Uses Netscape forms to facilitate communications with headquarters.

- Allows global account teams to share information securely.

- Provides an easy-to-find repository of sales tools and reference materials.

- Includes links to competitors' and customers' Web sites.

- Accesses and distributes a daily news feed on the industry.

SHORTENING THE LEARNING CURVE FOR SALES REPRESENTATIVES

The biggest effect from Cadence's point of view, is shortening the learning curve for a new sales representative. One of them says that he "learned in two days from OnTrack what it took months to learn [at a previous company]." When referring to Cadence Design System's ROI, IDC said, in its 1996 ROI study, "For a new sales rep, each month lost to training is a month of not reaching quota." After surveying the sales force, reductions in the time to become a fully capable sales representative ranged from two to four months. With 40 new representatives hired in the first year, and 40 planned for each of the next two years, reducing the ramp-up time for new sales representatives will have a substantial impact on additional profits to Cadence.

To calculate the value of this shortened learning curve, International Data Corporation focused on the additional initial profit generated by a new sales rep that was now able to meet quota in two months rather than the four months it took before the implementation of OnTrack. That profit came out to be $2,463,395!

A sales support system at Hewlett Packard does similar things. There a sales representative starts by entering the names of the products that a customer might be interested in. The system feeds back potential questions, answers, product descriptions, and system configurations. This is another example of getting the key information to the salespeople in a form they can use at the time they need it.

SETTING UP KNOWLEDGE EXCHANGE NETWORKS

Wang Software went through quite a process to grow their intranet sales support system, creating culture change out of an information problem.

When Wang Laboratories went through bankruptcy, it unloaded a lot of debt, along with 7000 employees. That left Wang Software about as lean as could be—understaffed, in fact. The field sales operation functioned on a kind of ad hoc basis, and support, especially information, was scarce. Continuing complaints from the field about not having the information to make sales drove the company to take action.

In charge of sales operations was Ralph Jordan, and the problem fell in his lap. He and Neena Mathur, the project manager, decided on two key goals for the new system they were going to design. It would have to get the right information from corporate to the field when the representatives needed it. And it would have to allow them to share their experience, insights, and information with each other and with the company.

They called the intranet they developed the Wang Knowledge Exchange. Putting the project together meant overcoming a number of internal barriers. One of these was a boss who felt Lotus Notes was a better solution than the intranet Jordan wanted and needed. Another was the need to go to outside vendors rather than using the corporate IS staff. The development process itself was riddled with problems, glitches, and bugs.

Oh yes, and, when the vendor contracts were signed, Jordan and his team had less than a month to bring the project together. They rolled the bare-bones system out at the annual sales meeting. There were 200 documents on it. Then they set about really developing it.

Sales representatives sent e-mail about how the system should work. Every suggestion got a reply.

What was going on was a culture change. At Wang, as at lots of other companies, you produce information once and then people use it. But, with the new system, authors of information were accessible and could expect questions.

Some of the keys were involvement along the way by all sorts of people who would participate in the new system. There was a lot of internal selling and persuasion. There were training sessions. Those who participated with suggestions and content were praised. Contribution to the Knowledge Exchange was made part of job descriptions. And just to apply a bit more pressure, other information sources, like newsletters, were discontinued.

One effect was to make cooperation an important and desirable attitude in sales and elsewhere at Wang. Another was the considerable benefit of getting information to the field when it's most helpful. *WebMaster* magazine quotes Wang sales rep Jeff Hausdorf, "I can be in a hotel in Dallas on a Thursday and download data sheets for a presentation for the next day. Plain and simple, I wouldn't have been able to do that [before Knowledge Exchange]. It's like the information chain has been cut down to one link."

These are global approaches to a companywide sales support process. We also forced several specific applications involving trade show support, front-loading the sales call, driving customers to a retail site, and using Web-available information to support a sales process.

TRADE SHOW PLANNING USING THE NET

Probably the most complex and star-studded trade show in the world is the Paris Air Show. Every couple of years, the world's aerospace and defense firms get together in Paris to show off their gear and woo the buyers of their expensive and sophisticated systems, up to and including heads of state. It's something like a normal trade show on steroids when it comes to a need for preparation and sales.

Because Lockheed takes part in a number of trade shows—of which the Paris Air Show is probably the kingpin—Lockheed has developed, on their intranet Web site, a section for trade show assistance. It starts with a huge contact database listing of all the shows, which business units are going to participate, and which individuals at the business unit are responsible for which products. People planning for the show can get lots of information here. They can download the actual graphics for the panels that are going to be in the show, which can help them save time and maintain the proper corporate look in their materials. They can find out what other business units are going to bring, so that effort isn't duplicated. If they don't see a photograph they need right away, there's access to the corporate photographic archives which contain over 5000 photographs of Lockheed Martin products and services, along with caption information, so that pictures are properly and accurately identified.

The Internet is also used to coordinate show planning and schedules, sometimes with a minute-by-minute schedule for top executives and their contacts with possible buyers.

DIGITAL SUPPORTS SALES ACTIVITIES WITH ITS WEB SITE

On a less grandiose scale, consider Digital Equipment Corporation. Digital sells different kinds of computer equipment, and some of it is quite sophisticated. Digital has used its external Web site as a way to front-load the sales process. Here's how it works.

Visitors to the Digital Equipment site who are interested in purchasing a system have access to thousands of product specification sheets, information forms, and other information. In addition, they can actually prepare their own quotes, good for 60 days, for a Digital system. This supports sales in a couple of ways. The first is that the basic kinds of information sharing that go into a system purchase are actually getting done in an automated way without the sales representative needing to be present. At the same time, if customers or prospects are interested in quotes on Digital's computer equipment, that information is also provided by the sales representative making the call. It can become a sophisticated point for follow-up and leads.

This works in other situations as well. Stanford Federal Credit Union has a number of "calculators" on its Web site. People who are interested in a mortgage loan can use the mortgage loan calculator to see how payments work out and whether they might qualify. Lots of that browsing happens at night, after 10 P.M., and on weekends, when the credit union isn't open. But the information about who's been checking out mortgage loan possibilities among the credit union membership can produce a solid lead for a loan officer to follow up on Monday.

OK, what if you sell some stuff at retail, or what if you sell an individual personal service? How are companies like that using the Web and Web technology to be more effective?

PROVIDING INFORMATION TO SET UP RETAIL SALES

Take a look at Goodyear. They make tires. They're the ones with the blimp. If you visit Goodyear's Web site, you'll find the blimp and a whole lot more.

First, there are the kinds of things that help you establish

Goodyear in your mind as an expert on tires. There's the usual array of information about what products are available and what their features and benefits are. But Goodyear has gone one step further and put a "tire school" on its site.

At the tire school, visitors can find information about wear factors, tread depth, and what kinds of tire patterns are best for specific situations. More knowledgeable consumers, who understand when they need a more sophisticated or expensive product, are more likely to buy it than if they feel they're being sold by whatever salesperson happened to be available when they walked in the front door of the store.

In addition, Goodyear, like other large retail companies such as Wal-Mart and Saturn Automobiles, has a store locator program to help people find a local dealer. Support sites such as Vicinity.com provide a support for Web sites that want to have store locator functions that result in simple maps. A "store locator" is a search engine program that allows site visitors to easily search and find store locations by entering zip code, city, or state they want to find a store in.

Other small retail stores are finding a way to support their sales on the Web by actually making sales at that point. Even in a small or relatively unsophisticated store, a Web site can be used to take orders for the kind of reorder merchandise that most businesses have. A music retailer, for example, might use a Web site as a place to take reorders for guitar strings or frets. In this case, the customer would already know what they're getting, have a relationship with the store, and find the Web a convenient way to order, sometimes at times when the store is not open.

Another powerful sales support technique is strategy the "bet you can't eat just one" principle. A great example of that can be found on the Web site www.platinumrule.com. This site was developed by the Expertise Center, located at www.expertcenter.com and founded by one of the authors of this book, to help Dr. Tony Alessandra support sales of his book *The Platinum Rule*, www.platinumrule.com, which is about how people interact in business using some basic social styles. Want to find out what your style is? Just go to the site. The site gives you the opportunity to check out your own style as well as the style of others and to receive some advice.

How does that help support sales? In this case, the Web site is being used as a way to show people how the technique in the book and other training support materials can help them be more effective. They get the opportunity to "try it before they buy it." And that makes it more likely that they'll buy.

Then, of course, there are all the standard reasons why a Web site helps sales for individual consulting practices. The site is available 24 hours a day, seven days a week. It allows people to find the information they're interested in on their own time and in their own way. It allows the consultant or author or expert to put up on the site far more information and greater variety than could be put in a press kit and to reach several specific niche groups.

In its Customer Profiles, Netscape Communications reports, "In large global corporations, it can be challenging to share timely information across the enterprise. For a pharmaceutical firm like Eli Lilly & Company, the ability for all employees to easily access vital company information can provide a significant competitive advantage." Lilly—headquartered in Indianapolis, Indiana—develops, manufactures, and sells pharmaceutical products in 150 countries worldwide.

"We have 27,700 employees around the world. It's often difficult to keep people informed about what's going on in the company," says John Swartzendruber, of Lilly's Internet services department. "People often don't know what is happening in other departments because they can't find the information."

With the advent of the World Wide Web, Lilly saw a powerful technology that might help alleviate some communications challenges. The company formed an Internet services department to use the Web to create an internal virtual information network. The result is ELVIS—the Eli Lilly Virtual Information Service. "The goal of ELVIS is to make information easily available to everyone who needs it," says Swartzendruber. "It's an internal distributed information system based on Internet technology."

Imagine the shipping and the printing costs that Eli Lilly's marketing department saves when it needs to distribute new sales information to 300 salespeople around the world, not to mention the competitive position it gives the salespeople in an industry where product updates and challenges happen daily. With pre-Net systems, when a customer needed certain details about drugs, the salesperson had to take valuable selling time to track it; now it is seconds away in ELVIS's searchable database.

A Web site doesn't have to be a big deal in terms of hardware and technological sophistication. Consider the Pritikin Diet Centers. Pritikin is well known in the United States for its diet and exercise programs intended to extend a vigorous life. To the rest of the world though, Pritikin is something of an unknown. The sales challenge is to generate referrals from professionals such as physicians, dietitians, and exercise physiologists. Pritikin makes increasing referrals possible by letting authorized professionals access its database of articles about life extension. The articles help the professionals and create the image that Pritikin seeks as a helpful partner and a good referral.

The system runs on a single outside server and is managed by Pritikin's service provider. Not a lot of tech, but enough to extend and enhance a global sales reach.

SCANNING FOR OPPORTUNITY

Another way in which Web technology supports sales efforts in businesses is finding public information and getting it to people involved in the sales effort. One sales manager we know at a major electronics company does just that. He uses a clipping service on the Net to scour the newswires for stories about companies that might buy the components his people sell. When those clippings arrive in his e-mail box, he e-mails them, and with his comments, to the salespeople who work for him.

We also see individual salespeople using clipping services, news services like Pointcast, and the search services on public sites like Excite to keep up with critical industry and client information. One technique we've seen several people use is to set up a clipping file, or search criterion, for company names of key clients and prospects. It's simple and very effective.

From simple e-mail forwarding to elaborate intranets with sales support as their primary goals, businesses are using Net and Web technology to enhance and support sales.

TACTICS

Let's examine how our tactics apply to enhancing sales effectiveness.

THINK LINKS

As you think about the links that help support the sales process, think about who has the kind of information and the kind of knowledge that your salespeople need. Then, look at ways to forge links from them to the salesperson.

Some of those links might be on an "interrupt" basis. An e-mail system could alert a specific group of salespeople, through their desktop e-mail or through their digital pagers, that a key client is expected at the plant or the office tomorrow and could supply details about the schedule.

Some of those links will be on as as-needed basis. Databases that include information about client and buyer preferences or about complaint, maintenance, repair, or service histories can be made available so that salespeople can search them when and as they need them.

AUTOMATE

Try to automate the processes that get the information across those links. Searchable databases and knowledge bases mean that only the person needing the information is involved in the process of retrieving it.

CUSTOMIZE

And look for ways to customize material automatically. Give people the tools to tie bits of information together and share them with others. We discussed one of the best examples of this earlier in this chapter—Cadence Design System's OnTrack guide to its sales process.

One of Netscape's Customer Profiles on Cadence describes the OnTrack System this way: "The OnTrack system maps out each phase of the sales cycle, including how to work with Cadence's in-house consulting group and other corporate resources." Barry De-mak, manager of worldwide sales automation projects, said, "For example, one section points sales reps to Netscape-based forms that they can submit electronically to request a local seminar. This request is routed to the appropriate group at headquarters and kicks off the planning process for a seminar campaign. ... You don't have to be at Cadence for three years to know who to call to get something done."

Fujitsu Limited, an international electronics and computer technology giant, has one of the largest and most successful intranet implementations in the world. Pre-Intranet Fujitsu's sales division used to conduct all its information transactions using paper. Now they have a pipeline connecting their headquarters, dealers, sales offices, and related companies. The intranet application, named SARFIN, enables its many users to access it for sales information related to new products, pricing, sales strategies, dealer information, and competitor intelligence. Netscape's Customer Profile on Fujitsu reports, "The sales force can use the application to research sample business cases, access tools for making effective visual presentations, and evaluate product combinations to determine which Fujitsu products will work best for a customer's particular needs."

Another example of the customize TACTIC is the extranet that Financial Services Corporation has set up for its affiliates (independent field sales agents), which has everything from forums, where they discuss tough sales situations, to updated mutual funds and annuities available on the trading desk of their extranet system.

TRANSFORM

Transforming data into information and information into knowledge is a key tactic in supporting and enhancing sales. In most organizations, the knowledge that makes for a successful sale is out there in the heads of people who've been making those sales for a while. That includes knowledge about products and applications but also about buyers and their histories with the company. Find ways to make that knowledge available, either in raw form so that people can get it on their own, or by pointing them to the critical human resource within the organization that has the information or knowledge needed.

INSIDE/OUTSIDE

Inside your organization is the knowledge and information that resides in the people's heads. There's also access to the latest product or service information. Outside are a variety of information sources that your people can monitor for leads, competitive information, and background. One way to bring those together is to create your own newsletter for salespeople. Deliver it by e-mail or post it on the Net, but bring together the best from inside and outside.

An excellent example of the inside/outside TACTIC comes from the Snap-on Tools Company, a leading manufacturer and distributor of quality tools and shop equipment. It has implemented Netscape's software-based extranet system as the company's primary mechanism for information delivery to its approximately 4000 domestic dealers. Before developing an extranet strategy, Snap-on communicated with its dealers by sending out mailings and relying on its management structure to pass necessary information along to the field. Dealers can now go to www.snapon.com and, after entering a special password, access relevant business information on such areas as product and promotions, best business practices, and company news. Netscape's Customer Profile reports, "Visitors to Snap-on's extranet can also take advantage of discussion groups to discuss relevant business topics with other dealers in the organization. The extranet has also provided an easy means for dealers and technical representatives to offer feedback about the online offering, products and customer information."

CORE BENEFITS/BIG PAYOFFS

The core benefits and big payoffs in enhancing sales force effectiveness revolve around getting salespeople information when they can use it best. Go for depth of information on things like products, applications and client histories. Go for timeliness in the ways your salespeople get the information.

Remember that "usable forms" include more than just information. Usable forms include programs that help a sales representative work up a bid. They also include slide shows that can be incorporated into a presentation, pictures of equipment, sound files, and many other ready-to-use applications.

Top producers in a sales force are the people most likely to adopt anything that will give them an advantage. Use that to your own advantage. But watch for the downside of this: If you can't show them an advantage they understand, they'll be reluctant to go with a new system since they're already doing well with the old one.

START NOW

Start now. Put the information you already have in forms that your people can get to at their convenience. And start bringing together the key sales knowledge that's out there in your organization so that it's available to all in the future. You can start now to enhance your sales force productivity by implementing some of the following Net-based applications:

- Marketing and sales tools management system—A one-stop application for sales news, sales presentations, document templates, and other marketing materials, in many document formats.

- Contact and project manager application—Used on any sales cycle, this is a handy way to manage your customer contacts and collaborate with other team members (both inside and outside the firewall) on major sales initiatives.

- Sales discussion groups—A sales hotline designed to support your sales efforts and ensure the best customer service, provide salespeople with easily accessible hypertext links, e-mail, or chat room meetings with other company personnel to answer sales questions and expedite the sales process. You can enable salespeople to quickly get answers to customer questions and requests 24 hours a day, 7 days a week via an extranet, and intranet or FAQ documents linked to a public Web site.

- Customer information about customers and their strategies, sales forecasts, sales reports, promotion calendars available on an extranet.

- Webcasting like Pointcast with customized reports on your target industry delivered via RealAudio/Timecast updates.

WALLY AND JEFF'S ENHANCING SALES FORCE EFFECTIVENESS LESSONS LEARNED

1. Demonstrating the use of Net software can support the user (whatever the user's job position—sales rep, executive, engineer, administrator) will accelerate the use of the system. There's really no better way to get people to use the system than to show how it delivers immediate, tangible benefits.

2. A good hook for getting salespeople to use the system is to make it possible for them to get information fast on their performance and commissions.

3. Cultural barriers can be a large issue, especially in "non-high-tech" companies where sitting in front of a terminal all day is not what they do. It is important that you feel out specifically what your employees want and need in a Net technology–based system before you move ahead and set up a new infrastructure.

4. A "10-second" sales-oriented patience-level performance of the system is one key to acceptance by the user. When your Internet system works faster, you will notice a sharp increase in the number of users.

5. Choosing to hire an outside developer to create its intranet application and associated tools frees up your personnel to focus their efforts not on managing a software project but on defining the process and the capabilities needed in the solution.

6. Just because your software is easy to use doesn't mean your system will be. We've seen a couple of people fall

into the trap of thinking that because users were familiar with the browser, no training was necessary on a new system. Remember that you have to show people the best ways to use the system for performance results.

7. Don't go for perfection. Instead, design a process and infrastructure that can satisfy 80% rather than 100% of the sales situations. This strategy will help a company in two ways. First, it is often more effective to refine a system after gaining experience than to attempt to design the perfect system from the beginning. Second, creating a process that can address all possible exceptions is more often than not an exercise in futility.

8. Use the Net to prepare the way and do many of the things that your salespeople used to have to do face-to-face. That makes each sales call they actually do that much more likely to be productive. It will also help salespeople see the benefits of an intranet quickly.

9. Use Net technology to help your salespeople do their routine paperwork routinely so that they can spend more time on sales and less money on postage.

10. Use the networking capabilities of Net technology by setting up ways for experienced salespeople to share information and the lore of the business with newer salespeople. This can be the biggest payoff in sales support, but remember that there needs to be some payoff, tangible or psychological, for the experienced salespeople to share their knowledge.

11. Whatever system you put in place for your sales support, we recommend that you include ways for field salespeople to communicate and share with each other. That sharing and discussion is often a way to transmit the lore of the business to newer people and help them climb the learning curve more quickly.

12. Net technology gives you ways to make your alliances work more effectively. Perhaps by putting together a virtual team to assemble a multifirm bid. Again and again,

we've seen simple, quick projects as an excellent way both to demonstrate the value of this technology and to give people experience using it.

13. Incorporate in your sales meetings and newsletters praise for, and success stories about, sales representatives who use the Net technology to compete to be top producers.

14. Use your Web site as an interactive brochure to support your "teleselling" phone calls.

CHAPTER 7

ENHANCING SERVICE DELIVERY

Companies whose "product" is a service have always had the twin problems of making their offering clear to prospects, clients, and customers and of dealing with the fact that what they offer is very often anchored in a personal relationship. Those two problems haven't gone away, but a few critical challenges have been added in the last two years.

CRITICAL CHALLENGES IN ENHANCING SERVICE DELIVERY

Today's businesses must enhance their service delivery to compete effectively for market share. What are the key challenges? There are four primary challenges that can be solved using Internet technology. These are:

1. Delivering information and knowledge in ways other than showing up face-to-face.

2. Increasing the speed and responsiveness of your ser-

vice information delivery system, often over markets that continue to expand geographically.

3. Keeping the quality of service going up while your costs go down.

4. Competing effectively with the new and different channels of competition challenging your market shares.

Recognize, to start with, that lots of service is really knowledge wrapped up in a delivery system. The first critical challenge is to find ways to deliver that knowledge and information other than showing up face-to-face or through traditional communication media like the fax or the telephone. If your service is actually an information product, then your demands to deliver information can be affected by daily changing facts like interest rates, and distribution of this information may be controlled by strict guidelines, such as regulatory and governmental laws imposed in the financial services industry.

The second critical challenge is to increase the speed and responsiveness of your service information delivery system, often over markets that continue to expand geographically. And your information service may need to be available 24 hours a day, 7 days a week.

Service delivery firms are often prisoners of their own success. Over the years, they get good at providing high value from the customer's perspective. The problem with that is that the customer has come to expect it and to expect an increasing level of value. Providing that increased value can often send costs skyrocketing. The third critical challenge is to keep the quality of service going up while the costs go down.

The fourth critical challenge for service delivery firms is that their competition isn't coming from the places they used to expect it. In the old days, accounting firms were pretty much accounting firms. Banks were pretty much banks. Management consultants were management consultants. But, in today's business world, where boundaries are blurred and categories are loose, that's not true anymore. Today, a bank may sell securities like a broker and offer advice like a management consultant. An accounting firm is likely to position itself as a management consultant for its clients and offer products and services that, years ago, it would have left to the bankers and the brokers. And just about everybody has gotten into the consultative selling game.

The result is that many of the strategies that used to work still do, but it's harder to implement them. Service businesses face the same kinds of challenges that manufacturing businesses do. Their clients want things customized. They want things quickly. They want things when they want them.

SOLUTIONS

Let's see how some of the organizations we talked to when we were doing our research for this book are using Net technology to meet the challenge of enhancing service delivery.

MORTGAGE SERVICES VIA EXTENSIVE NET SYSTEMS

Jerry Gross, executive vice president and chief technology officer of Countrywide Home Loans, Inc., chuckled, "You could say that our effort here at Countrywide was born out of my penchant for a great lifestyle and being lazy."

Jerry doesn't like voice mail. He doesn't like handling paper. And, several years ago, he was looking for a way to communicate with his division and the rest of the company from his house in Malibu on weekends or from an airplane or from wherever he happened to be at the moment. The result of that discomfort, that penchant, and that quest was the major Net initiative at Countrywide Home Loans.

Jerry started out by adopting a lot of Lotus Notes technology. And that was good; it gave people a way to share information. But then he discovered the Net. As he puts it, "I discovered that there was a whole other world out there of subscription lists, and people on e-mail, and on this thing called the Internet."

It didn't take Jerry long to realize that the Internet was going to change the way business was done. And not just his business but the business of everybody he dealt with. As Jerry put it, "Within a matter of 90 days, I realized that it was going to change the face of commerce. And I just realized, in discussions with people here and elsewhere, that e-mail was only the first piece of it, and then I stumbled onto the Web and, from that point on, my lot has never been the same."

So Jerry went to the people at Countrywide. He said, "Hey, hey, I found this great thing called the Internet and we should set up a domain name." Then, he smiled, "They said, 'What the hell is that?'"

At that point, Jerry was pretty much the driver for the company. He went ahead, and the company set up countrywide.com, but this was way back before the Web was really on most people's radar screens. It was before Netscape even existed.

Jerry was virtually alone with his enthusiasm right then. And there weren't many places he could go for help. So he learned on his own by experimenting. He got a copy of Mosaic, and set up a little Web site on his computer at home. Then he used that site to experiment with ideas about how his business and the Web would come together.

REDUCING FAX DELIVERY COSTS

The first big insight was that this could be a great cost-avoidance strategy. One immediate application came to mind.

"On a daily basis, multiple times a day, we would fax out to these hundreds of correspondent lenders our prices for loans." Jerry went on, "The fax cost was rather high. It ran into seven figures on an annualized basis. It was huge." But, Jerry reasoned, if Countrywide had a Web site, it would be like publishing the pricing information. There would be real-time pricing that correspondent lenders could get whenever they wanted it. That was a big benefit for lenders, and a big benefit for Countrywide because it eliminated a lot of fax costs. How much? The old fax cost system was running into seven figures on a yearly basis. And today? "I would say it dropped seven figures down to five. I mean it's below five. We just sit back and we still pinch ourselves."

But that was just the tip of the iceberg. Business costs plummeted, but there were many other big benefits to be had. Jerry realized quickly that what was going on was that a system like this began to tie the lenders and Countrywide together in a new way.

The Countrywide Web site, called Platinum Lender Access, offers a huge amount of data and information and knowledge to the 500 Countrywide partners around the country. That data includes loan statistics and account histories and interest rates. And it's available to anyone with access to the site, using a browser.

Jerry Gross and Countrywide see that as just the beginning.

REDUCING TIME AND COSTS OF DELIVERING CUSTOMIZED APPLICATIONS

"In the beginning, we saw that the business-to-business opportunities were there for cost reduction. But this quickly evolved to ... my God, I can communicate with anybody at anytime and so very quickly ... we need to connect to anybody, anywhere, anytime, and do anything, and allow them to connect to us and to get whatever data helps them be part of our enterprise." Relationships were improving, costs were dropping, and the speed of decisions was turbocharged. As Jerry puts it, "You have a transaction that used to take 30 days that now can take literally 30 minutes."

That led to the idea and the concept of beginning to extend out toward consumer applications. "All this was happening before most people were on the consumer bandwagon, and there were a lot of naysayers. There were folks, first of all, who were saying, Well, this business-to-business thing isn't that big, and then when the business-to-business applications started to really cook, they talked about how consumers would never use the Web. And then they would use the Web, but security would be a problem, and so forth."

Jerry's idea was different and far-reaching. "It's been a tremendous source of marketing opportunity for us and a source of business. Our strategy now is that every application we have—back-office, front-office, management reporting application—we're really evolving that into a public application." Countrywide is looking to maintain its strength where it is but to extend its business out to the ultimate consumer. Jerry thinks that that provides two key benefits. He thinks that starting with an "outsider" in mind forces you to develop applications that are easier to use. He also believes that working this way means that he saves money because he has to prototype only once.

GETTING PROACTIVE ABOUT SECURITY

Now, that raises all kinds of security issues. While the media may have overblown the level of security threats on the Net and the Web, the threat is still real. And it's a particularly important factor to anyone dealing with financial data or privacy data. Countrywide's solution? "Hack yourself," Jerry suggests. " ... it's not a question of IF you're going to get hacked, it's WHEN you're going to get hacked or attacked." Countrywide literally hires people to try to break into its system. That keeps the company realistic.

As Gross puts it, "The fact of the matter is that we feel there are certain transactions that we cannot do yet over the Internet." From his history, you know that Jerry doesn't mean that they won't ever do them; he just means that right now they're not possible. That realistic perspective is the core of the way that Jerry Gross and Countrywide Home Loans have worked—that and a strong customer-oriented approach.

In the case of Countrywide Home Loans, the user approach is driven from the inside. It was Jerry Gross who got interested in the Net. It was Jerry who built the Web site on his own computer. It was Jerry who said "Let's have a domain name." But always with applications and users in mind. At Stanford Federal Credit Union, the stimulus for technological development came from a different direction.

A CREDIT UNION IN FRONT OF THE PACK

How does a relatively small credit union turn out to be the first financial institution to let people do financial business on the Web? You'd expect it to be one of the giants like Bank of America, or Citibank or maybe one of the "innovative" banks like Wells Fargo.

Instead, though, the first financial institution to do real business on the Web was the Stanford Federal Credit Union. They were letting customers do real account transactions when other financial institutions were just thinking about it or even saying that it was too dangerous. How that happened is a unique story of business development using the Net.

It all started back in 1985, ancient times by Internet standards.

That was the year that Warren Marshall took over the reins at Stanford Federal Credit Union (SFCU) in Palo Alto, California. Things were not good at the credit union just then. Its reputation was pretty bad, and people in the campus community weren't returning Warren's phone calls. His introduction to the magic of the Internet was the discovery that he could reach almost anyone with e-mail and get an answer, even from people who wouldn't call him back.

Since e-mail was a fact of life for many members of the Stanford community, the e-mail started coming back with other information and requests beyond just simple responses. People asked the credit union to handle an account transfer for them. Or they asked for a balance check or for information on a car loan. Soon, staff was assigned to check the e-mail box and take care of whatever business was there. In response, SFCU set up a system to handle e-mail based on the service needed.

HOME BANKING ON THE INTERNET

In 1993, SFCU went to home banking but only on the Internet. Most financial institutions started "home banking" by requiring special software and having people dial a special number. Not SFCU. The process was handled using a program called Telnet over a leased line. The computer handling the business was isolated as a security measure.

At about this time, all sorts of people were discovering the Web, and Stanford was a hotbed of Web activity. Web pages were going up all over and for all kinds of reasons. It was at about this time that a group running a project called Portfolio out of the Stanford Library approached the credit union about including information on credit union rates and such on the library Web page. They had been entering the information themselves—keying all the rates manually. Creating a link to SFCU put the rates on the library page without need to rekey the information. In response to their complaints about rekeying information, the process was automated.

A FULL-SERVICE FINANCIAL WEB SITE

More amazements were to come. One day, Marshall got a call from a Stanford Ph.D. student. He really liked the credit union services, he said, but he thought the presentation (the interface) was really awful. Then he made an offer. "I've put up a page with how I think things should work," the student said, "Why don't you check it out?" Marshall checked it out using his own password and account number. "I was astounded," he says, "There was this great Web page, and it worked with our system. My first thought was that we had a security problem." That wasn't the case. The Web system was just tacked on as a front end to the Telnet system that was already in place. Soon, the Web interface was up and running.

"It was really an adventure," Marshall recalls, "It seemed like I was being contacted by someone in the community every couple of days. They'd tell me what they wanted, and we'd try to make it happen. Sometimes, they even told us how to do it."

The result is a full-service financial Web site for the Stanford Federal Credit Union. But that's not all. The concept of community that's fundamental to the credit union movement is carried out in strategy. And the strategy of the credit union is played out on the Web.

Early on, Marshall and his board set a target of servicing $1 billion of mortgage loans. That's a lot for a $160 million credit union. "Frankly," Marshall says, "We didn't know quite how it was going to happen."

The Web helped. In 1995, the credit union set up Mortgage Mart to help people who wanted to obtain a mortgage loan. For many people, buying a new home and financing the purchase constitute the largest financial undertaking of their lives. Mortgage Mart was designed so that people could check out what size loan they qualify for, look at different payment schemes, and gather information about the home-buying process. And checking out who's been using those loan calculators provides leads for lending officers.

Stanford Federal Credit Union and Countrywide Home Loans present two very different ways of developing the use of Net/Web technology. One was driven by an internal champion; the other kept looking around to find that members were pulling development along. What they have in common, besides dealing in financial transactions, is that both follow a strong strategic vision that calls for being responsive and helpful and delivering the service that their customers want in the most efficient way possible.

LEVERAGING KNOWLEDGE USING THE NET

Probably the ultimate service delivery firm is the consulting firm. And one of the largest and most respected, and certainly one of the oldest is Booz-Allen & Hamilton, based in McLean, Virginia. The firm was founded in 1914 and has evolved into one of the top management and technology consulting firms in the world.

Recent years have been good to Booz-Allen & Hamilton. Revenues nearly doubled in the period from 1990 to 1994. As with most consulting firms, that meant that the staffing was doubling, too.

Expansion like that brings two kinds of problems right away. One of them is simply integrating people into the practice. The second key challenge is that things are bigger and harder to coordinate. And all this is going on at a time when clients increasingly expect higher immediate value and payoff when a consultant shows up on their doorstep. It boils down to finding ways to locate the information and knowledge needed on a client project quickly, regardless of where it resides and who has it. Then that knowledge needs to be leveraged into a profitable client application.

Years ago, that might have been easy because the consultants pretty well knew each other and had known each other for some time. They probably also had a good idea who the various clients and industries were that Booz-Allen worked with. That's no longer true in a fast-changing worldwide environment.

Booz-Allen's answer to the challenge was to set out on the ambitious project of developing a firmwide knowledge program. That started by setting up a chief knowledge officer (CKO), who had four key responsibilities.

The CKO was responsible for managing research and development activities that revolved around creating or sharing new knowledge. The CKO was charged with building an infrastructure to make it easy to share knowledge and information. Along with that went the charge to design and implement processes for sharing, collaborating, and using knowledge and, finally, to create changes in management communication processes so that companywide behavior would change to meet the other objectives—a pretty daunting set of objectives.

Booz-Allen & Hamilton went with Net/Web technology because of the open systems standards. It could be used by people with a variety of platforms, and it could be integrated with lots of other technology. That made it easy to implement and easy to use, and it reduced implementation costs on the technology side.

Two kinds of knowledge users within the firm were identified. The first of these were senior people, who already had a good knowledge base and a developed consulting practice. They knew a lot about clients and industries. What they were interested in was cutting-edge applications and new ideas.

The other group that was going to use the system was at the opposite end of the experience spectrum. These were the new people, junior partners and others who were coming onboard quickly. They needed quick access to client and industry knowledge and the ability to attack a project without having to reinvent wheels that Booz-Allen & Hamilton had not only invented but had perfected years before.

The system Booz-Allen & Hamilton developed and called Knowledge On-line (KOL), delivers three kinds of knowledge to the firm's 2000 plus consultants. The first of these is static content, which includes data and information about a variety of topics. It's the kind of information a consultant would normally dredge up on a basic background search at the beginning of a project. It also includes routine administrative items, such as calendar items, business news, and human resources information.

The second key area of knowledge that Booz-Allen & Hamilton identified is applications that support business activities. These include searchable knowledge databases that are organized around the key competencies and specialties of the firm. And it includes training.

The third key area is access to experts. The searchable knowledge database has links to job histories, résumés, and other information about people in the firm and outside who can provide expertise quickly to support Booz-Allen & Hamilton's consultants in more effectively servicing their clients.

These help people at both ends of the experience spectrum. Newer members of the firm can get up to speed quickly on an industry, client firm, or type of problem, making them more productive sooner. More senior members of the firm can use the system to help put together project teams, develop subordinates, and plot strategic direction.

The payoff at Booz-Allen & Hamilton has been huge. Return on investment is estimated to be 1389% per year, with a payback period of 0.19 years—a couple of months. In the calculations, performed by International Data Corporation, of Framingham, Massachusetts, the ROI is due primarily to the time saved by using Knowledge On-line's system compared to the previous, informal methods of gathering information, data, and knowledge. The intranet system that Booz-Allen & Hamilton has put in place allows a relatively new consultant to quickly get hold of the information, knowledge, and people necessary to be productive in servicing their client's needs.

That leads to another benefit, which is subjective but still powerful. With Knowledge On-line's system, Booz-Allen & Hamilton consultants are able to show up at a client's ready to produce. That's a key competitive advantage in the consulting business.

Historically, consulting has been something of an apprentice trade. A new, young consultant worked with an older consultant and learned about the clients and the industries and mined the knowledge that was in the older consultant's head. As time went on there was a certain handoff of clients and projects and increasing responsibility. That was based on a relatively stable size and geographical proximity. With the KOL intranet system, it's possible to share knowledge and insight quickly and effectively and to move consultants up the learning curve rapidly. That, in turn, leads to expanded business opportunities because Booz-Allen removed the limits on the number of knowledgeable people. Sounds pretty wonderful.

But there is a fly in this ointment—something called *culture*. The cultural issue here is that consultants don't like to share information with each other if that information and their knowledge is their internal competitive advantage. In fact, Alan Dutta, who was instrumental in setting up the Booz-Allen & Hamilton system and is now with Silicon Valley Internet Partners, calls this kind of information sharing "an unnatural act."

What Booz-Allen & Hamilton discovered was that it's not enough to have the technology in place. It's not enough to make the right choices about which servers and which software and which training programs to use. That's all-important; but it's also important to pay attention to other, cultural issues.

Booz-Allen's answer to this was to build on the natural inclination of people in the consulting business to be interested in content. Early on, the firm realized that most of the content was going to come bubbling up from the consultants and not be created by the formally appointed knowledge managers. That meant providing an easy way for people to put content out there, in effect, to show off.

Attention to team building and top management attention to eliminating barriers were important parts of the effort. And practical incentives were offered. Publicizing the value of the knowledge base and the value of contributions was just the start. Consultants who participated in sharing knowledge on the system were rewarded. Providing formal rewards for participation and incorporating knowledge creation into consultants' performance appraisals had a major effect as well.

In the case of Booz-Allen & Hamilton, we see an ambitious attempt to get at a knowledge-sharing system and a recognition of the intense human factors that go into making a system like this work. No technology system, no intranet, stands alone. It works instead through the human beings that make up an organization. Therefore, paying attention to things like compensation, reward, and value systems is as essential as picking the best software.

According to International Data Corporation's 1996 ROI Intranet Report,

> KOL 2.0 consists of a main Web page that provides access to eight areas of information—which, taken together, support knowledge and information sharing throughout the firm. The information in any of these eight areas is no more than three mouse clicks away:
>
> - Knowledge—A searchable knowledge database with links to job histories, résumés, and project records
> - Business Operations—A listing of calendar items, business news, and HR information
> - Skills and Methodologies—Informative and interactive training materials
> - KOLaborate—Ability to provide threaded messaging capabilities

- Office—Links to local office home pages
- Practices/Teams—Searchable knowledge database organized around Booz-Allen specialties
- External/Résumés—Ability to search and download staff data linked to job histories
- Idea Mart—Selection ideas, project results, and expertise for clients and other external entities

When first entering KOL, the user logs onto the system, thus identifying the user and the user's privileges. Each user's view of KOL is dynamically created based on the person's position in the firm. For instance, only officers and principals have access to client and financial information. The Oracle database contains all of the business processes and rules needed to create the pages dynamically.

Booz-Allen & Hamilton's service delivery enhancement applications provide us with an excellent example of what many companies use intranets and the Web technology for, that is, to enable them to cut costs, boost profits, and enhance operations.

ANSWERS ON THE WEB FROM ERNIE

Booz-Allen's Knowledge On-Line is one of the most sophisticated firmwide knowledge systems we've seen but, in one sense at least, it's playing catch-up to rival Ernst & Young. That firm has extended consulting into the virtual world with a service called Ernie.

Ernie works like this. A company subscribes to the service for $6000 per year, and that buys access to the private part of the Ernie Web site. Ask a question and add some information to help categorize it. Then, pick the one of nine topics that's closest to your concern and send the message on its way.

Ernst & Young will route the query to "the appropriate professional," who will prepare a personalized reply. That works fine for fairly simple questions. In fact, some may generate instant answers from a database of previously asked questions.

For clients who have more complex needs, the firm has rolled out the Ernie Business Analyst, which will provide a report, such as a market analysis, for a separate fee.

This virtual consulting should have two benefits for Ernst & Young. First, it should extend the market for its services to companies that can't or won't pay for individual, face-to-face consulting. Second, tracking the questions themselves should provide a high-quality window on the concerns and needs of the small to midsized businesses the service is aimed at.

TACTICS

Let's look at our tactics and how they apply to enhancing service delivery.

THINK LINKS

Think about the various links where people gather information about the service or those cross-boundary information sources that might add value. For example Booz-Allen & Hamilton has links on its intranet, KOL, to the company's personnel capital, which includes best practices, proposals, reports, decision support, collaboration, and engagement management. Users can search for subject information about work performed by the consultants, for planning new projects and for identifying which of Booz-Allen's human resources are the right experts to use. In order to do this, a search will link to work-related documents which have dynamic hotlinks to the consultant's résumé, clients involved, client's profile, staff involved, and a description of that engagement and related engagements.

AUTOMATE

Look for ways to automate the try-it-before-you-buy-it, bet-you-can't-eat-just-one marketing types of strategies. As you do that, look for ways to cut costs ruthlessly. The service descriptions, and even the delivery of service, have been incredibly paper-intensive. Eliminating paper and the passing of it from hand to hand can have a major impact on your bottom line. To achieve this, you can use Net applications such as:

- An extranet with searchable information that employees, business partners, and suppliers can access to enhance collaboration and provide solutions for customers.

- Online technical or service support provided through a FAQ document, discussion forums, or e-mail.

- Product and service description pages via Web hyperlink.

CUSTOMIZE

Countrywide Home Loans used Net technology to customize its service delivery system—which was previously done by fax, phone, and "snail mail"—by setting up and implementing an extranet called Platinum Lender. Platinum Lender lets Countrywide's bank and mortgage partners point a browser, after they enter their secret password and identification number, check loan status, account history, or interest rates.

TRANSFORM

In service delivery, look at all the options for transforming data into information and information into knowledge. Look for opportunities to pull key insights, understanding, relationships, and guidelines from the little personal relationship pockets where they exist into the general pool of available information and knowledge.

INSIDE/OUTSIDE

The principle of inside/outside here involves looking for services that you can deliver over the Net. At the same time, use the Net to help you find out what services most matter to your customers and clients and how they want them delivered.

Stanford Federal Credit Union (SFCU) enhances service delivery for its customer base—which consists of the Stanford community that is related to the university—with the Deals on Wheels Program. Located on SFCU's public Web site (at http://www.sfcu.org/wheels/), the Deals on Wheels Program lets any SFCU member obtain a preapproved car loan and purchase a new car or truck via the Internet. Once a member's loan application has been approved, SFCU submits the vehicle request to Auto-By-Tel, which sends the request to one of over 1400 participating dealers who will assist members nationally. The dealer will call the member directly within 48 hours with a competitive price quote. This credit union service eliminates the haggling and hassles often associated with buying from dealerships. Subscribing dealers uphold consistent high standards for customer service and satisfaction. The service costs the consumer nothing and often saves buyers thousands of dollars. By using SFCU's online purchasing program and online financial program, its members can experience an easy, hassle-free way to buy a new car.

CORE BENEFITS/BIG PAYOFFS

Begin by looking at what you already do with fax and mail. Your core benefits/big payoffs are likely to come from moving those to the Net/Web. A key in this area is to look for ways to increase the information or ease of sharing critical information. If you put the information most valuable to your customers online, and they get used to finding it there, the Net/Web will be where they look first.

START NOW

Start now to identify the information components in your services that can move quickly to the Net. Begin looking for actual service delivery options over the Net/Web.

WALLY AND JEFF'S ENHANCING SERVICE DELIVERY LESSONS LEARNED

1. Stay flexible. Most of the companies that we've seen use this technology wound up doing things they never imagined when they started their projects. Possibilities will open up for you all over. Just make sure to keep your eye on the reason you're doing all this. It's easy to get seduced by the technological tricks and lose sight of the bottom line.

2. Consider where the highest quick payoff or the greatest benefit will be for most users. Then use that to sell the project or to demonstrate benefits and the need to expand it. Jerry Gross combined his knowledge of the technology with his drive to develop Countywide Home Loans' first practical application of Net technology by replacing daily fax correspondence with e-mail. When we spoke to Jerry, he said, "There was all the marketing potential and there was all the electronic commerce potential, but I felt initially that, with e-mail coupled with Web technology, there was the possibility of tremendous business-to-business cost reduction."

3. The Web spreads fast and you need to move quickly to gain control over grassroots projects that are developing. If you're being pulled by staff or customers, this can be especially important. There's always going to be a tension between a local unit or individual control and the need for a common corporate image and style. Many of the companies we interviewed for this book, such as Booz-Allen & Hamilton, Countrywide Home Loans, and Stanford Federal Credit Union, combined the pull for fulfillment of service needs from their customers with solid business planning to develop a step-by-step process to choose the deployment architecture of the service enhancement that Web technology offered them. See Chapter 11 "Making It Happen in Your Organization," and Chapter 1 "The TACTICS Action Planning System," for specific guidelines to build your business plan.

4. Be sure to identify the differences in the needs of different users. That may call for different content or different delivery systems or both. Don't get too cute with graphics, Java, and Shockwave applications if most of your remote users access you via dial-up services and lower-speed modems.

5. Consider that most of the applications and processes you run internally can also be run by your customers or

clients. Developing your systems with that in mind should help you develop more usable systems. Making content submission easy was critical to the long-term success of a dynamic knowledge store like Booz-Allen's intranet, KOL.

6. When moving to the Net and Web be especially careful if your organization's culture has rewarded information hoarding and made it a source of power. You'll have to deal with that when you try to get people to share information on a Net.

7. The success stories we've seen often include someone who's been able to create a simple model of what change was all about for the organization. That makes it easier to sell and to implement.

8. When setting up an extranet or allowing access to proprietary information via your public Web site, we cannot stress enough that you evaluate the security risks early in your planning and develop your strategy to handle the potential issues and problems that *will* arise from time to time. As Jerry Gross said,

> Our view is that it's not *if* you're going to get hacked, it's just a question of *when* you're going to get hacked or attacked. So we've made investments both in technology and in people to constantly monitor our Networks and our electronic commerce transactions. The fact of the matter is, we feel that there are certain transactions we cannot do yet over the Internet and there are some transactions we can do, but it's all got to be planned from a realistic perspective.

9. Use Net technology to expand your geographical coverage. Once you've worked out an effective delivery system for the kind of service you deliver, you may find that it's one small step to move toward expanding your market geographically. Net technology enables you to deliver many components of service as easily around the world as around the corner.

CHAPTER 8

FULFILLMENT AND DISTRIBUTION

Fulfillment and distribution are the functions of the business that get products and services from where they start out to where they finish. In recent years, this has been a hotbed of business improvement, with businesses looking hard at their logistical processes and beginning to use more and more outsourcing techniques. The Net can help you here. That's because large portions of the fulfillment and distribution process involve information flows as well as flows of goods across geography.

CRITICAL CHALLENGES OF FULFILLMENT AND DISTRIBUTION

The online tools of the Internet can help you address the following four key challenges of fulfillment and distribution and, by doing so, improve your competitive position.

1. Use fulfillment and distribution as a competitive advantage by not only delivering faster but moving beyond recipients' quality expectations.

2. Enhance the overall and specific relationships in the fulfillment and distribution process to form productive partnerships and strategic alliances.

3. Meet demand-driven distribution requests so that you are more responsive to your customers while reducing your costs.

4. Reduce your overall fulfillment and distribution costs.

The first key challenge is to make logistics—the art and science of moving resources around—into a new competitive advantage. Forward-looking firms have seen logistics as a way both to cut costs and to improve customer satisfaction by delivering higher value.

The second key challenge emphasizes enhancing the overall and specific relationships in the fulfillment and distribution process. Many years ago, this process was seen as several distinct items. A manufacturer dealt with fulfillment and distribution in terms of shipping goods to a wholesaler or distributor. That wholesaler or distributor saw fulfillment and distribution in terms of shipping goods from its location to a retail customer or contractor. And retail operations saw fulfillment and distribution as getting goods to the individuals who bought them.

That's changed in recent years. As business strategies have become more concerned with relationships and partnering, business managers have started looking at the entire chain, running from the original producer to the final consumer. That chain has gone by several different names. We refer to it as the *value chain,* but others have called it the *supply-chain.* Dennis Passovoy of Amicus calls it the *food chain.* Whatever you call it, it's a critical part of your business, the part that gets the goods to the customer, and it's one of the major opportunities you have to improve profits while improving value.

Many times, businesses that would be your competitors if they were nearby can be allied with you in your value chain when they're geographically distant. Foster productive strategic alliances that will enable you to make your fulfillment and distribution more effective and more efficient while reducing costs and meeting demand on time.

Meeting the challenge of demand-driven distribution, which is the supplier side of just-in-time inventory, means managing the flow of information in such a way as to be more responsive to your customers while at the same time reducing your costs.

The fourth key challenge is to reduce overall fulfillment and distribution costs. How can we build on the premise that the more we automate the flow of information, the more we can save the costs of employee time and deliver faster than our competitors?

SOLUTIONS: A LOOK AT THE WHOLE SUPPLY CHAIN

What's a supply-chain? Think about the entire process of how a product reaches the end user. It begins with the sources of raw materials. Those materials are shipped to a manufacturer, who turns them into finished goods. The goods move to wholesalers or retailers and on to the final purchaser. That's the supply-chain—the whole chain of events and transportation from raw material to final purchase. The best formal definition that we've seen of a supply-chain is that it is a "set of interlinked processes through which products reach end users."

There are two key parts of that definition. The first is that it is the entire chain through which products reach end users. When GE looks at its Trading Process Network (TPN), it takes in the entire chain for a particular business unit, beginning with the original manufacturer, through the various processing and distribution points, all the way to the end user. Viewing the entire system gives GE and others practicing supply-chain management a way to spot the potential in relationships and efficiencies and opportunities to craft strategies to make the entire process more efficient and profitable.

Businesses like GE are finding that, if you pay attention to the entire chain, it's possible to streamline operations, increase efficiency, and save money. The consulting firm A. T. Kearney recently completed a study of the potential impact of supply-chain management on the pharmaceutical industry. It estimates a potential for $30 billion in savings in that industry alone.

POTENTIAL RELATIONSHIPS AND NEW EFFICIENCIES

Once you've laid out the supply-chain (or chains) for your business, look for ways to make it work better. You may find some help from several industry initiatives.

This idea of supply-chain management has lead to an initiative called the supply-chain operations reference (SCOR) model, a cross-industry framework for improved supply-chain performance. The objective is to define common supply-chain management processes and match them against best practices and bench-marked performance data.

The SCOR model was announced in November 1996, and the first initiative for the council that put it together has been making it known widely. The SCOR model analyzes best practices and how they work in the supply-chain system.

That leads us to the second key part of the *supply-chain* definition. Supply-chain management is about interlinked processes. It's a recognition that the way a product is designed and packaged has a bearing on how it's delivered to the final user and that the order form used by the original equipment manufacturer can have a bearing on the cost savings for the distributor in the middle of the chain and the retailer and end user at the far end.

That's what makes this supply-chain management concept so incredibly powerful as an application of Net and Web technology. Net and Web technology provide a way for companies along the chain with different kinds of computer platforms and different levels of technological sophistication to make use of the efficiency gains and profit enhancements that supply-chain management can provide.

That's actually like the original promise of EDI (Electronic Data Interchange), only more so. The original idea of EDI was that if certain kinds of data were handled in the same way throughout the supply-chain, major cost efficiencies could be gained. That's true, but EDI has proved successful almost exclusively for small, stable communities of trading partners, especially those with a dominant partner who can enforce standards. On the other hand, Net/Web technology can be used by a broad variety of companies.

GETTING LOWER PRICES

When we spoke to Bruce Chovnick, GE Information Systems' vice president of Internet consulting and services, his comments were pretty straightforward about the limitations of EDI. He said,

> One of the dilemmas is that a very low number of companies can benefit from the kinds of productivity that you've got if they have to use EDI. So, last year one of the things that we did for ourselves and our customers was to lower those barriers, by developing a product which definitely takes a Web-based front end, and Internet-capable front end and brings that as the user interface. ... Now I can present to you everything that you need on a browser-based interface, you can do the turn-around documents, everything else and you're really now part of this electronic community, but your barrier to entry is so much lower, all you need is a browser and a connection to the Internet, and have joined that community.

The basic concept here is to take the principle of EDI—shared information moved automatically along the supply-chain—and make it work with the Net/Web. General Electric's Trading Process Network, which began primarily as a cost-cutting move, is a secure Web site (www.tpn.geis.com) that was set up to automate purchasing by GE's lighting unit.

There have been big payoffs just from the purchasing side. Since mid-1996, the average purchasing cycle has been cut in half from 14 days to 7. In addition, the prices being bid turn out to be 10–15% lower than those bid through non-Web sources. General Electric thinks that's because bidders aren't sure who else is bidding and, consequently, shave things a bit closer. The data and the bids come in standard form. They can be integrated with manufacturing processes. As products move out the door, important information is available about the products as well, to flow down the chain along with the goods to wholesale distributors and to retailers.

SAVINGS IN TIME AND PAPER COSTS FROM TPN

When we asked Bruce Chovnick if he had heard any hard numbers or ROI results from the companies that are implementing GE's Web-based distribution and fulfillment system, he said, "I was with a very large company last week, and I asked them if they had done an ROI on their investment, and they said no, but they recently did a cost/benefit analysis that basically said they're going to save more money just in the paper they distribute to their trading partners or their distributors or their dealers than they are in what it's going to cost them to put an electronic version up." And that's without adding the benefits of speed and ease and the savings in time.

BRINGING EDI TO THE WEB

General Electric isn't the only company with the idea of putting the concept of EDI on the Web. Several companies are coming out with solutions. Premenos has released a program called WebDox to do the job. Major EDI players are in the game, too. Harbinger has Harbinger Express and St. Paul Software has Web EC, and Advantis and Sterling Commerce are rolling out products as well.

These companies and others are moving to adapt the core idea of EDI to a Web environment. Others are looking at the Net/Web itself as a starting point for analysis. We'll examine the three basic steps in a typical supply-chain. And we'll look at manufacturers, wholesale distributors, and a retailer.

IMPROVING RELATIONSHIPS WITH WHOLESALE DISTRIBUTORS

Johnson Controls is a major maker of the controls used in industrial processes and construction. The company was founded way back in the 1880s after Professor Warren Johnson invented what he called "the electric telethermoscope" to help the janitors at Wisconsin State Normal School regulate the room temperature in classrooms without barging in and out and disturbing the students and, probably, Professor Johnson.

That beginning tells you a couple of things about Johnson Controls today. Just like the founder, the company is into inventive problem solving.

A major market for Johnson Controls is the heating, ventilating, and air conditioning market, where the supply-chain runs through wholesale distributors to contractors working on job sites.

Johnson Controls wanted to do two critical things. First, like most businesses, it wanted to cut the cost of doing business and improve its efficiency and thereby its profitability. Second, it wanted to increase the quality and strength of its relationships with its wholesale distributors. As a way to meet these objectives, Johnson Controls wanted to make it easier and more profitable for key distributors to do business with them. They saw Net technology as a way to do that.

Gerry Cellucci works on the initiative for Johnson Controls. He works out of Toronto, Canada. The first thing Gerry did was to find out what other people were doing.

"We were looking for a kind of best practices," he says. The people from Johnson Controls paid particular attention to excellent examples of Net/Web use by wholesalers and manufacturers. They felt that the best strategy they could follow would be to provide their distributors with a way to become more profitable. That would allow Johnson to use more cost-effective technology at the same time it hit the goals of improving relationships and adding value.

FORMING A NETWORK WITH MANUFACTURERS AND DISTRIBUTORS

Research on best practices took two forms. The first stop was the literature, articles were read and case studies digested. Then the researchers went out and looked at some good operations, those of top manufacturers and distributors in many areas, including companies like GE and Marshall Industries.

Next came the question of how to implement the strategy. At this point, Pareto's law, the 80/20 rule, kicked in. According to Cellucci, "We decided to start with our top distributors, the ones that provide 80% of our revenue and profits."

Then Johnson got those distributors together at a meeting in Palm Desert, California, and talked about what it wanted to do. Speakers were brought in from distributors who've done it, such as Rob Rodin from Marshall Industries, and the distributors were asked what kinds of things they needed.

Johnson Controls wasn't about to rely on exhortation to sell its network to the distributors. In addition to showing the distributors the advantages they would have from Net/Web technology and supply-chain management, Johnson sweetened the pot by providing incentives for the distributors to use automated order-processing systems to place their orders.

Essentially, Cellucci says, there are two sides to this supply-chain business. One of them is the sales side. That includes all the things that go with what's usually called electronic commerce, like sales and transaction processing and payment settlements. The other side, and the one we're concerned with here, is the logistics side. That includes EDI (and its Internet/intranet variants), automatic inventory replenishment, order tracking, and remote shipping. The logistics side is really covered by the logistics buzzwords that have been floating around distribution, such as continuous replenishment, sales activated settlement, electronic order management, category management, and electronic product information.

One of the distributors for Johnson Controls is Minvalco Corporation in Minneapolis. Minvalco had already set up a Web site to provide information for contractors. It had also begun engaging in some limited EDI but it wasn't sure that there was a really big payoff in that. It seemed as though the Web might offer more opportunity at lower costs.

Ed Landt at Minvalco liked what he heard from Johnson. He saw Johnson's strategy as one that would benefit them both. Minvalco would be able to save money on ordering and processing costs for the products it buys from Johnson. Marketing and sales should benefit as well.

What about Johnson? There are some cost savings to be sure, but there's also a stronger relationship with a key distributor. Tying in key distributors with information and process links strengthens the current relationship and makes switching less likely.

The idea is for all the parties to benefit, including Minvalco's customers, who should get faster or more flexible service and more accurate and complete information.

A TOP EXAMPLE OF ELECTRONIC COMMERCE AND INTRANET/EXTRANET USE

Marshall, a distributor of electronic components headquartered in El Monte, California, has been one of the leaders and top examples of electronic commerce and intranet/extranet use in American business. As a distributor sitting in the middle of a two- or three-step supply-chain, Marshall's challenges are to receive products effectively and then to market down the supply-chain. That includes matching its systems to those of suppliers, making supplier information available to customers, and automating all of its processes as much as possible.

The Marshall system is set up to allow electronic ordering. The electronic ordering system is hooked directly into a robotic warehouse process that automates order picking, packing, and shipping. United Parcel Services has a site inside Marshall's warehouse that facilitates shipping. That enables reduced cycle times, greater efficiency, and the cost savings that benefit from automating processes that used to be done by hand.

That's not all for Marshall, though. Marshall is also using its intranet and extranet to provide additional value in both directions on the supply-chain. For example, in early 1997, Marshall set up a Web site that enables design engineers to actually do some computer-aided design online. This is a benefit both to its suppliers, who are often manufacturers, and to those of its customers who use components in their own manufacturing processes.

Marshall uses its education, news, and entertainment network to provide training and industry news to suppliers and manufacturers alike. And the company continually strives to makes its processes more automatic and easier to use while making the technology that enables the processes as transparent as possible to the user.

OUTSOURCING DISTRIBUTION AND FULFILLMENT SERVICES

Sometimes, some of the automation that we're talking about here happens through outsourcing. For example, the Federal Express Corporation offers its large customers services that go beyond the shipping function (absolutely, positively overnight) to include additional logistics functions, including order picking and fulfillment.

FedEx does this for one IBM division. Parts "from IBM" are stored in a Federal Express facility. In fact, the parts are shipped there directly from the original manufacturers. When orders come in, they go through Federal Express, which handles the fulfillment, order processing, and shipping. From the customer's perspective, the parts are coming from the International Business Machines Corporation. From the logistics perspective, they're coming from Federal Express.

One of our clients is looking into putting together a consortium of industrial distributors that handle the same kinds of goods but in different parts of the country. As one of the principals put it, "The bottom line is that it doesn't matter where we ship the product from; it only matters that the right product gets where it needs to be on time."

SUPPLY-CHAIN PARTNERS

For companies at the front end or in the middle of the supply-chain, the idea is to make things easier, more effective, and more profitable for people further along the supply-chain while increasing efficiency and profitability. To understand how that might play out, let's take a look at the end.

FOOTLOCKER STORES AND THE NEW BALANCE COMPANY

We'll start with a model. The model is based on EDI and used by the Footlocker stores and the New Balance Company, which makes several shoes, among them Elite Runners.

Before handling the system electronically, a retailer had to anticipate demand as much as six months in advance. Bad guesses could cost retailers thousands per store while slow movers languished on the shelf and sales of hot items were lost. For New Balance, the solution was to set up an EDI system for large retailers such as Footlocker. The system uses a private value-added Network that allows retailers to place an order from an electronic catalog. That speeds both the ordering process and the delivery. Utilizing that automation system has enabled New Balance to go from its largest account's eleventh-most-profitable vendor to its fifth-most-profitable.

All that's fine for a big retail chain such as Footlocker. It doesn't work so well for smaller retailers, and that's where the intranet/extranet solutions can come into play. In this case, it comes in the form of a system that works over the GE Information Systems' TPN and costs small retailers just $300. That compares with several thousand in minimum start-up fees for a standard EDI system.

NATIONAL SPORTING GOODS ASSOCIATION AND THE NATIONAL SHOE RETAILERS ASSOCIATION

Lots of small shoe retailers would like to have some of the automated options that larger retailers have. In the footwear industry, two trade associations, the National Sporting Goods Association and the National Shoe Retailers Association, put together a program called Shoe and Sport Talk (SST). Here's how it works.

The program provides a small retailer with three key features: Universal Product Codes, Electronic Data Interchange, and e-mail. The work for certifying suppliers, matching systems, and passing on codes is handled by SST. All the retailer does is sign up.

For a cost of $50 per month SST provides UPC codes and the EDI connection for average volume, over average pays more. Even so, this is far less than it would cost a retailer to set up such a system on its own. It's also easier. And, because trade associations are involved, so are most of the manufacturers.

The only downside to a system like this one is that it's a separate system from the other basic Windows programs that the business may be running. In the next few years, though, you'll probably see these systems move to the Net/Web to pick up the advantages of open platforms and a common interface.

APRIA HEALTH CARE AND KAISER PERMANENTE

Sometimes, the initiative to automate the supply-chain comes from two key partners. Apria Health Care is a preferred supplier of respiratory therapy and home medical equipment for Kaiser Permanente, one of the nation's largest health maintenance organizations (HMOs). They've linked their computer systems to provide an array of benefits to both. When a Kaiser Permanente member needs respiratory therapy or home medical equipment, the order for that is entered directly at Kaiser. It's transmitted immediately to Apria. There, a customer service representative is alerted to the arrival of the order through an interrupt message on his or her screen. The rep then gets back to Kaiser to confirm any details that are necessary.

Once the material is delivered, confirmation moves over the electronic system, and so does billing. According to Stephen Plochocki, president and CEO of Apria, the system eliminates the need for phone calls, faxes, duplicate data entry, follow-up requests for missing information, and numerous other activities that can hinder prompt delivery of service to patients. It also ensures more accurate and prompt delivery of patient services because orders can be transmitted to Apria only after all necessary patient, clinical, and authorization information has been entered.

KNOWING YOUR CUSTOMERS AND HOW THEY BUY

For wholesalers in the middle of the supply-chain, there's sometimes a special problem: They don't want to be in the business of making basic consumer sales. When that's the case, a different strategy is in order. The R. E. Michel Company is a heating, ventilating, and air conditioning wholesale distributor in Maryland. Steve Neathery has been responsible for setting up its Net and Web initiatives.

According to Steve, everything begins with a simple question, "What's the point of being here?" *Here* can mean "in business at all." So, Steve points out, Web strategy is tied to business strategy, and that means that you have to know all the basic things: Who are your customers (and who aren't your customers)? What do they really buy? How do they do it?

For R. E. Michel, that means understanding the contractors who buy from them and install equipment. According to a survey in the December 1996 *Refrigeration Service and Contracting* magazine, these contractors have three approximately equal buying patterns: 35% like to call or fax their order in and then have it delivered; a similar percentage prefer to just drop by the counter and place the order and pick it up all at the same time; a slightly lower number, 30%, call or fax the order in and then pick it up. The best prospects for using an online system are the phone/fax order placers. Shifting to online ordering should make things easier and more profitable for the wholesaler and the contractor. The next step is to figure out how to do that.

Based on some research we've done, we'd say that a key will be understanding that the contractors who are online use the services at night. Why? Because, during the day, they're on the job site. That means that a system that will work for them will have enough information and be easy enough to use to allow contractors to place their orders when there's no one there to help. That's the kind of system Neathery is out to create. He doesn't think it will be that hard. His advice: "Don't underestimate the skills of your contractors"—especially your top contractors.

Neathery also points out that, if you have a public Web site, you have to realize that individual homeowners will find you and want to place orders. When that happens, driving the individual consumers to local dealers is the strategy of choice. The results aren't in yet on how this particular balancing act will come out, but it's the kind of problem many wholesalers and retailers will face as more and more business connections are made on the Net.

It turns out that the key to good fulfillment and distribution, good supply-chain management, is the same as the key to good business—knowing your customers and giving them value—in this case, concentrating on the part of the business that gets the product to them. One key point here that you should look for, and expect to see, is integrated solutions that are designed for the Net environment. Here's an example.

INTEGRATED SOLUTIONS

Hops are important to Heineken, and so is HOPS. The former is an essential ingredient in beer and has to be chosen with care. The latter, HOPS, is the Heineken Operational Planning System, and it's important to getting Heineken's beer to you quickly.

HOPS is based on a product from American Software for supply-chain planning. It's Net-based and it generates order and replenishment recommendations for individual Heineken distributors based on a number of criteria: past sales, seasonal trends, geography, the

weather, and so forth. Distributors can interact with the system using a standard browser.

Without HOPS, fulfillment and distribution worked this way. A
district manager at Heineken USA would plan an order with a distributor. The order would be faxed to Heineken's U.S. headquarters
which, in turn, would transmit it to the brewery in Holland. Ten to
twelve weeks later, the distributor got the beer.

With the HOPS system, here's how it goes. The system generates
a "forecast order" every month. The distributor checks out the order on a secure Web site and makes any changes that are necessary.
At that point, the order is entered automatically into the Heineken
system. And the beer? It arrives in four to six weeks—less than half
the old cycle time.

The HOPS system represents some trends that we think are important. First, there's the management trend toward considering
and planning for the entire supply or value chain. Second, there's
the movement toward using computer technology to automate
those processes for which automation works. Finally, there's the
movement toward using Net/Web technology to make sophisticated supply-chain and distribution management available to businesses for which traditional EDI is not the right choice

TACTICS

Let's look at our tactics and examine how they apply to fulfillment
and distribution.

THINK LINKS

In fulfillment and distribution, the links turn out to be pretty obvious. They're the links between the different parts of the value chain.
Ask yourself,

> What kinds of information need to flow along those links?
>
> What kinds of information would make your channel
> partners more effective?

Financial Services Corporation (which we spoke about in Chapters 4–6) has a trading desk within its extranet where rates of the mutual funds and annuities are regularly updated, which, in turn, become valuable information for FSC's field affiliates to use with their respective customers. We've found, when working with clients, that a good way to ask these questions along the value chain is to start with this question, "What could we do that we don't do now that would make a dramatic difference in the value we provide or in our profitability?"

AUTOMATE

As you automate processes along this chain, think about ways of extending functions and applications that you have in your internal operation to your other channel partners. That's a good strategy to pursue because you've probably developed them fairly well already, and all you'll need to do is to adapt them to delivery in the new technology.

Start with the premise that information should be keyed once and then passed along in digital form across Net connections so that people don't have to key again. Look for ways to automate all the processes that go with getting the goods from one place to another, including the ordering process.

Federal Express offers a classic example of an automated fulfillment system. FedEx gives people access to its global package tracking system on its public Web site. This allows customers to track their own packages en route to their destinations. FedEx has saved millions of dollars by cutting back on the time its customer service department previously had to dedicate to answering customers' phone inquires about the status of packages.

CUSTOMIZE

Customizing is important in fulfillment and distribution. There are usually two ways to consider customization in the value chain. The first is to view customizing in terms of the type of user. For example, a manufacturer might think about the different types of information that need to be available for end users and for wholesalers. The second way to approach customization up and down the value chain is to identify the needs of particular companies or groups of companies, such as premier distributors.

The system Marshall set up to allow electronic ordering is a good example of using Net technology to automate its fulfillment and distribution process. By combining its electronic ordering system, which is hooked directly into a robotic warehouse process that automates order picking, packing, and shipping and by having a UPS site inside its warehouse Marshall Industries not only reduced cycle times but also cut costs while facilitating an efficient shipping process.

TRANSFORM

Transforming data into information, and information into knowledge, is important to consider here. We see a tendency for companies looking at their value chains to concentrate almost exclusively on operational information—order tracking, for instance; but looking for ways to share the kind of information and knowledge that make their partners more effective can pay big dividends as well. For example, consider how Heineken uses its Heineken Operational Planning System (HOPS) to generate order and replenishment recommendations for individual distributors, so that they receive their orders in less than half the time it took using pre-Net technology. As a basis for these recommendations, HOPS calls up data on distributors' past sales and combines that with other data, such as seasonal trends, weather, and geography. HOPS transmits that information to distributors, enabling them to make knowledgeable decisions about their ordering needs.

INSIDE/OUTSIDE

Inside/outside is key here. Look both ways along the supply-chain to find opportunities to apply Net/Web technology. Consider relationship building as a key part of what you're doing. Look for ways to foster alliances by using Net technology.

CORE FUNCTIONS/BIG PAYOFFS

Core functions/big payoffs in fulfillment and distribution come at two levels. First, there's the operational level. You'll find the same sort of cost savings and service enhancements here as in other areas of business. But there's also a strategic level. Pay attention to your choice of the channel partners with whom you establish Net/Web connections. They're your partners; their success and your success will be linked.

General Electric and Netscape have used both the inside/outside and the core functions/big payoff TACTICs by forming a strategic alliance team to further strengthen the potential solutions of business-to-business electronic commerce. General Electric Information Systems is utilizing Netscape open-platform software to create extranet solutions for its customers, such as enabling manufacturers to extend their legacy order entry, order tracking, and inventory management systems to their suppliers and distributors. This enables manufacturers to establish just-in-time inventory, save on warehouse space, and reduce manufacturing cycle times.

START NOW

Start now to stake out your territory and to forge the best alliances possible. Your competition will be moving in this arena, if they aren't already. Make sure your organization can compete. Start now by implementing the appropriate distribution and fulfillment technology application for your organization. Consider such Net applications as:

- Linking systems you already have, like EDI or warehouse automation and your Net/Web efforts.

- Setting up links across the Web between sources of information in different locations, such as manufacturer's files and distributor's order systems.

- Providing access to your extranet—a key relationship-building device.

- Using your public Web site as the front end to more private applications.

- Establishing a tracking system for your customers so that they can track product shipping status as in the Federal Express example in the "Automate" section of the TACTICS Action Planning System.

- Outsourcing the setup of your Net system's architecture. (Many associations and companies, such as Amicus Networks, are developing sophisticated solutions for companies in specific industries.)

WALLY AND JEFF'S FULFILLMENT AND DISTRIBUTION LESSONS LEARNED

1. Look at the whole chain. Look at the whole chain. Look at the whole chain. Whether you call it the supply-chain or the value chain or the food chain, there are benefits to be had by looking at it whole when you streamline your processes. Looking at the whole chain will help you identify the areas where the biggest improvements can come so that you can start there. Remember that your value chain is really a set of relationships. Look for ways to enhance those relationships. Examples in this chapter of how Net technology can help you implement this lesson are Heineken's HOPS system, the GE Information Systems Trading Process Network, and Amicus's explanation of the "food chain" in the financial services industry.

2. The EDI model is a good but limited one. Take the basic concept—enter the data once, use coordinated systems—then pick the technology that will work best for your organization. Expect that there will be Net- and Web-capable software that will do many functions of traditional EDI, but be careful of trade-offs.

3. Be sure your firewall is secure and your Network infrastructure solid before rolling out critical data. It should

be as reliable and transparent to users as making a telephone call. Test for any leaks in your Net system.

4. Net and Web technology provide a way for companies along the chain with different kinds of computer platforms and different levels of technological sophistication to make use of the efficiency gains and profit enhancements that supply-chain management can provide. This is a major benefit that has special application here in the value chain.

5. Pareto's law (the 80/20 rule) still applies on the Net. Start by setting up and enriching your relationships with the trading partners who are most important to you.

6. Involve all stakeholders in your fulfillment and distribution network, plan early, and don't forget to plan capacity ahead of demand.

7. Make sure your employees are trained in how to communicate and sell your Net technology applications. Without understanding and trust, the greatest fulfillment and distribution system in the world won't be used.

8. Cost-cutting benefits are often a good way to sell the need for an intranet to internal people who need to approve it. But don't neglect the potential for productivity enhancements and enriched relationships.

9. Don't forget to tie your systems together internally as well as externally.

10. Check out industry or association solutions to supply-chain management. If the basic work has already been done, you can implement faster. Just be sure that the "best industry solution" is also best for you.

CHAPTER 9

CUSTOMER SERVICE

It's not just the complaint department anymore. Back when some of us started in business, that's what customer service meant. It meant the place where people call to tell you that your product didn't work, your service was lousy, or your people were rude. Somewhere along the way, a transformation occurred.

We began to think of what used to be the complaint department as a way to add value in business. And, thus, "customer service" was born. The change to thinking of it as customer service is more than semantics. It's a recognition that the sale doesn't stop with the actual purchase. Instead, it continues through use, and the service that supports that use can be a true force to add value. That concept was probably better for business, but it certainly made things harder.

Three key challenges have grown out of this shift toward customer service in the last several years. With these come an increasing need in business to deliver value and service as part of the equation, a need that makes customer service far more important than it used to be. And they come at a time when increasing competition and cost pressures have been mounting as well.

CRITICAL CHALLENGES OF PROVIDING HIGH-QUALITY CUSTOMER SERVICE

The three major challenges in customer service that the Net can help you deal with are how to:

1. Add value to your product or service.
2. Reduce costs of providing customer service.
3. Increase ease and responsiveness of supporting customers.

SOLUTIONS

A first critical challenge relating to customer service is that this service is now expected to do a variety of things besides handle complaints. In some industries, what we're calling customer service also includes the functions of the help desk—the place people contact for technical support or advice on how to use the product. According to the market research firm Dataquest, personal computer hardware and software vendors handled more than 200 million customer support calls in 1995 at a cost of over $4 billion.

MAKING HAY OUT OF CUSTOMER COMPLAINTS

According to Jeff Bork of Scopus Technology, headquartered in Emeryville, California, 82% percent of people who have a complaint or problem successfully resolved will buy from a company again. That means that just handling the problem effectively has an impact.

On the other hand, only 37% of those that never connect to have the problem solved will buy again, so getting them to connect is important, too. There's a measurable correlation between contact and future sales. And the key is making it easy for them to contact you and get their issue handled.

Using the Web as a contact tool can improve the odds that people will get hold of you and present their problem. It has the additional benefit of handling customer service and other inquiries at a far lower cost than a call center.

Customer service departments routinely gather data about the kinds of calls they get and feed the data and information to the sales force and the product development teams in the company. Out of that comes a demand for the customer service department to add value. They do that by sharing information but also by the highly professional and personalized way in which they're able to handle calls.

Before the Net, you had to discover in advance, or at least guess in advance, what information other employees, suppliers, or customers were going to need. What you usually did was to send them a bunch of information so that they would have it when they needed it. It was "just in case" information.

With the Net, you can provide a broad array of information and links between that information that help people get precisely the information or mix of information they want when they need it. You can put together custom information solutions or let them put together their own custom information solutions. That increases the quality of service and that becomes a way to add value and differentiate your company from your competitors.

SAVING CALL CENTER COSTS

The second challenge grows out of the first. Customer service is an incredibly people-intensive part of the business, and those people have to be good. For the most part, it involves people who answer telephones and give answers to people or who respond to mail inquiries and send back answers. Net technology gives you some alternatives to that.

With Net technology, your customers or clients get the answers themselves using technology that you provide. When that happens, you don't pay. You don't pay for employee costs. You don't pay for the 800 number inbound or the postage outbound. In short, you don't pay for the average $20 per call moving through a customer service call center. That's all well and good, but people-intensive equals costly in today's business environment. So the second customer service challenge the Net can help you with is the challenge of reduced cost.

The savings can be dramatic. Dell Computer currently has some 20,000 customers a week downloading support files. Those people used to have to talk to a technical support person. Thousands more check on their orders using the order status checking feature on Dell's public site. The savings: about $500,000 per month.

The third customer service challenge is responsiveness. People want customer service that's responsive. They don't want to have to hunt for it, they don't want to be put on hold, and they don't want to talk to people who don't know any more than they do. Net technology can help you meet the responsiveness challenge. Using the Net, you can provide information at any hour of the day or night. Using sophisticated support tools, you'll be able to give people the information they need when they need it.

One of our clients makes an industrial product that has a basic information sheet. They've discovered over the years that when they ship the product, they will, over the lifetime of that product, ship an average of 7.2 information sheets for it. That's because purchasing takes one for its files, and maintenance needs one, and they need one in the plant manager's office. And, then, when maintenance uses its sheet, it gets all greasy and stuffed in the bottom of somebody's locker, so it has to be replaced. The problem is that it often doesn't need to be replaced until the next time it's needed. Today, with a Web site, our client can have that product sheet available immediately. People can get it when they need it.

Companies especially known for their customer service, such as Nordstrom, even empower their people to solve problems that aren't created by the company or by the product and services it sells. It turns out that Net and Web technologies are great ways to meet all these customer service challenges.

Part of that can be done publicly. More businesses are using their public Web sites for product support and customer service than ever before. The marketing research firm Techtel reports that, in the 12-month period ending in June 1996, the percentage of companies that offer product or services support through the Internet nearly doubled, from 15% to 29%. That brings it up to about the same percentage as those using the Net for advertising.

ADDING ENHANCED VALUE IN SECURITIES

At times, if you're like most of us, all these challenges may seem a bit overwhelming. A lion's share of them can be solved by implementing public Web sites or setting up intranets and extranets. Here's what we found out when we talked with Stan Witkowski of Prudential Securities and asked him how he was passed the technology ball to run with.

Stan has lots of titles at Prudential Securities. He's an executive vice president. His work description is client strategic initiatives. And he's also the director of mutual funds & annuities in sales marketing. Prudential does about $8 billion worth of mutual funds sales and about $1.4 billion of annuity sales annually. So this is pretty heavy all by itself.

Stan's been in the security business for a long time. He was with Shearson for a total of 24 years before he hit Prudential a couple of years ago.

When he arrived at Prudential, he'd already known Chairman and CEO Wick Simmons for a number of years. He came onboard without a really clear job description, but Simmons gave him a list of 35 employees and sent him off to find out about the company and its challenges. It took about two weeks to get that done. Then the two had lunch.

It turns out that there were two agendas at that lunch. Stan's agenda was to present all the neat ideas he'd had and all the proposals and try to see what Wick would buy into. Wick's agenda was different.

Partway though the lunch, Wick leaned across the table and said, "Stanley, Stanley, Stanley. We need to compete in the '90s based on a platform of technology. We need to embrace these new technologies. And we need to build the things that will help us access our marketplace better, capture market share better, and help the productivity of our key people ... I need you to work on that. So where do we get started?" According to Witkowski, Wick Simmons got up, bid farewell, and left him sitting there.

At that point, Wick had a big smile and Stan was, well, puzzled and worried. He had his challenge. As he describes that time, "There's nothing like embracing technology right for the wrong reason. But I was either going to embrace it or, no kidding, look for a new job."

SETTING UP A CROSS-FUNCTIONAL TEAM

The first thing Witkowski did was put together a cross-functional committee that he called the Technology Advisory Group, TAG for short. That wasn't just important for technology, it was important because Witkowski was new to the company and didn't really have connections to infrastructure and knowledge that he would have had if he'd been onboard a long time. He told the company that what they were doing was a strategic initiative for the company. In two years, he wanted them to have a significant impact on the business. The impact had to be in areas that were usable and practical—they had to make a real difference. Finally, they had to be profitable. There was going to be a budget, and they were going to work within it, and what they were going to do in addition to being practical was to help the bottom line.

He started by looking at an array of things that the TAG could address. One of them was automating some of the order entry system. As he puts it, "This wasn't cutting-edge technology, this was catch-up technology." But catch-up technology had to be in place before Prudential could move out to the cutting edge.

Then he started talking about having Web sites. At about this point, some challenges started coming from the members of the group.

Now, there are lots of training courses out there about how to deal with conflict, and they usually set soft prescriptions, but anybody who knows Stan Witkowski knows that he's a pretty straight-ahead guy, especially when he's on a mission, and he was. "I stopped talking. I looked at these people, and I said, "Look, we're going to do this. If you don't believe it, you're invited not to come to the next meeting, which we're going to have in three weeks. By the way, Wick Simmons, the chairman, will be here in three weeks to address this group.'"

Then he went on to tell them other things—that his responsibility was to get the funding and do that kind of work, and that theirs was to help achieve the initiative. And so, Witkowski and his group were off and running.

THE FIRST FULL-SERVICE AROUND-THE-CLOCK BROKERAGE FIRM ON THE WEB

Prudential Securities' first Web site, VBO, which stands for Virtual Branch Office (www.prusec.com) came up by September 1, 1991. That gave Prudential an experience with Web-based technology and set the stage for the next item, which was Prudential Online. According to Stan, "We said we'd be up September 1; we were up September 1. It's actually been a big success for us. Once we were able to establish that, I wanted to drill down a little deeper, and we were the first full-service brokerage firm to have a site—known as Prudential Online—which allows our clients 7 days a week, 24 hours a day to access their accounts."

Now, all this was moving pretty fast but, in order to fully appreciate the customer benefit Net technology provides, you need to hear it the way Stan put it to us.

Let's say you're not in the financial services business. You work hard all day in your office. At the end of the day, you go to your car. It's six o'clock in the evening. You've had a long day. You turn on the radio, and what do you hear? You hear the market's up or down 100 points. Which is not atypical anymore, OK. And you get into your house and everybody welcomes you, the family and your wife, and you have dinner and you open up the mail, and it's eight o'clock at night by now. You have a quiet moment. What do you want a solution for? I would suggest you want to solve, well, how am I doing. The market goes up or down 100 points, how am I doing? And what are your choices? Not good, eight o'clock at night. Number one, you can't really get your broker at eight o'clock at night. Number two, the evening paper—it's tedious to try to pull all your stocks and mutual funds and eyestrain out of the paper. Or, number three, look at your statement, but that's 30 days old.

How would you like to be able to sit down at your Web phone or your Web TV or your computer and, with a couple of keystrokes, up comes your VBO; one click and you're into Prudential Online, and there is your account. It tells you right there what your value is that day. And then, if you click again, it will tell you what your asset allocation is that day. How much is in stocks and equities, bonds, mutual funds. You click again, and it will show you what your equity position is. You click again, it will show you what that research report on that stock that was up 10 points today is about. You can click again, and it will tell you if they got your check that day and if your dividend came in. And, oh, there's the name of that mutual fund I own that I couldn't think of today. OK, you did it in 50 seconds and you get off. That's it, you're off. And you're satisfied.

With extranets like Prudential Online, you don't have to play telephone tag three or four times to reach your broker. Stan says that it is all about access and control for the customer. If Prudential can provide that, then customers can handle a lot of their own customer service. For Prudential, that frees up brokers for more productive time while improving customer satisfaction. The danger, of course, is that it can turn into loyalty based on transaction efficiency rather than on relationships, and that kind of loyalty is harder to maintain.

TEAMING UP WITH NETSCAPE TO CREATE AN INTRANET

The next step was to have an intranet that Prudential calls PSI Web. On November 4, 1995, Netscape Communications Corporation and Prudential Securities Incorporated announced that Prudential had licensed Netscape client and server software to create an intranet connecting clients, financial advisors, and the firm's internal resources throughout the United States. Netscape Navigator client software, the Netscape SuiteSpot server family, and Netscape Fast-Track server software are the products that would be used.

One of Stan's closest associates in Prudential's Internet project, Bill Anderson, executive vice president at Prudential Securities, said, "Through our intranet, we will be able to provide our 5700 U.S. financial advisors with strong ability to communicate with clients and to share information. We expect it to reduce costs, increase productivity, and enhance internal communication with important corporate resources. This new license provides Netscape software to all 17,000 employees' desktops at PSI."

STANDARDIZING AN E-MAIL PROGRAM

The Web wasn't the whole deal. There was also the matter of an older, but in some ways more popular technology, e-mail. Prudential has about 18,000 employees and, at that time, it had at least five different forms of e-mail which, according to Stan, "is like having no e-mail at all. If you don't have a common platform, you've got babble. " So Stan and his TAG set about making sure Prudential Securities had a uniformly proficient e-mail platform.

So, OK, now Prudential is roaring along in big corporate initiatives, but how does it get all those 18,000 people onboard. How does that get them to be part of the electronic village? The answer is to help them buy laptops.

A LAPTOP IN EVERY ACCOUNT EXECUTIVE'S TOOLKIT

Witkowski asked Bill Anderson, formerly with IBM, to go negotiate a deal with IBM for a couple of thousand laptops. They're nice machines, loaded with lots of software and an NT operating system. Some of the software is off-the-shelf, like ACT Contact Management, and some of it is proprietary. The laptops would normally cost about $6700, but Prudential subsidized $2400 of that, so the out-of-pocket cost to Prudential people who what to buy the laptop was about $4300. The entire package included preinstalled software, training, and an extended warranty.

Witkowski: "If they drop it in the parking lot, we sweep the pieces up and send it to the FedEx location. Back comes either a new machine or a fixed machine." That's putting the system in place and making it easy to use—almost bulletproof. The idea is also to make it easy for representatives to work.

Prudential Securities has jumped on the idea of automating a lot of its customer service. That immediately introduces benefits and new competitive challenges.

CUSTOMER SERVICE ON THE WEB

How do you make your customer service operation even more effective using this technology? Let's look at IBM for a great example.

You start out by just moving some of your customer service operations onto the Web. That seems simple, but it can have a great big impact.

IBM did a study at its Atlanta Call Center to determine what the difference was between handling a given volume of calls strictly through a telephone call center and handling them through a Web site. The results of the study were dramatic. Essentially, 10 to 12 people can handle the same call volume using a Web site as 20 people could if telephone were the only way to handle the queries. That's a 40% saving right away—less than that if part of the load is still handled by employees taking calls.

CUTTING COSTS OF PACKAGE TRACKING CALLS

You can see comparable numbers from examples like Federal Express. Reliable industry estimates are that it costs Federal Express about $8 to handle a package tracking call with all the expenses included. When those calls are handled through the Web site, the cost drops to pennies.

So, OK, you start out by just putting stuff on the Web. If your company handles lots of routine inquiries, you'll get big benefits right off the bat. Most people who've run a customer service operation know that lots of questions recur again and again. That's true if you're selling computer equipment or actuators for air conditioning equipment or almost any kind of consumer product.

There are probably 50 to 100 questions that cover almost 80% of the inquiries that would normally come in on the telephone. That's what we've found in client situations that we've analyzed. Once you know that, you can let your customers get those answers themselves, eliminating the need to call a help desk. The savings can be dramatic since, as estimated by the Gartner Group, of Stamford, Connecticut, companies that run a call-in help desk spend, on average, $2743 per user per year on the function.

What Is the Process for Delivering Customer Service Using the Net?

We've discovered a fairly straightforward process that companies seem to follow in moving customer service to the Net/Web. Like many of the other techniques here, it starts simple and goes for the big payoffs first.

STEP 1: START BY PUTTING UP FREQUENTLY ASKED QUESTION FILES.

Part of your strategy here is to get customers to go to the Web first when they have a question. Increase the possibility that they'll contact you and you'll increase the probability that they'll buy again.

Be sure to have a simple e-mail connection for questions that extend beyond your frequently asked ones and give people an alternative way to contact you, like phone and fax.

STEP 2: ADD AN INFOBOT FOR EACH SPECIFIC QUESTION.

Then, go further. A next step here might be to add, for each of the specific questions, an infobot that sends an e-mail with information to people almost immediately on their request. This has two benefits:

1. There's the benefit of people getting the information they want.
2. The second benefit is a bit more subtle. It involves the expectation you set up for people, that when they go to you for information, they get a quick response.

Now, since you know that no frequently asked question file can answer all the possible questions, you need to deal with the fact that many of your answers will not completely handle a customer's individual problem. Here's how to do that.

STEP 3: ADD LINKS TO OTHER RESOURCES ON YOUR INFOBOT MESSAGE.

In the message that you send on your infobot, include some other places people can go for more information. That might be a particular part of your Web site, or might be another Web site. In any case, your objective is to give people the answer to that question as completely as possible with your first answer and all the references you provide.

Remember our TACTIC to automate as much as you can. The more people can do for you in this process, the more profit impact your move to the Web will have.

STEP 4: CAPTURE AND AUTOMATE CUSTOMIZED CUSTOMER SERVICE RESPONSE.

Now, let's look at stepping up your level of benefit. Think about what happens when somebody asks a question that calls for a custom response. Your customer service representative or your technician prepares a response, maybe several pages worth, and sends it out to the customer. Now what?

Now you need to capture that information. You're really looking for two kinds of things. You want to capture your response to the query. That means you want to get it into a database or, better yet, a knowledge base, so that other representatives can use the material the next time the question is asked. If you've captured your responses over time, you build an excellent database that your internal reps can use. If you'd like to look at a good way to do this, check out the main Lotus Web site and then follow the links to customer service. What you'll see there are the results of replies to questions that people have asked over time. Those replies have been put (in this case) into a Lotus Notes database that can be queried through an HTML interface. All that is technical jargon meaning that, if you've got your Web browser, you can get an answer out of a database that's built using a different kind of technology.

You can expect to see more and more of that as time goes on.

At this stage in the process of using this technology to improve your customer service, you set up a basic response mechanism, deal with frequently asked questions, and develop the way to capture your questions and responses to new questions as they arise. Remember that one of the things you're trying to gather here is the way your customers ask their questions. For almost any customer service operation that's one of the big challenges—not just having the answer but knowing how the question is going to be asked. So, be sure to capture that as well.

STEP 5: ADDING ADVANCED INTERACTIVE TOOLS WILL MAKE THE PROCESS AS MUCH AS SIX TIMES MORE PRODUCTIVE.

At this point, you've had some major increases in productivity and profitability. But the best is yet to come. Look at what you can do with advanced interactive tools to make this process as much as six times more productive.

These are ways to connect your customers (using an extranet, for example) or just general users to databases that you already have. Using tools like IBM's Net.data, a customer with a query about an order, for example, can check a proprietary database.

When that database is checked, a report is generated that's turned into an HTML page that's unique to the particular inquiry. The HTML page is seen by the customer.

Let's stop and look at that IBM example. It begins with customer service being handled through a call center. So the first step in the strategy is to substitute some online customer service for the call center strategy. Then, as technology develops, IBM and others are going to look at ways to customize the customer service.

Different companies will do that in different ways. Federal Express, for example, is planning to give key customers access to the same customer service database that their own people use. If the company follows its normal rollout pattern, a limited form of access to the database will ultimately be available to all customers.

The ideal, of course, has every customer able at any time of the day or night to get a precisely customized solution to a customer service question. That might be fully automated with no human intervention at all, but it might also involve human intervention at the point where it's needed. At that stage, the people who become involved are top-grade, well-trained customer service representatives who can bring to bear their knowledge and experience, perhaps supported by a corporate knowledge-based Internet system.

AN EXTENDED INTRANET WITH A NATIONAL NETWORK OF FINANCIAL REPRESENTATIVES

Horner, Townsend & Kent (located on the Web at http:// www.htk.com), a subsidiary of Penn Mutual Life Insurance Company, set up an extended intranet with its national Network of more than 1200 financial representatives. C. Ray Smith, executive vice president for sales and marketing, said, "HTK's objective was to establish an extraordinary resource for our 1200 financial representatives, giving them the information and communication support they need to offer world-class customer service."

Horner, Townsend & Kent is using Amicus Corporation's Tool Belt technology at its intranet/extranet-based Web site. The HTK extranet includes:

- An electronic forms service, enabling site users to print any HTK forms on demand
- Information about products and services
- Procedures for doing business with HTK, including information about commissions, licensing and registration, and compliance issues
- Hypertext hotlinks to preferred sponsors or sources of information about markets and breaking news
- E-mail capabilities
- Company updates

Up to now, we've been talking about big companies. What about the smaller companies?

HOW SMALLER COMPANIES PROVIDE CUSTOMER SERVICE

Some of the tools we've talked about here seem out of reach if yours is a smaller business. The good news is that there's a race for software companies to develop applications that can provide sophisticated solutions to smaller businesses. Your job is to look for these off-the-shelf applications. There are more every day.

TRACKING SOFTWARE FOR SMALL AND MIDSIZED TRUCKING COMPANIES

One quick answer here is that lots of firms are lining up to help provide off-the-shelf customer service solutions. One of those is Illinois-based Payne Corporation. Its product is a computer system called LoadTrack, which is aimed at small and midsized trucking companies and other carriers.

To understand the importance of this, we have to go back several years. It was in the 1980s that CSX, then the Chessie system, became the first transportation company to allow customers to track their own shipments. The service was made available in the form of a proprietary system, to its very best customers. Federal Express was early on this bandwagon as well. The very first Federal Express tracking by customers was enabled by proprietary software given to preferred customers.

Over the next few years, large carriers, such as Roadway, Consolidated Freightways, and American President Lines, all made it possible for their main shippers, and then for all their shippers, to check on shipments. That gave them an advantage over the smaller carriers, who didn't have the computer power or sophistication to do the same thing. LoadTrack is designed to help those carriers compete.

We see this same trend in lots of other areas besides customer service. Software firms are lining up to provide security packages and transaction packages and EDI packages and groupware packages, all to help smaller companies. You can expect that trend to continue as the market for these services mushrooms.

ONLINE PROFESSIONAL SUPPORT

The Credit Union Executives Society (CUES) started working toward setting up its Web site in August and was live by January 1996. Barbara Kachelski, senior vice president of membership for CUES, said,

> ... there were four things we wanted to accomplish. One, we wanted to establish some type of a forum for our members to contact each other because we know that not everybody has networking access through conferences or through their local area. Two, we wanted a place for job postings where professional societies and people can turn to when they want information about job openings. Three, we wanted to have some marketing presence on the Web, some demonstration of what CUES is. And, four we wanted to have other credit union Web sites available so that members could look at what the technology was that was being used by their peers.

One of the unique online services CUES provided for its membership is a "members only" LISTSERV called CUES Net. In order to access this area of its Web site, members need to have user I.D. and a special password. CUES members can subscribe at no charge to this accessible e-mail venue to "discuss" important timely issues with fellow credit union executives. They're able to get answers to critical questions daily by e-mail. CUES was kind enough to give us special access to an archive of these e-mail discussions. What follows is a list of the kind of topics CUES members were able to discuss and get timely information about to enhance their overall member (customer) service. The list included:

- Auto loan recapture
- Virtual meetings
- Excess deposit insurance
- Bankruptcy charge-off policy
- Visa Card access for home equity loans
- Home page and home banking

- Credit union boards on the Internet from LIST CUES
- Check cashing ATMs from LIST CUES
- Cost justification of technology
- Today at CEO network
- Employee empowerment
- IRA investments
- PC home banking
- Mortgage lending

Consider what topics your business partners, distributors, affiliates, or strategic alliances might like to discuss in a special area of your Web site. They might also want to refer to an archive where the group wisdom is stored for future reference when needed.

The Credit Union Executives Society also enhances its members' operations online by providing upcoming conference listings, a form to register for conferences and pay by phone, fax, or mail. It also offers a job posting area on its Web site that allows credit unions to submit positions available and for members to submit positions wanted.

Those applications are going to find their way into the one- and two-person business, the small consulting firms, retail stores, and service businesses. But, even now, those firms are using Net technology to handle inquiries more effectively.

ENHANCING CUSTOMER RESPONSIVENESS WITH A LARGE DEALER NETWORK

Extron Electronics, established in 1983, is a leading manufacturer of computer-video interfaces, switchers, distribution amplifiers, computer-video scan converters, and high-resolution cable. Educating the market is inherent in Extron's corporate philosophy. In order to provide the most current information on video, multimedia and professional audiovisual industries, Extron offers dealers and customers educational seminars, newsletters, instructional videotapes, and the biannual *Handbook of Computer Interfacing*. In addition to these support materials, Extron sales, technical support and engineering departments offer state-of-the-art customer service and 24-hour technical support on weekends. This commitment to service and education is the cornerstone of Extron's S3 philosophy, which stands for service, support, and solutions.

Just as Extron's products meet the specifications of new and changing technology, its approach to customer service and customer accessibility has followed suit. Extron has set up EXTRON-WEB, which was developed so that customers could reach Extron on the World Wide Web. Extron's home page provides new product information and accessibility to product literature. Customers also have an opportunity to contact Extron employees through e-mail and, recently, Extron instituted a new service called WebCall. It can be accessed off Extron's public Web site and is designed to have a *human*—they say, "Talk to a Real Person from Extron"—return the call. Imagine that, off their Web site, you can access WebCall, and Extron will call you on your terms, when you want a callback, and on its dollar. When we talked to Gary Kayye, the vice president of sales and marketing, he said, "WebCall is just another customer service–oriented feature we are providing to enhance our responsiveness to our customers."

SMALLER COMPANIES CAN USE MAILBOTS, TOO

One very effective tool being used by lots of small companies is called an autoresponder, or an e-back system or a mailbot. This tool is a little bit of software that allows a person to request information and receive it immediately and automatically via electronic mail.

Lots of small companies have discovered that the majority of the service calls and information requests they get center around a few key issues and questions. To deal with these, they've adapted a technique learned from the Internet called a frequently asked question (FAQ) file. These files, which are made available on Web sites and via autoresponders, supply answers, when they're needed by clients or customers, about the questions they're most likely to ask. Result: For the customer, prompt information; for the company, greatly lowered customer service costs.

Just like the big guys, smaller businesses utilize technology to raise the power of customer service while driving the cost of providing that service.

TACTICS

Let's look at our tactics and how they apply to customer service.

THINK LINKS

When you think links in relation to customer service, start by thinking about how to link more of your customers and clients to your operation. Then, determine how far you want those links to extend.

A good question to ask is, "What kinds of tracking, follow-up, or help systems are we using internally that we could allow our customers to use?" E-mail access to your company or a "WebCall" that lets customers tell you when they want to be contacted by a real human being as Extron Electronics has done.

Many financial services, like Northern Trust, The Dreyfus Corporation, Prudential, and Community Credit Union in Dallas, Texas allow customers to access their accounts online using a password system in a secure part of their Web sites. Once customers have accessed their accounts, they can check their account status, such as checks cleared and current balance; they can pay bills, check on current stock prices, review their investment portfolios, and apply for loans and credit cards to manage their financial affairs personally.

AUTOMATE

Once you've answered the links question for customer service, start asking about how you can automate the function. The cost savings here can be astronomical. For example, McDonnell Douglas's commercial aircraft manufacturing division, Douglas Aircraft, distributes aircraft service bulletins internationally to its customers. The average bulletin is 25 pages, and some customers receive four or five a day. Customers can now access this information using a unique password, which is stored on Douglas Aircraft's secure server.

Horner, Townsend & Kent uses an extended intranet as an electronic forms service, enabling its financial representatives to print HTK forms on demand.

Another example of customer service automation that's been used many times is Federal Express, which provides one of the biggest and best hard-dollar savings examples. It doesn't matter which reference source of FedEx savings figures you use—there are several out there—FedEx is saving a ton of money on order tracking alone.

CUSTOMIZE

With links and automation dealt with, look at ways to customize your operation. That really should take two forms. The first is to allow those inside your Net, your staff and your trusted partners, to have access inside your firewall to information in a form that's most helpful to them. Then, look at ways to customize the customer service process from the customer's or client's point of view.

You can store all your customer information on an intranet so that all qualified internal employees can use it to better serve your customers. This information can be customized to include such information as customer's names, products or services they use, customer history, problems they have had, things they want more information on, and any quirks they have about how they like to be communicated with.

TRANSFORM

Transforming data into information and information into knowledge is a big part of using this technology and customer service. We see companies building knowledge bases about their products that they use internally and then extending the use of those knowledge bases out to their customers. Usually, that happens first with trusted partners and then moves out to the customer population as a whole.

INSIDE/OUTSIDE

Looking inside/outside can pay off big with customer service. Inside, you'll find answers and the knowledge to provide more answers. Get that material together and into a form that's usable. Publish as much as feasible. From outside, you'll find out what the questions are. Keep track of what your customers and clients ask. And make sure you put the new answers to their questions into the same form and place in which you put the older ones. Keep building that information and knowledge file.

CORE BENEFITS/BIG PAYOFFS

Core benefits/big payoffs start by putting a link to frequently asked questions (FAQs) on your public Web site that responds to the typical questions your customers have and providing an e-mail contact for more specific questions—set up infobots or mailbots to automatically send information that people request to their e-mail addresses. Attention to customer requests will help you prioritize the customer service material you put on the Net/Web. Set up e-mail discussion groups or forums focusing on the various needs and challenges of your customers.

START NOW

Start now because the payoffs are almost immediate. Then, move along to make your system more effective and profitable. Start by providing customers with information on your public Web site like product brochures and detailed specifications available as Web pages or as e-mail automatically sent to your customers via your mailbot. Provide customer support training via the Web using hyperlinked documents and graphics-based scenarios that explain how other related customers have implemented your product or service to meet similar challenges. Consider setting up an extranet for your affiliates and field salespeople to access all the product, customer history, technical support, and "archived group wisdom" information needed to respond quickly to their customers needs, questions, problems, and concerns.

WALLY AND JEFF'S CUSTOMER SERVICE LESSONS LEARNED

1. Using the Web as a contact tool can improve the odds that people will get hold of you and present their problems. It has the additional benefit of handling customer service and other inquiries at a far lower cost than a call center.

2. Make sure the information that flows through your customer service operations makes it to your intranet and from there to other people who can use it, such as sales and product development. The whole idea of the Net is to make information available, but making that happen often means doing more than just putting information systems in place. It usually involves looking at the business processes that generate and use information and then making sure that the technological system links them.

3. Make sure that the private, sensitive information about your customers that comes via your intranet or extranet is protected and made available only to qualified employees.

4. Use e-mail, forums, and e-mail discussion groups to serve your customers by collecting future product or service requests.

5. You have to start from wherever you are. That may mean that you have to put "catch-up technology" in place before you get to the cutting-edge stuff.

6. No matter where your project starts or what it entails, it still has to be run right. In some form, you'll need participation and buy-in and endorsement and a plan and a budget.

7. Make sure your field representatives have the technological equipment they need to access your intranet/extranet customer service information and know how to use it.

8. The next few years will bring major advances in the ways we'll be able to customize information for both internal and external users. Make sure your systems people are on the lookout for these advances. But don't leave it entirely up to them. Make it part of your job to check out other company's public sites (especially your competition's). When you see something that works well, tell the people responsible for implementing your network about it and see if it will work for you.

9. As you look at options related to customer service, consider ways to improve your responsiveness and increase its relevance and to reduce your costs using Net technology.

10. Consider giving customers, employees, and business partners access to an expert's advice through chat rooms to which you invite special guest speakers to share their ideas and experience on specialized applications of your products or services or areas of related interest to your customers.

CHAPTER 10

LEADERSHIP

Since ancient times leaders have done three things.

First, leaders establish the vision and direction of the group or organization. Consciously or unconsciously, formally or informally, leaders establish the organizational identity and the direction that the organization will take operationally. They help their organization move into the future.

Second, leaders communicate purpose, values, and goals. It's through the tools of communication, some formal and some informal, that leaders get things across. Without core values and ideas about purpose and direction, this communication is hollow. But, without communication, all the important things are impotent.

Often, the first two activities start with following the advice of Deming: assemble a cross-functional executive leadership team and "formally" document the vision, direction, purpose, values, and goals into strategic long-and short-range plans of action.

Third, leaders maintain the thrust of action toward achieving the objectives and goals of the business. Leaders know that it's not enough to send out a directive or an e-mail memo. It's not enough to make a stirring speech. What's necessary is making sure that, day after day, with unremitting diligence, the purpose is defined, the direction laid out, and the communication received. Today, much of the day-to-day operation of this process throughout all the functional areas of a business is carried out through project teams.

All this has been true since the first human being put together the first hunting party and led it out onto the plain. But today's challenges have some unique elements.

CRITICAL CHALLENGES OF LEADERSHIP

Today's business leaders are charged with six primary challenges you can use Internet technology to solve:

1. Communicating the vision and direction of the business in a way that gets the buy-in, ownership, and support of the employees, who are often independent, intelligent, and opinionated.

2. Facilitating merging cultures from vision, direction, and values to policies and procedures in a way that can quickly ramp their productivity to meet the demands of the marketplace.

3. Create innovative ideas, strategies, and tactics to meet the rapidly changing, hypercompetitive demands of the environment.

4. Implement project teams, especially in organizations where the team members are geographically spread out, that achieve their objectives at the least cost.

5. Enhance the free flow and access of daily need-to-know information in a business environment in which current information is your primary combative asset.

6. Create and actualize strategic business plans that incorporate finding and implementing cutting-edge Net technology systems that ensure your ability to compete and survive in the information age.

Today—suddenly, it seems—purpose and direction often need to be established with people of different cultures and values who live in different places and work on different time schedules. In the case of many of today's business organizations, what's involved is creating a new set of purposes, values, and direction from a set of older purposes, values, and directions.

Sometimes, as in the case of a Lockheed or a Columbia/HCA, organizations have been brought together quickly and need to be formed into a single entity. Sometimes, as in the case of Prudential Securities, the organization needs to change the way it's doing business, abandoning established and successful tools and techniques for new ones.

Many of today's workers are scattered about and don't often—or ever—see each other face-to-face. The last few years have seen the rise of the virtual workforce and the virtual team.

All this happens in a world where communication moves more rapidly than ever, where information—both accurate and inaccurate—is more available, and where scrutiny by governments and regulatory bodies increases almost daily.

Leadership is never easy, but one industry in which it seems especially difficult is the aerospace and defense industry. Let's consider the situation faced by Lockheed or Boeing or any other major aerospace company.

SOLUTIONS: CHALLENGES OF THE AEROSPACE INDUSTRY

Let's start with the complexity of what they make. Aerospace products are complex, using millions of parts and subassemblies. The quality of those parts has to be top-notch, and so the purchasing function is critical.

Many projects in the aerospace industry are carried out jointly with other firms. Some of those firms may be competitors in other situations. Still, the companies need to work across company lines effectively and efficiently to bring the project in on time and under budget.

While all this sharing is going on, a great deal of the information that's shared is highly confidential. Some of it is military classified, but even what is not is important for competitive advantage and therefore very closely held. Security is important.

Scrutiny? You'd better believe it! In aerospace, you've got two kinds to be concerned with. First, there's the government. A lot of aerospace work is done on government contracts, and so government regulators are everywhere looking around, checking into things, and watching what you do. But there's also the scrutiny of the press.

Think of just about any big cost overrun story you can remember from the last several years, such as the $600 toilet seat. It won't do, after the fact, simply to justify how the company met the military specifications and why those specifications called for special construction, there's the need to tell the story out front to journalists and the public as a whole.

There's geographical spread. Company units, subcontractors, partners, and vendors scattered around the globe but needing to work together. And let's not forget an array of craft, trade, and professional workers, all with strong opinions about how things should be done.

Aviation and aerospace companies may constitute a good leading indicator of what will happen for other firms, especially manufacturing. If most companies are going to engage in joint projects and become more global and be more regulated, then the companies that are already working in that environment can give the rest of us an idea of what to expect.

The aerospace industry is a great place to look for examples of how technology can enhance leadership in difficult leadership circumstances. When aerospace giants Lockheed and Martin Marietta joined to produce Lockheed Martin, it was yet another step in the history of one of aviation's great firms.

Lockheed Martin joins two of the great names in aviation history. Lockheed has been around since 1926 and is responsible for many top innovations in aerospace. It's the home of the famous "Skunkworks," and it's the firm whose designers, like the legendary Kelly Johnson, turned out airplanes like the P-38 Lightning, the SR-71 Blackbird, and the stealth fighter.

Martin, which is famous for the Pan Am Clipper and the Martin Flying Boat, was founded in 1917 by aircraft pioneer Glenn Martin, and it has grown, merged, and adapted over the years.

The two firms, with all their units, history, and culture merged in

1995. If you want an idea of how fast all this has happened, consider that, on the morning we interviewed the people at Lockheed Martin for this book, one of the participants needed to check just how many companies Lockheed Martin had at the moment. The answer, by the way, was 84.

Now these companies come from all over with different kinds of histories and, as you might expect, different computing platforms and policies. That diversity provided the impetus for where Lockheed Martin chose to start when putting its intranet system together. As Bill Buonanni, director of World Wide Web initiatives, puts it, "… with such a diverse computing environment, it was vital for us to find a tool that would work across multiple platforms."

Lockheed Martin decided to use Netscape SuiteSpot as the basis for a companywide Lockheed Martin Network (LMN). For a place to start, Lockheed Martin chose business policies and procedures. If you're going to bring people together with a common purpose and direction, one of the ways you do that is by providing them with a large shared base of things they do the same way. In most companies, like Lockheed Martin, that includes basic policies and procedures, and that was a great place to start.

The intranet provides policies and procedures for all of Lockheed's business units and functions. It also does lots of other things. Job opportunities, personal information, and other things are easily shared on the Net. A future events calendar keeps people up-to-date on what major events are going on that are going to affect Lockheed and any given unit of the company. Special applications, in manufacturing, sales, and marketing, are all available for people concerned with them. Earlier, we've talked about Lockheed's support for trade show sale efforts.

Netscape specifically talks about some of the applications Lockheed Martin has used with LMN in "Lockheed Martin Merges Systems with Netscape SuiteSpot," a case study report. The network delivers both policies and procedures for every business area within Lockheed Martin, including finance, human resources, business development, corporate communications, and legal. It also hosts a variety of other applications, including:

- Future Events Calendar, a section that lists all marketing events. Employees can add events to the calendar and indicate which events they are interested in attending.

- Job Information System, an application that allows employees to see what jobs are available, submit résumés, and apply for jobs online. After applying, employees can continuously check on the status of their applications via LMN.

- Trade Show Archive, a section that helps employees build a tradeshow kit, including all the necessary presentation material. Because Lockheed Martin has over 80 businesses, this section helps ensure a consistent look to all of Lockheed Martin's materials by providing employees with specific style guidelines. From this section, users can access information about a particular show, choose from an archive of photographs, and then begin designing and developing collateral materials for the show.

- Lights On, a special section available to intranet users in Lockheed Martin's Information Systems Center in Florida. As part of the facility maintenance activities, lights go out at 7 p.m. but, through LMN, employees working late can enter a code to turn the lights back on in a particular area.

The dollar payoff on this has already been enormous. According to International Data Corporation's 1996 ROI study, "The Intranet: Slashing the Cost of Business," Lockheed Martin got an ROI (return on investment) of 1505%. And, in the area of savings, IDC reports "Qualitative Yearly Benefits" of $1,807,838 direct reduction in staff time, $3,699,144 in productivity gains, $9000 in communications, and $966,000 in mainframe upgrade.

The biggest payoffs really haven't even begun to hit yet. Those payoffs are the ones in joint projects. Those are a key leadership challenge, particularly in the aerospace business, where the projects are a lot bigger than in other industries.

In aviation/aerospace, three, four, or more large companies need to work together to produce a single product. In addition to the key players, there are a host of subcontractors. If they're going to work together, you have to keep them on the same page, and you have to keep them focused, and you have to keep them communicating. It turns out that Net/Web technology is an excellent way to do that.

The people we talked to at Lockheed Martin describe this as Generic Project X. At Lockheed Martin, like any other big aerospace firm, there are 10 to 15 of these going at any one time.

When Lockheed Martin starts a project, the first step is to create a Web site for it. The number of people who have access to that might be 20 or 200, and that creates certain security problems. Each participating company has its own portion of the Web site. There's also a need for programwide information. That's where action items and checklists and calendars would be.

When requests for information (RFIs) go out, a portion of the Web site might be devoted to requests for information responses. The same would be true for responses to requests for proposals (RFPs).

You can't have a project like this without a ton of meetings. Some of those are likely to be virtual and some physical, but they all produce minutes. And the minutes or notes of those meetings wind up on the Web site as well. It's at about this point that some of the benefits of Net and Web technology begin to take hold. Notes, data, and information that are already in digital form can easily be shared across a variety of platforms using this technology.

Once that stuff is out there and sharable, it's easily searchable with standard search and database tools. In addition, there's the power of linking. Data sheets, meeting minutes, and a variety of other documents, data, and information pieces can easily be cross-linked. The idea is to get the information out there and to begin to link it up. That makes it possible for people who are involved in the project to get the information when and as they need it and to post up their own information, reactions, and insights.

There's another piece to this as well. One of the challenges is to figure out exactly what form you want stuff to be in. That's solved in the beginning by some joint decisions about what form different documents will be in. For example, all the presentation materials might remain in Power Point, a Microsoft presentation program. There would probably be an agreement that certain documents would remain as document files in a particular word-processing program such as Microsoft Word. That takes away the need to convert all the documents to HTML. There's a clear trade-off here between the linking power of HTML and the workload necessary to convert everything over. On massive projects like those in aerospace, you get a bit of both.

There's also the challenge to make this easy. There are lots of underlying technologies that the tech people know really well; a good example is file transfer protocol (FTP). There are a couple of ways for an organization to use FTP to make files (such as word-processing files) available. One way is to teach people to use FTP. The other, and what Lockheed Martin and other companies do, is to make the FTP technology transparent. What that means is to use tools that make it possible for a user to drag and drop, or click and get information that's not available in an HTML file. The rule here is that the easier you can make it for people to do something, the more likely they are to do it.

All this needs to be handled securely. The details of the security are best left to people who are experts in the field, but it is important for you, as a leader, to understand that security is important and requires some expert input. On large and complex projects, what often happens is that a combination of security technologies is employed. On smaller, simpler, or less sensitive projects, perhaps a simple password or authentication process might be in order.

Let's stop for a minute and look at what we've got here. Basic purpose and direction and a large body of common information and practice are put in place using the Net so that they are accessible and available to all. Special applications and joint projects get special attention with special Web sites and security systems.

One of the things that happens here and in other leadership applications is the formation of effective teams. Teams are formed in two ways. The first way is that the boss assigns the team. You usually see that in the early stages of a complex project like Generic Project X. The team is put together based on particular skills and the needs of the project. Then they need to work together.

Other teams form naturally throughout the project. There's a need for two or three engineers to discuss a particular design issue, and that turns into a series of meetings.

There are lots of sophisticated conferencing and whiteboarding technologies out there for bringing teams together, but one of the simplest is the use of regular e-mail. A technique we've seen over and over again is for a group of people working on a project to simply copy each other on all the electronic mail messages related to the project. They might follow a classic brainstorming format for this. First, the key question or problem is posed, and then people respond to it without any judgment being offered. Then there's a period of idea review and consolidation and critique, followed by decisions. The process, though virtual, mimics what goes on in the physical world. It has some specific advantages, though.

One key example is that this method is asynchronous. People come to the project and work on it and share their ideas as it works for them in their work flow. That makes it possible for people in widely dispersed geographical areas to share ideas with each other without the need even for time coordination, let alone travel and its attendant costs.

The second big advantage of virtual teaming using electronic mail is that people can look things up in their own files. They can use their material to spark ideas or to gather information or to marshal arguments, depending on what stage of the process they're in.

A third advantage, and one that we've discovered only since we've been working with e-mail virtual teams, is the cultural advantage. It turns out that certain groups are culturally reluctant to participate in classical brainstorming in a physical environment. Think about what's involved there. In a classic brainstorming session, people are shouting out ideas in a verbally assertive way. For some people, who have been raised to be quiet and differential, that can be a real problem. What can easily happen is that some of the best ideas don't get shared because the person who has them is unwilling to participate aggressively enough to be listened to.

With virtual e-mail teams, that problem doesn't exist. Research done by Sproull, Kiesler, and others points to two key findings. People are able to participate in virtual e-mail teams in their own way, one that's comfortable and culturally appropriate for them. And, the effect of rank seems to disappear.

Most businesspeople have taken part in idea sessions held with a senior person in the room. In the physical idea sessions that we conduct, we have a little consultant's trick that we use to determine the role of rank. Before the process actually starts, we ask a simple question like, "When do you people want to break for lunch?" If all eyes turn to the senior person in the room and everyone waits for his or her response, we know that authority is going to be an issue in our session. Research on computer-mediated idea sessions shows that the rank queues disappear after a brief time. That means that there's a greater flow of ideas and a wider reach of the ideas. And the result, according to Sproull, Kiesler, and other researchers, is that virtual teams often come up with more aggressive or wider-ranging solutions than their physical team counterparts.

Virtual teams and regular communication become a way to provide leadership to a workforce that is scattered all over. By some estimates, there will be 55 million virtual workers by the turn of the century. That doesn't count expatriate workers (those working in countries other than their own) or workers in different countries (citizens of that country) whose primary contact with the company is electronic.

To pick just one example, it's become common practice for software firms to have development work done in India. The country is English-speaking, and the workers are educated and sophisticated, but they don't get paid as much. A network applications developer with five years' experience in India may earn $10,000. In the New York area, that same experience level would probably command $65,000 in salary alone.

Regular communication is part of the key here. That communication can be either on a functionally or departmentally specific level or on an enterprisewide level. Tektronix, for example, publishes a regular HTML document every day with critical information for its engineers. This includes news, updates, technical information, and pointers to good Web sites. It's specific to the design function.

A VIRTUAL OPEN-DOOR POLICY

Quaker Oats, on the other hand, publishes a daily e-mail message to all its e-mail–connected people. Employees of Quaker Oats were quick to dub these messages "oat mail." The daily e-mail message includes information that employees ought to have, including pointers to information available via e-mail and on Quaker's Web site. But there's another, and more interesting part. What's going on, in addition to basic communication is an electronic version of an open-door policy. One of the hardest things to do in a large geographically dispersed organization is to keep the people in touch with one another.

In many businesses, the founder or CEO tries to visit every location at least once a year. Even for the most energetic, like Wal-Mart founder Sam Walton, this can get to be a bit much as the number of locations expands exponentially. There's also the "corporate king" effect. The CEO arrives and is escorted through a series of encounters by staff members. He or she meets with carefully selected groups of workers. Generally, the bigger the organization, the more highly orchestrated the visit.

Quaker Oats gets around that by having an electronic open-door policy. It works this way. Quaker employees can ask questions in a variety of ways. They can use voice mail, the e-mail system, or (heavens, how neanderthal!) a handwritten note.

The questions and the answers are integrated into the daily electronic newsletter. The communication process is open and responses are quick—usually within a few business days. Quaker Oats has also used Oatmail to distribute surveys or just get reactions to business developments.

Note that anybody can ask anything and get an answer. If you try that, you're sure to be tested on it. Note, too, that the effect of having the top executives paying attention to all these questions is not limited to the people who ask the questions but is felt by their bosses up the chain of command. Those people pay a lot more attention to what they're doing if they know that the CEO might be looking at it at some point. And each question gives the CEO an opportunity to clarify the vision, the purpose, and the direction.

It's really an electronic version of the kind of informal communication that John Kotter highlighted years ago in his book *General Managers*. Kotter noted then that most effective general managers don't use formal memos and such as their primary method of communication. Instead, they seize the opportunities offered by chance encounters, meetings, and functional communication as an opportunity to present their agenda and values. That's what's going on at Quaker Oats.

BOOSTING PROFIT MARGINS AS A CORE BUSINESS STRATEGY

That brings up another essential point. Leadership utilizing this technology is not leadership using only this technology. We've talked about Marshall Industries several times in this book. Let's look at its development of Net/Web technology and how that's intertwined with other business efforts.

According to Vice President Bob Edelman, the story has to begin with the business back before the Internet and World Wide Web were an important part of anybody's thinking. That's because one dominant characteristic of Marshall Industries' approach to electronic commerce is that it is enterprisewide and strategic.

So, let's begin the story around 1990. At that point, Chairman Gordon Marshall and new CEO Rob Rodin were confronted with a business problem that many have faced. The problem was pretty simple. While Marshall had been successful for years, it was successful in an industry that was beginning to change radically.

Marshall Industries is a $1 billion-plus distributor of industrial electronics based in El Monte, California. It's part of the semiconductor business. In 1990, that business, which had been in high-growth mode, was beginning to mature. Industry margins were dropping, and pressure to reduce costs was increasing.

At the same time, Marshall Industries was what Edelman calls "suboptimized." It was made up of lots of different pieces, but the pieces often worked quite independently. Warehousing had its own concerns, as did the field sales force. And the people who handled administrative operations had goals that sometimes conflicted with both.

Just as in lots of businesses, what often happened was that the people in the individual specialties cranked up their efforts for their own best interest at the expense of other interests and perhaps the interests of the entire company. As Edelman points out, it was a perfectly rational system.

"We would want them to do one thing, say, concentrate on a particular product line," says Edelman. "But people would look around and realize that they would make more money or get more praise if they did something else. So they followed their own best interests."

So, Marshall and Rodin took a look around for an answer. But it wasn't the Internet, not yet. The Internet would be a part of the answer that falls into an overall business solution.

Like many other businesses, Marshall Industries took a look at Deming's quality principles for improving both quality and innovation. It decided that that was the place to start because that would make a major change in the company. That change took Marshall in the direction of being a highly customer-responsive company delivering top quality in as efficient and profitable a way as possible.

The first step was education. People who worked for Marshall across a range of functions were educated in the Deming principles. But that wasn't enough.

Step two was to modify the compensation program. At that time, Marshall was like most industrial distributors. Compensation programs tended to reward effort in narrow spheres, and large commission rates on the sales end served the interests of the sales force over those of the company and its customers. The compensation program that Marshall put in place in 1992 is still around today. It simply pays people a salary plus a share of corporate results. And it allows people to concentrate on the customer and on making good business decisions. It's part of what Edelman describes as a need to align the company structurally with its purpose.

The result of the quality principles and the change in the compensation program was that people began to make good business decisions. They made those decisions in a variety of areas, in human resources and operations, and with an enterprisewide perspective (including both people and technology) and it's here that the Internet technology story begins to kick in. As more employees were trained and empowered to make decisions and decision making began to move to the front line, information flows became more important. Decision makers needed a constant flow of helpful and timely information. It appeared that this new Internet technology would provide Marshall with the help it needed.

It was 1993 and the Internet was not yet on the cover of *Time* magazine. Sure, people were e-mailing back and forth, and several businesses were connected. But this was not yet a widespread interest. Nevertheless, at Marshall Industries, it was decided, in early 1994, that this was going to be a business-changing event in which they must participate if they were to be more effective. Company leadership saw Net technology as a way to carry out their vision. They kept a steady focus on the need to reduce costs and increase efficiencies and make sales more effectively. The mating of technology and strategy produced one of the very first corporate Web sites in July of 1994.

The idea behind Marshall's first Web site and everything since, according to Edelman, was "electronic commerce in its broadest sense. Not just selling, but creating intimacy with the customer." We should add that this intimacy is actually a strategy of providing value to customers through their relationship, not just through their transactions.

That search for intimacy and a broad look at commerce began almost immediately with serious and continuing efforts to get information back from the people who visited the site. "We saw right away that we didn't want people to just get information from us," says Edelman. "We wanted them to interact with us so that we learn things about them and they learn things about us." That led to various technological ways for visitors to tell Marshall what they thought. They could share suggestions, make requests, give reactions. It also led to some of the first focus groups very early in the development of the Web site to find out what purchasing agents and engineers wanted from a supplier like Marshall.

FOCUS GROUPS AND DIRECTED CONTENT

What was learned from those focus groups has become a driver for changes in the design of the site. Bob Edelman calls the idea *directed content*. There are two principles of directed content. The first is that the visitor needs to be the one in charge of managing content. That means having enough of the right information in enough forms and accessible in enough ways that the visitor makes key choices about what content to experience.

The second principle is that the technology that allows that management of content must be transparent to the user. Visitors don't need to know if what they're getting is coming from a Lotus Notes database or an SQL search of a database on a remote site or a document that was originally prepared in Microsoft Word. They click and they get the result.

Right now, that means that Marshall is one of the only distributor sites on the Web that connects visitors directly with supplier information by virtually searching over the Internet. On most other sites, there are spec sheets or pointers to manufacturer or supplier sites but no direct contact.

In the beginning, the site had product information only. Then more information services. In 1994, Marshall began integrating databases with its Web technology to provide custom solutions and active notification. By 1995, Marshall was beginning to offer the news services that would ultimately become the Education, News and Entertainment Network.

By the end of 1995, Marshall was providing a broad array of information in dynamic form to its customers as well as news and information to the industry at large. It was taking orders and responding to inquiries using Net technology. But it still wasn't enough.

AN EXTRANET FOR MORE EFFECTIVE PARTNERSHIP

Bob Edelman again: "What we had was fine for spontaneous users and for regular visitors, but strong business partners need more than that. That's why, in early 1996, we began looking at an extranet." Edelman is quick to point out that all this was driven by normal business purposes—the need to reduce cycle times, to provide quick response to competitive initiatives, and to link information inside the company with key partners along the supply chain.

An intranet was already in place for employees, where they could gather information for commercial purposes and also get training on a variety of issues, including human resource and personal growth items. It was time for an extranet to link the strong business partners and the internal people, and for even more innovative uses of the technology.

One good example is in the way the extranet and order tracking can be pulled together. Marshall uses a robotic picking system to automate warehouse operations, and UPS has a presence right in the warehouse in El Monte. Warehouse workers use Java scripts to check status on orders, and that information is available in real-time over the extranet to anyone authorized to get it.

NET SEMINARS FOR EDUCATION, TRAINING, AND COMMUNICATION

From a studio in El Monte, Marshall's Net seminars help meet goals of education, training, and communication. The company can offer audio and video as well as pure information based on customer needs. Edelman is quick to point out that *customer,* as used here, has the broadest definition. It includes customers both inside and outside the company and people who may be customers for information but not yet for products.

The method of delivery is constantly improving. Marshall has recently discovered that more than 50% of the users of its training facility are coming in on lines of 56 kilobytes or better. That allows a degree of use of multimedia that would not be possible if their connections were of lower quality. Note that this is the opposite of the challenge faced by Ann Yakimovicz at Columbia/HCA Healthcare. In Ann's case, the Net-deliverable training needed to be scaled down to meet the limitations of lower bandwidth connections and less sophisticated machines. In both situations, user needs and capabilities drove the training design.

Marshall has used its Net to train suppliers, employees, customers, and others as part of its normal course of doing business and making itself the supplier of choice. Marshall has become so good at it and gotten so many requests, that it's starting to offer training services outside its normal supply chain through its ENEN subsidiary.

Marshall also uses its Net as a daily news service, a kind of electronic industry headline news—again, more value for visitors, a way to differentiate Marshall from other distributors, and a reason for people to keep revisiting the public Web site.

In all this, the company has been fairly eclectic in its choice of technologies. As you listen to Edelman talk, you become aware that Marshall pretty much uses whatever works. Oracle databases and Lotus Notes exist side by side because they work well together and both are set up to work with their robotic order picking system. Real Audio Netcasting is part of the mix because it works.

Evolving Uses of the Net

Bob Edelman thinks that an actual blending is beginning to happen. "It's becoming possible," he says, "for it not to matter whether our customer is coming in using Notes or a standard Web browser or a 3270 terminal." That fits in with a future of the Net that is cross-platform and cross-technology. So what are some of the new things that Marshall is up to?

One really interesting innovation is an entertainment site called IKON Kids. It's set up for kids less than 10 years old to talk to adults about how they experience the Net. The idea is that this is the generation which has grown up with the Net. It's the generation that assumes that it's actually normal to check your e-mail a couple of times a day and make telephone calls from your car. Marshall Industries is convinced that it will learn from IKON Kids about where its development should be going. That's one kind of driver.

From Marshall's standpoint, the idea of the Net includes continuous evolution to meet the needs of a changing enterprise and customer base. The news service, training, and IKON Kids are part of that. So is a new service that provides engineers a place on the Web to actually do some fairly sophisticated design work.

Commenting on generational issues, Edelman points out that, although a lot of commerce is digital, there are people among Marshall's customers who will not be comfortable in that mode but need the regular paper trail of prior years. "You have to be able to accommodate both," says Edelman.

There's constant development and change on the site. Both content and context change frequently, sometimes more than weekly. And new versions, or generations, of the site are introduced as driven by need and customer abilities and enabled by technology.

The future? Probably a flatter site is the prospect. The idea is that people should get things easily, in a more customized way, and more quickly without having to drill down through several levels of information. Marshall's sophisticated database and agent technology are likely to make all this possible.

One of the reasons we've chosen to cover Marshall Industries in this chapter on leadership is that it's one of the few companies we've seen that has integrated the Net and Web into its strategic thinking and operations. This technology is how Marshall does business, both internally and externally.

THE INTERNET AS A STRATEGIC PLANNING TOOL

Netscape Communications reports in its Customer Profiles, "Rockwell International, a Fortune 100 company that is a leader in industrial automation, semiconductor, avionics and communications and automotive component systems, has standardized on Netscape Navigator client software and is using Netscape SuiteSpot server software as the enabling technology for its main corporate Intranet. In addition, Rockwell is using Netscape software for many of its department's intranets across the company."

RWEB, Rockwell's main intranet, was created to serve as a key information resource for employees with information and applications, including:

- Rockwell Vision, featured at the top of the RWEB home page to unite the company under one vision statement by Chairman and Chief Executive Officer Donald Beall. Rockwell used RWEB as a means to help roll out the vision statement to the entire company.

- News Section, which contains all the current press releases, current and past HTML issues of Rockwell's newspapers, and other company news.

- RWEB Information, which contains employee, company, and community information.

  Using the RWEB, Rockwell employees can

- Access company policies and procedures.
- Join special-interest group discussions covering everything from object modeling to pricing and contracts.
- Read Rockwell's internal newsletter.
- Find in-depth information on key customers.
- Get information from the U.S. Patent Office.

- Track a Federal Express or UPS package.

"Rockwell's goal is to be the technology leader in each of our markets," said Scott Nelson, manager of internal communications at Rockwell. "Part of the secret to our success is a core philosophy based on sharing information and expertise among our business. Netscape's cross-platform, open Internet technology is a key ingredient in enabling us to do just that."

Carolyn Drake, executive vice president of Fort Knox Federal Credit Union (FKFCU), started off her interview with us by suggesting that businesses concerned primarily with creating their own Web pages may be missing the boat and that she sees a greater advantage in "using information that's on the Internet as a strategic planning tool," that is, "using the information of others."

The credit union's adventure with Net technology started off like that of many of the people we interviewed. At a strategic meeting with senior management when the topic that they were kicking around was the Internet, Carolyn Drake said, the question at that moment was, "Is it a tool or a toy?" The group wondered where the credit union belonged on the Net, whether development of its own Web page was practical, and if it was something the members would want. Carolyn said, "In order to answer that question, we signed several of our senior managers up to Internet service, put them out there and said, 'Play with it, look at anything you want to, learn to use the Internet, see what people are doing on the Internet, and borrow the best of what you see out there, and then come back and talk about it.' We began to do that, and we found that it's like the world's library—many things that we were spinning our wheels accumulating research material on is there with the flick of a button."

Fort Knox Federal Credit Union has been diversifying a lot and opening new branches in recent years. It started out as primarily a military and civil service credit union; then their sponsor, Fort Knox, went through cutbacks and lost over 7500 jobs in the last year. In order to sign up and serve new members (customers), FKFCU has been reaching out to outlying communities and has been doing strategic planning to determine where they should branch.

Carolyn reports, "We opened two storefront branches in the past year. And some of the things you would want to look at in that type of strategic planning would be the economics of a given area, the demographics, what the competition is in that area, and we have found virtually all that information through the Internet. Rather than run to the library or run to the chamber of commerce, for instance, in adding low-income communities, we've used the Census Bureau information off the Internet."

From the FDIC page, the credit union has been able to pull a profile on any banks in the area it is targeting and to determine their loan mix. It was then able to incorporate in its strategic plans whether a competitor was serving the consumer needs of that area or was primarily a real estate lender. This let FKFCU decide if there was a niche in that area where their products would fit. How does this enable the credit union to cut costs and boost profits? If you consider the costs of opening up a new branch operation and having to close it six months later because the business just isn't available in that area, you can get a pretty good idea how much the Internet is worth to FKFCU.

With the Internet, FKFCU can pick directions for expansion, deal with a difficult business environment, and cut the risk of key strategic decisions. It used the Net both to help create its vision and to implement it.

Let's look at how some other companies we've already talked about have blended Net/Web technology with strategy and purpose.

In some cases, the strategic need was to align technology with the marketplace. We saw that at both Prudential Securities and Countrywide Home Loans. And, in both of those cases, the change was driven from the top.

But also, in both cases, technology was put in place to support the leadership issues. In the case of Countrywide, we saw an emphasis on sharing and getting information out to people in the branches that helped bring everyone onto the same page and give them ways to share their own experiences.

In Prudential, we saw a major corporate initiative to underwrite the acquisition of technology—through subsidizing laptops—for members of the organization.

At Columbia/HCA Healthcare, one of the major drivers of leadership strategy is the training function. By providing high-quality, common training and learning experiences to people up and down the hierarchy, Columbia is driving a commonality of vision, purpose, and direction consistently.

At Booz-Allen & Hamilton, the strategic idea and leadership emphasis are to support collaboration and sharing of knowledge to maximize opportunity. Under that banner, the development of a shared knowledge system using the Net becomes the technology that enables the strategy.

And take special note: In all the cases that we've outlined, there was hard-dollar return on investment, which is independent of the strategic examples, whose value is harder to measure.

TACTICS

Let's look at our tactics and how they apply to leadership.

THINK LINKS

Leadership is about links and information. But the leadership challenge when you start thinking links is a bit different from the challenge for the others we talk about in this book. As a leader, you need to understand that every link is a potential for communication.

That means that you can start from either end of the link. Start by thinking about who it is you need to communicate with to do your leadership job effectively. Donald Beall, the chairman and CEO of Rockwell International Corporations, communicates his vision and direction with a link off both Rockwell's public Web site's home page, at http://www.rockwell.com/, and the intranet, RWEB, home page.

When we think of how Rockwell extends its leadership links, three sections on its site map immediately come to mind. First, under the Home Section off their public Web site, they have links to Welcome, What's Hot, Did You Know ..., Contact Us, Site Search, and Legal Disclaimer. Then, in the Current News section, there are links to Current News, Press Releases, Quarterly Earnings, Reports and Dividends, Rockwell in the News, and Rockwell Perspectives. And, finally, in the About Rockwell section, there are links to Rockwell At-a-Glance, FAQs, Science Center, Rockwell Global, Rockwell Video, Corporate Responsibility, Key Executives, and Rockwell History.

The Corporate Responsibility link in the About Rockwell section describes what being a responsible corporate citizen at Rockwell means. The Rockwell Perspective link in the Current News section contains the text of Donald Beall's presentation, "How and Where R & D Partnerships Make a Difference: An Industry Perspective." In this presentation, Beall clearly illustrates and communicates the qualities of leadership needed for effective research and development partnerships.

Lockheed Martin exemplifies leadership with links of its Corporate Overview section to Our Values, Lockheed Martin Leadership, A History of Mission Success, and Lockheed Martin Corporate Ethics & Business Conduct. The Our Values section is a collection of essays by Norm Augustine, the resident and CEO of Lockheed Martin, which communicates the company's values in the areas of ethics, mission success, and teamwork.

While this kind of visionary leadership communication is important, it is equally important for leaders to make sure that there are communication links that make their leadership vision, values, and goals happen. And don't forget to look at who needs to communicate with whom in order to be most effective. Work to establish links there as well.

For example, National Semiconductor uses its internal Web as a catalyst to stir employee innovation and enhance collaboration and efficiency. It's internal Web provides a selection of complementary communications alternatives to telephone, e-mail, and videoconferences. In his interview with Netscape, Tim Stuart, information services consultant for National Semiconductor, said "The Web helps to bridge time differences. You can publish something and let someone draw from it after you go home. It's better than dragging someone out of bed for a conference call," he says. "If we can give people a new way to communicate and make that communication richer, then we can make better products faster and more efficiently."

Don't stop, though, with the links that you establish. Look at the links that are already in place, and think about how you can either make them more effective or use them more consciously to establish values and direction. E-mail discussion groups and newsgroup

forums are active areas where employees from different departments and widespread geographical locations can get together to
discuss problems, issues, and concerns while they share their expertise and brainstorm innovative solutions to the daily challenges
they face.

Communicating with unremitting diligence is a necessity for effective leadership. Repetition, it has been said, is the mother of
learning. It's also the mother of leadership.

AUTOMATE

As you automate, look for ways to automate routine communication functions so that they happen routinely. Consider ways to incorporate key slogans, mottos, and short value statements in all
your basic communications. Those can be on the headers and foot-
ers of internal or external Web pages; they can also be in the signature line in your e-mail. Lockheed Martin provides a link to
Lockheed Martin Shareholder Direct, which offers an option to subscribe to its e-mail list to receive news releases automatically about
earnings, dividends, and corporate news.

CUSTOMIZE

As you think about customizing, think about giving people information that they can use in whatever their function is in your business.
Your leadership messages and overall communication need to
stress the commonalities and linkages. Leave the people in the
units to improvise and adapt because they certainly will.

TRANSFORM

Throughout this book, we talk about transforming data into information, and information into knowledge. You still have to do that as
a leader, but you have another transformation task as well.

You have the task of transforming vision into action. Look for opportunities in the way you use your intranet, extranet, and Web site,
and your internal electronic communications, to move people toward actions. You want them to put one foot in front of the other in

pursuit of your organizational goal. Many companies are offering their employees training on how to participate effectively in a virtual team and providing them with tools like whiteboards, regular news releases, and information forwarded by cutting-edge push technology like Pointcast that customizes the news delivered to you from the Net and other Net application tools, to enhance their collaboration and the implementation of their ideas.

INSIDE/OUTSIDE

Today, inside/outside is more than ever your job in leadership. Other employees represent the company, but leaders *are* the company in the view of many outsiders.

There's another key leadership challenge here. That's the challenge of bringing outside cultures inside when you've got situations like those at Columbia/HCA and Lockheed Martin and Boeing. Look for ways to use the Net/Web to communicate and reward the behavior that's consistent with the culture you want. For example, you can establish a regular real-time chat, or e-mail discussion group to which you invite internal or external "experts" to share their experience and success stories with your employees in areas that relate to your employees' daily challenges and work activity.

CORE FUNCTIONS/BIG PAYOFFS

Core functions/big payoffs in leadership come from those other two C's we've talked about throughout this book: culture and communication. Use the power and reach of this communication tool to concentrate on the culture you want to have. And don't assume this will happen in isolation.

Everything else in the organization is about culture, too—the topics you cover in the newsletter, how your compensation plan is structured, who gets promoted—use the Net/Web to help make changes there.

START NOW

Start now. Actually, with leadership, you don't get a choice. If you're in a position in the hierarchy at any level, you don't get a choice about being a leader. That's because people will watch what you do, listen to what you say, and act on it. Your only choice is the kind of leader you turn out to be. The communications power and reach of the Net will help you do that, but it can magnify your warts as much as your good points.

Leadership today is really beginning to revolve around two things. First are the things leadership has always revolved around—getting the organization moving in the right direction, with everybody participating meaningfully and keeping that energy going.

Leadership today is also concerned with how to bring in, use, and develop this exciting and effective Net and Web technology to make the corporation more effective. That's what we cover in the next chapter.

WALLY AND JEFF'S LEADERSHIP LESSONS LEARNED

1. Vision and direction of the business can be communicated by setting up intranet Web pages or sending out company newsletters via e-mail or the Web with long-term, weekly, and daily messages; by setting up a virtual open-door policy using e-mail; and installing an e-mail discussion group.

2. Use Net technology to facilitate merging cultures by providing on Web pages the information on vision, direction, and values and possibly setting up a searchable database to find policies and procedures that relate to specific functions and situations.

3. Use newsgroups, e-mail discussion groups, training on the Net, and surveys to give your business a forum where employees can create innovative ideas, strategies, and tactics to meet the rapidly changing, hyper-competitive demands of the environment.

4. Implement virtual project teams using e-mail, white-boards, forums, Webphones, and other online tools, such as real-time chat sessions, to cut down on the costs of traveling to a central meeting location or using faxes and telephones.

5. Companies that successfully use Net technology incorporate the implementation of this technology into their regular business and strategic planning process.

6. Determine who owns your intranet, extranet, and Web site. Have a Webmaster in charge who has a team of champions driving the ongoing implementation and management of the growth of your company's use of the Net. Make sure it is driven by solid business goals.

7. As a leader encouraging people to change and adopt your intranet, extranet, or Web site as part of their everyday working life, remember the golden guideline of culture change, "Give your employees training and knowledge about how it can be valuable to them, ask for their ideas on how to use the Net innovatively, encourage and reward participation, and your employees will take ownership and they will change. Mandate it and they will fight you every step of the way."

8. Many nontechnical senior and middle managers have not mastered the skill of typing because they have always had secretaries and will not use a computer for fear of being embarrassed. Win their support by giving them the training and understanding necessary to "look good" when they model what you want the rest of the front-line troops to do. If you don't win their support for your Net technologies, they will unconsciously send out the message that the Net is a waste of time.

9. Many managers are used to hoarding information to establish their power base with their employees and won't use the Net for fear of losing control because they believe that informed employees are harder to manage.

This belief system must be addressed in helping them understand how to manage effectively in a networked enterprise.

10. To foster collaboration on the Net, you must provide leadership role models, praise for collaborating, and hoopla about successful collaboration efforts from leadership and incentives.

11. Establish advisory boards or forums consisting of managers and employees from the various functional units of your business to set fair use Net standards and guidelines in all areas.

CHAPTER 11

MAKING THIS HAPPEN IN YOUR ORGANIZATION

OK, you've read the examples, looked at the TACTICS, jotted down lots of good ideas, and stuck Post-it notes all over the book. What now? Now it's time to turn the ideas you've got into actions that improve your business's bottom line.

When clients come to us with a project, we take the time to outline for them what they should do, in what order, and what they should watch for. That's what this chapter is about. Imagine you're one of our clients, and let's go through the steps.

THERE ARE LOTS OF WAYS THESE PROJECTS GET STARTED

In our consulting work and in our research, we've discovered that projects can start in lots of different ways. From our observations, here are the main ways in which people begin to use Net technology. Each one has unique challenges. One of them is likely to be the way your business is beginning its transition into using Net technology.

THE CHANGING TECHNOLOGY BEGINNING

Sometimes the technology people in your organization are the ones who bring up the idea of using Net/Web technology strategically. For Susan Wood, at Financial Services Corporation, the idea to begin using this technology grew out of a major systems change project. Financial Services was in the process of changing its computer system to make it more effective. Specifically, it was moving from a command-oriented "green screen" to a graphical user interface.

In the course of doing the analysis of how the system should look, the systems people suggested looking at Net/Web technology. If the technology people bring you this as something they should be exploiting, it will be your job to connect this with strategy and to apply TACTICS to use it effectively for business.

THE "VOICE OF GOD" BEGINNING

Sometimes it's the boss who drops the project on you. That's what happened for Stan Witkowski. He got what we called the "voice of God" approach. Stan's boss had looked at a number of strategic issues. He was aware of the emerging Net and Web and sensed their importance for the future of Prudential Securities. Basically, he said to Stan, "You want a project? Here's a really big one. Make it happen."

There are a lot of benefits to getting your project started that way. With top management onboard, it's easier to line up the resources you need and to get people to participate. But there are some dangers as well. This kind of project, when handed over by the boss, tends to be an "up or out" project. As Stan Witkowski told us, he was either going to make this work or be looking for another job.

If the boss lays the project on you, make sure you know what he or she really wants and knows. Make sure that the commitment is really there and that the resources will be available when you need them.

Then, as Stan Witkowski did, bring that boss in at crucial points to make the point to everybody involved that top management is really behind this.

THE "FROM THE TOP" BEGINNING

What if you're the boss yourself? Then, your responsibility is to be clear about what you want and support the project as it moves along. It will be your job, as the crucial leader, to attend to the issues of making sure that your Net/Web project supports strategy. It will also be your job, as leader, to do "the leadership thing."

You'll need to be visible in your support. You'll need to be doing that buttonholing of people in hallways that's important to communicating your ideas. You'll need to make sure the project is on key agendas and that key players are informed and onboard. You'll need to use everything at your disposal, including personal visits, e-mail, and anything else to get the message across that this is important and critical to organizational success.

THE CHAMPION BEGINNING

There's another way in which these projects seem to happen. Sometimes there's a champion. Think about what happened with Jerry Gross. Jerry saw the potential right away for his business, but he wasn't in a position to just make it happen. He had a clear idea of what needed to happen and how. The problem was that nobody else did at that point. So what did he do?

If you're the champion, then you need to be constantly working on the details and constantly running up the flag. Jerry, you'll recall, went off and put together a Web site on his home computer. That gave him an idea of how it would happen and what the technology was capable of. And he kept coming back to the company with ideas, reasons, and benefits. That's how the champion moved this along.

THE SPONTANEOUS IDEA BEGINNING

Sometimes Net/Web projects just start happening. That's what happened at IBM. All of a sudden, IBMers were putting up Web sites. They were doing this inside the company and outside the company. The Web sites had lots of different looks and functionalities. The challenge for IBM and your company, if you've got a lot of volunteer Web site projects springing up, is to try to control to the appropriate level. That's something that's easy to say, but very hard to do. In IBM's case, the answer was to develop a no-excuses toolkit so that everybody had access to the tools to make the site look like IBM, and no excuses for not doing that.

At the same time, IBM, along with many other companies, chose to give their people as much freedom as possible to exercise their own initiative. The strength of the Net and the Web is that it gives people information, and information is power. That power is diluted, or sometimes even eliminated, by overcontrol. The trick is to get some balance.

THE WELL, WE'VE GOT A WEB SITE BEGINNING

Sometimes the question involves putting together pieces that already work but that don't work together. Dell Computer had a fine public Web site. Adding the ability for customers to check on order status made it more effective. Many companies get themselves into intranets/extranets by considering features that they want to add to their public Web sites.

THE HOLY COW, WE'RE ALREADY DOING THIS BEGINNING

Some organizations, maybe yours, already have an intranet or extranet but have never used those terms to refer to it. Both Texas Instruments and Hewlett Packard were in that group. The language may help you to explain to others what you do or to see more possibilities, but the real question is how are you using this technology to boost your bottom line.

THE PROCESS

Regardless of how your project gets started, we've found that there's a basic six-step process that almost every project goes through. Here are the steps.

1. Assess your starting point. In this step, you'll determine where you are on the way to tying your whole business together with Net/Web technology.

2. Put your team together. In this step you'll assemble the

team that will get the project done and determine how the members of that team will work together.

3. Do the basic strategy and TACTICS analysis. This will give you a good idea about how to proceed.

4. Develop your plan. Here's where you clarify your objectives, resources, and timelines.

5. Implement your plan. As you do that, you'll need to pay attention to many things, among them design issues, culture concerns, security, and budgetary issues.

6. Deal with the changes that will happen. You need to stay on top of changes in your organization and its culture, as well as changes in technology and your customers' capabilities.

STEP 1: ASSESS YOUR STARTING POINT

Ultimately, you want your information strategy and technology to support your organization strategy throughout your company and all along your value chain. For most companies, though, that's something to be worked toward. Do a quick assessment of your situation. This analysis will give you some basic direction and give you ideas about who should make up the project team.

Look inside first. Here are some things to consider.

- Are you already in a client/server environment? Networks in business often consist of client machines that use programs, data, and other applications provided for all the clients on the network by a server.

- Do your people routinely share files, use e-mail, and send information to one another electronically?

- Do your people have access to the Net?

- Do they use browsers either at work or at home?

- Are your administrative and marketing documents in digital form?

Lots of positives here usually mean that you will have a good base of expertise to draw on from inside your company. It should also mean that you can move fairly rapidly with project implementation.

- Do your people use groupware?
- Does your company use EDI?
- Does your company use a proprietary computer system to coordinate operations?

Yes answers to these questions give you both information to build on, as well as cautions. ... Being already familiar with groupware and EDI will help your people learn to use Web tools that perform similar functions more quickly. But beware of financial or psychological investments in older technology that can be a barrier to change.

Now, look outside.

- Do you have a Web site?
- Have your people seen it?

Most companies begin their involvement with Net/Web technology with two things: e-mail and a Web site. Think for a minute about what each do for you in the public arena.

Both Web sites and e-mail let you extend your reach all along your value chain. They make it easy for you to share information as well as having it available for people when they want it.

If you haven't got an intranet in place, imagine that same ease of use and brain-friendly functionality working for you inside your business. Here's the vision that Tom Thomas, vice president and chief information officer of 3Com, has for his company's intranet: "... support virtually every function in the company, including sales and marketing, customer service, manufacturing, engineering, product development, electronic commerce, and systems development. It will span our many global locations and incorporate our external site on the World Wide Web."

Intranets let you extend the ease and functionality of the browser to internal information. Extranets let you get that same ease of use for information you want to share with others.

In a fully networked enterprise, you can connect anywhere throughout the world using a simple Web browser to perform such daily practical business activities as:

- Collaborating on developing and delivering products or services customized to meet your customers' needs in less time at less cost.

- Providing forms on demand that can be changed to meet the needs of any particular interaction and be made instantaneously accessible.

- Making a quick search for best practices, frameworks, business intelligence, competitive data, comparative analysis, business tools, and techniques to help solve client problems as well as locate the leading experts on a topic.

- Strengthening your business relationships by providing responsive customer support.

That is the promise of corporate extranets.

Your quick starting-point assessment should leave you with an idea of what direction you should be moving in, along with a rough sense of how fast you might be able to move. The next critical step is to set up a cross-functional project team.

STEP 2: PUT YOUR TEAM TOGETHER

We've found it best—and our research for this book underlines this—to undertake Net/Web projects using cross-functional teams. The nature of these projects seems to demand this since they involve flows of information between functions. Here are some guidelines for putting together a team.

To make up a good team, you need three things: interest, expertise, and power.

You want employees with interest in the project. They might be the champions, like Jerry Gross, of Countrywide Home Loans, or they might be the people who are already running volunteer projects. They could be functional managers who've got an interest in what this technology can do. Look also for the people who may benefit the most. They generate interest in the project quickly once they see the benefits for them.

You want employees with expertise. Technical expertise is a part of that. You want people who understand Net and Web technology and your organization's information system. For one of our clients, that meant two people—the director of information technology and the consultant who had helped develop the databases the client was using.

In addition to technical expertise, you want functional expertise. Make sure you involve employees who understand your key business processes. If you're developing an extranet, you should consider team members from outside your company but along your value chain.

Your team also needs power in some form. That can be awareness of the political climate or the ear of the boss. Remember how Stan Witkowski went about using the power he had but how he also brought in the CEO at key moments. In many organizations, involving people from many different constituent or stakeholder groups is important for managing the team's power.

Your core team size should be under 15, which makes for good discussion, but also effective decision making. OK, you're thinking, how do I involve lots of team members and still keep the group small? The answer is to think of three rings of involvement. We call them core, consulting, and commentary.

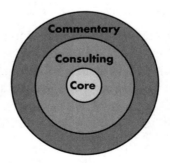

Figure 11.1 The three rings of involvement in virtual teams.

As illustrated in Figure 11.1, the *core* ring, at the center of the bull's-eye, is the team responsible for managing the project and for making key decisions and recommendations. They should bring interest, expertise, and power to the project and should be able to make it a top priority and devote time to it. Outside the core is the *consulting* ring. Business professionals here have interest, expertise, and power but often do not have the time to make this project a top priority. Their commitment is to respond to questions and to comment on decisions and discussions. The outside ring is the *commentary* ring. This can include interested people with whom communication is fairly easy.

These projects present excellent opportunities to use virtual teams, which can contribute expertise from all areas of your business. In a virtual team project, a great deal of the sharing of ideas, impressions, and information can be handled using e-mail or, if there's already an intranet in place, an internal Web page devoted to the project. Net technology has many other tools to offer, such as e-mail discussion groups, forums, whiteboards, and real-time chats, which can enhance your virtual team's creativity and productivity.

STEP 3: BASIC STRATEGY AND TACTICS ANALYSIS

Once you've got the team together, give them some homework to get up to speed. Have them read this book, check out articles about how this technology can be applied and talk to others in the industry. Then, use our strategy questions, listed below, to begin your formal analysis.

- What is your strategy?
- What are your key business processes?
- Who are your suppliers?
- Who are your customers?
- Who are your partners?
- Who is your competition?

There's more detail on these questions in Chapter 1 on our TACTICS Action Planning System. Once you've got a handle on how the Net/Web project will connect with your business strategy, apply the TACTICS Action Planning System to think through how you can tailor the implementation of Net technology so that it fits your business.

• Think links

• Automate

• Customize

• Transform

• Inside/Outside

• Core functions/Big payoffs

• Start now

Some of the business professionals we interviewed who have "been there" offered the following advice.

Tod Fetherling, director of interactive marketing, Columbia/HCA Healthcare talks about specific linkages that are strategically important and that Columbia/HCA will use its Net to enhance: "We just want to strengthen our relationship with our vendors and allow the clinicians who are actually in the day-to-day patient care to have access to the best information about the tools that they're using to deliver quality patient care. That's the number one goal. "

Fetherling links development to a specific goal. Bob Edelman of Marshall Industries provides perspective on how your project should support your strategy: "The key drivers for the project should be business purpose and customer need. The original move to the Internet, as well as all the planning and innovation that have happened since, are firmly anchored in Marshall's business model which is a customer-driven model. Marshall started with changes in the business and then used IP (Internet protocol) to help support, drive, and enhance those changes. ... You also have to look at things from an enterprisewide perspective, taking into account people and technology and purpose and goals."

That's the message from Chris John, president, Resource Financial Group as well. "It depends upon the purpose for which they want to set it up. I mean the Web is just a medium. Some people want to use it for marketing and advertising, other people want to use it for services delivery medium. I think it depends. It's like asking someone, How do you suggest using pen and paper effectively? It's just a medium."

STEP 4: DEVELOP YOUR PLAN

With your team together and the basic analysis done, it's time to get on with the job. Start with a good project plan. But don't overplan. There seem to be two general ways of getting a Net/Web project under way. Some groups want to plan it all out in advance. Others want to just jump in and try stuff. We agree with Ian Campbell of IDC: "Higher ROI seems universally to go to those who decide to implement now and fix later rather than those who spend massive amounts of time in design."

It's often a good idea to look for the applications that are easy to develop but that bring a big payoff. Many human relations and administrative applications fall into this category.

Many companies start developing an intranet with things like employee directories, employee benefits documents, and basic administrative procedures such as expense forms and travel vouchers. Usually, those are not only quick and easy to develop but they tend to have a big payoff. That's because they let one person (the one who needs the information) get it without help from the person he or she used to need (the person who located the document or explained the policy, for example).

Put the plan together in a way that makes sense for your organization, your objectives, your team, and your starting point. Susan Wood, of Financial Services Corporation, saw it as a five-step process for her company. Here are her recommendations.

1. Find the right resource—internal or external, it doesn't matter, but ... "It is the resource that can take you to where you would go if you knew it was there."
2. Select a group in the company to be first and let them be first. In our company, it happened to be marketing.

There are some very good reasons to let it be marketing. First of all, the information is easier to manage and deal with because there don't tend to be significant security issues. They tend to be a more open and innovative group so they're a little less worried about stuff. But whatever group it is, pick an area and say, "You guys get to go first," and let that team be first.

3. Set a time frame and go with it. One of the huge benefits that we had ... is we had our big awards conference starting May 23 in Aspen, Colorado. ... So, what we basically did was say what can we do between today and May 23, and that's what we'll have.

4. Keep it simple. The old "KISS," only I call it "Keep It Simple, Staff." It doesn't have to be complicated. It doesn't have to be sophisticated. Whatever you get out there initially, some people will like it, some people won't like it, but having something for people not to like sure beats having nothing.

5. And then I think the last and most important piece is plan to spend some time getting your users (whether they're internal, external, whatever) onboard. That may be less true today than it was a year ago, but ... once you go outside the traditional home office, it's going to take some time getting them onboard, getting them used to it, and getting them comfortable.

That's one way to look at it. Whatever your plan turns out to be, it should follow the guidelines for effective plans in any area. You should have clear and reasonable objectives. You should have the process mapped out and know where resources are coming from. And you should have a way to keep track of things as you go along.

Planning, however, is just planning. After you've sat back and congratulated yourself on a good plan, it's time to put that plan into action. We think you should move to trying things out as quickly as possible. Then, learn as things unfold.

STEP 5: IMPLEMENT YOUR PLAN

Even though many things will develop as you and your people use the system you've planned, there are some specific areas where pre-planning is vital to avoid problems. As you roll out your plan, pay particular attention to the four areas listed below to see if things are working as you expected. Make changes if necessary. The four primary areas to monitor are:

1. Design issues
2. Culture concern
3. Security concerns
4. Budget issues

Design Issues

Net and Web technology are very powerful in the ways they enable people to find and use information. For that reason, it's easy to slip into thinking that you don't really need to pay a lot of attention to design. Actually, the reverse is true.

One of the strengths of this technology is that it enables people to do things on their own. In practice, that often means "by themselves." What you're trying to do is set up functions that work for the people who need them, when those people need them, without having to have someone there to help them. That means paying attention to several design factors.

The first one, and maybe the most obvious, is to make help available. On an internal network, that can be a simple link on every intranet page that lets a person ask for help. Note, though, that this works only if you've got help in the form of an individual available all the time. Otherwise, help files set up as part of the intranet are usually the best solution.

Even if you do have systems people available all the time, you probably want to encourage people to use the Net on their own. For that reason, we strongly suggest building features into your intranet or extranet that let people find help on how to use the Net without calling on another individual.

Pay attention to navigation. On Web pages, internal or external, that usually means having navigation buttons at least in the top and the bottom of every page. It may mean using image maps to simplify complex navigational choices.

That's just a part of designing for ease of use. Another part is making the user's job as easy as possible. Jerry Gross thinks you do that by designing all your applications, even internal ones, as if they'll be used by consumers.

As Jerry puts it:

> Prototype it once. You're forced to make these applications easy to use because, if it's a public application, it's got to stand on its own. ... then if you reuse it internally, it lowers your training costs because then the metaphor becomes a transferable metaphor in terms of the online experience to the customer service rep internally. You don't have to retrain employees; they just say, oh, OK, this is a Web application, I get a customer calling in and asking me a question about *xyz* ... click click click, I've got the answer.
>
> Now, the concept back in the '60s and the '70s was you had applications that were only used in the back office. In the '80s, the applications moved to the point-of-sale terminal and the branch office and closer to the customer. Our view is that applications, using this technology, need to bypass all of these layers in between. Our goal is to build technology applications to the customer that's actually buying our goods and services.

Culture Concerns

In their marvelous book *Corporate Cultures,* Terrence Deal and Allan Kennedy offer a definition of culture that we like. They define culture as: "The way we do things around here."

In our own consulting with organizations on strategic issues, we've found that cultural barriers to change are often the most powerful because they're based on unconscious reactions. For that reason, you usually won't be able to argue people out of their opposition; instead you'll need to find another way.

"The way we do things around here" develops slowly. Behavioral norms develop because they work. They may be easier than what the procedure calls for. They may bring rewards. In either case, the reason why they were done in the beginning is lost by the time they've become deep-seated cultural norms. We say again: You won't be able to argue people out of their behavior. You'll have to find another way.

One way is to change the rewards system. Look back at our discussion of the Booz-Allen & Hamilton project. One major issue that needed to be resolved was the practice in Booz-Allen (and many other consulting firms) of hoarding knowledge so that individuals could use it for their own internal competitive advantage. The solution there was to revise the reward system so that it was good for people to share information. Still, change didn't happen overnight. It never does with cultural issues. Booz-Allen, though, gave public recognition to those who shared information and also tied employees' performance appraisals to that behavior.

Rewards don't have to be financial. Countrywide Home Loans simply set up a system in which information was available first to businesspeople who used the Net. Stan Witkowski let the team members and employees at Prudential know that the boss was watching.

Don't forget to publicize the successes of employees who use the system. That helps show others the benefits.

The other way to change cultural obstacles is to make sure that the new way is easy. Consider the purchase order application at Liberty Mutual. The system gave line managers more control, and that's a reward, but the system might have been dead in the water if it hadn't been easy to use. Instead, the automated purchasing system is easier than going around the system. Result: Managers are more likely to go to a preferred vendor.

Cultural issues are powerful, but they're best addressed, in our experience, indirectly. Incentives, including praise, promotions, and financial rewards, help. Publicizing success stories helps. Making things easy helps.

Security Concerns

One aspect of the Net and the Web that's gotten a lot of press is security. So, let's begin our discussion of security on all your applica-

tions of Net and Web technology by looking at the issues that revolve around a public site.

There are really two kinds of security issues out there: the actual
security issues and the perceived issues. Perceptions, formed by a
number of sensational media stories, concentrate on the presence
of evil hackers stealing sensitive information, including credit-card
numbers, from unwary businesses and consumers. There's just
enough truth in those stories to make them believable. There have
been significant hacking incidents, like the invasion of the Netcom
computers and the theft of credit cards from them. But, at least as
of this writing, there has been no documented case of a credit-card
number sent over the Internet being stolen en route. None. Not one.

What that means is that, if you're doing any business on your
site, or even internally, you need to deal with the perception people
have of security, not just its reality. We suggest for our clients who
have public Web sites and conduct sales or informational transactions on them, that they give people multiple ways to respond. That
means providing phone numbers, fax connections, and postal mail
addresses as well as e-mail responses. For anything that's deemed
sensitive, we suggest you use a secure server.

If you are doing information-gathering transactions, situations in
which people share information with you, such as their names and
e-mail addresses, then we suggest that you describe the purposes
for which you using that information, as well as mentioning any
purposes for which you definitely will not use it.

Now, what's reality? The first piece of reality you'll have to plan
for is that there are hackers out there. So the best thing to do is plan
that you will be hacked. Jerry Gross lays out his philosophy: "Security is a real concern. Our view is that it's not *if* you're going to get
hacked, it's just a question of *when* you're going to get hacked or attacked. ... So we've made investments both in technology and in
people to constantly monitor our networks and our electronic commerce transactions."

There's another security reality that you have to be aware of
whether you're setting up a public Web site or an internal one. That
reality is that your biggest security threats are the people close to
you. That means your employees, your customers, anybody who's
got access to your network. The first thing to be aware of is that

people share passwords, sometimes consciously, sometimes not. You won't ever be able to stop that completely, but you do need to set up rules, procedures, and other measures that stress the importance of security in areas where it's needed. You also need to try to get a system that makes it easy for authorized people to get information.

If you use an Internet service provider instead of having your own network, you need to be aware of security there as well. We found that very few Internet service providers have done any kind of background checks on their employees, even when those employees have full access to sensitive information on the provider's computers. For that reason, we recommend to our clients and to you that any Internet service provider who is part of your network be required to conduct full background and criminal-records checks on anybody with system or e-mail privileges. You should also consider having service providers bond employees with similar privileges.

Your security system needs also to have systems built in to determine if there is a problem. One area to pay attention to here is making sure that your systems people update the security features of the system.

Here's the bottom line on security. There is a real threat, but it's probably less than the dangers presented in the media. Your biggest threat will tend to be your people inside, but you need to balance security controls against ease of use. Finally, lots of security problems result from laxity, so rigorous attention to the procedures you have in place is probably more effective than looking for ever-better procedures.

Those are implementation issues that you can plan and watch for. They're ones you should prepare for. But there are other changes that will happen in your organization. They may be a bit more subtle and take longer to develop, but you should be prepared for them, too.

Budget Issues

Budgeting is always a concern for business projects. Even though implementing intranets (especially) and extranets can be done fairly inexpensively, it isn't free. Work out a good and realistic budget. As you do so, consider the following.

You may already have a good deal of the basic infrastructure in place. Use it if you can, but watch capacity issues carefully. We've seen clients who implemented a trial intranet, or a small scale one, who needed a major computer and communication investment to take it enterprisewide.

Watch out for personnel costs for maintaining your intranet/extranet. This usually doesn't take a lot of people—the staffing at companies like Eli Lilly and Sun Microsystems is in single digits—but it will take some.

Explore possible budget issues that grow out of increased workload. It may be possible to automate responses to information inquiries, for example, but you may choose not to because they really need to be supplemented by a human response.

Finally, keep an eye on the costs of success. In lots of organizations, budgets are set a year or more ahead and allow little flexibility to exploit success. Planning in advance for what you'll do if you're wildly successful will make it more likely that you'll get funding.

STEP 6: DEAL WITH THE CHANGES THAT WILL HAPPEN

One thing we can be sure of is that, once you start using Net/Web technology, changes will happen in your organization and environment. We've seen those changes fall into two main categories:

1. Leadership and operational changes
2. Technological and capacity changes

Leadership and Operational Issues

As a leader, you should be aware that organizations change when they start using this technology. The biggest change is that people now have the ability to make decisions and take actions that were probably more difficult before.

The result is that employees start making decisions and taking action. Your role as a leader, then, is to help them make better decisions and choices. If you're in an organization that has traditionally been top-down, you're going to find your pyramid flattening. We've found that talking this through with client executives and building it into the whole implementation process is usually all that's necessary.

One crucial decision that leadership will need to make is how much control it wants to try to exert over the changes that will occur. Eli Lilly had an intranet up and running before many of us had even heard the word. The person responsible for that is John Swartzendruber. Here's his perspective on this issue as delivered in *Web Week:* "Sometimes I feel like Dr. Frankenstein chasing his monster as it runs toward the village ... No central group can manage all of this. It's like herding chickens. ... Our philosophy is, we'll make decisions on the software and hardware environment but, other than that, people who are closest to the data and the ones supporting them should decide how the intranet develops. We don't tell them what they can and cannot do on the Web."

That approach has led to the development of a broad array of applications, from the very simple to the more sophisticated. In addition to the usual directories, manuals, and so forth, there are systems for paying vendors, purchasing applications, a virtual learning center, and a news feed that delivers news important to Lilly's people.

We can tell you, from our own experience as consultants facilitating culture change, that there are bound to be some very uncomfortable managers at Lilly as they watch the monster heading for the city. Part of the challenge will be to keep the resistant managers and employees productive as the world changes around them.

As people begin to take charge of their own applications and operations, the role of information systems (IS) changes. Before, when a manager brought a problem to IS, the response was, "How do I develop a solution for this?" But, for good effective intranets, the response should be different. Now, it should become, "How can I set things up so you can develop your own solution next time?"

Steve Telleen is probably one of the people best qualified to put this in perspective. He was instrumental in setting up one of the first corporate intranets at Amdahl, and now he's a partner in Silicon Valley Intranet Partners, a consulting firm.

> When you enable communication with an intranet, then it starts to break down the barriers inherent in paper systems. ... as that happens, as understanding of the Net and what it can do develops, it's something like a flower unfolding ... It's important for leaders to understand that this kind of system is not neat and engineered like a machine or a car. Instead, it's an adaptive, living thing. ... When you have the implementation of a broad-based Intranet type of system, you can be sure that something will change. The question is how to manage that change or perhaps whether to manage it at all.

Technological and Capacity Changes

Because technology in this area is changing so rapidly, you'll need to stay on top of things.

First, watch how changes in technology and capacity enable you to do more things. When Marshall Industries discovered that the people using its Net-based training had more capacity than they thought, they responded by adding some sophisticated technical features to the training.

Keep looking for technological applications that will help you do things better. In the next couple of years, we suggest watching for the following developments.

You can expect some agreement on standards for electronic transactions. Once that happens, you'll see an explosion in new products for handling payments, settlement, and other key functions. At the same time, competition should drive down the cost on these. There will be modifications in existing technologies, like EDI and groupware, so that they will work effectively in the Internet/intranet/extranet environment.

You can also expect to see development of a variety of products to link different internal functions effectively. Netscape has starting calling this breed of product *crossware,* but you'll also hear it called *middleware.* Keep watching for new ways to bridge the gaps in your system.

You can expect that more of the people in your value chain will be open to the possibilities of the Internet, their own intranets and sharing via extranets.

Right now the major move is for companies, large and small, to set up intranets or intranetlike applications. In the next few years, we'll see businesses increasingly extending their data, information, knowledge, and applications beyond the firewall with extranets. The future of building and implementing a networked enterprise as a competitive strategy to cut costs, boost profits, and enhance operations online is *now*.

What should you do? Whatever your organization or organization size, you should look for opportunities to use this technology to forge bonds with other organizations in your value chain. You should seek out ways to be more effective and help your people be more effective using Net/Web technology.

How do you do that? Use the TACTICS of Net technology.

Think links

Automate

Customize

Transform

Inside/Outside

Core functions/Big payoffs

Start now

If you build a strategy based on using the TACTICS Action Planning System to tailor and implement your business's Net technology, you can and will lead your business successfully into the future of our networked global business community.

Appendix A

RESOURCES

BOOKS

What follows are some resources we think will help you put the principles and ideas in this book into action. Rather than giving you a lengthy sort of listing, we've opted to present fewer resources but add comments about how you might use them.

The Fifth Discipline by Peter M. Senge is achieving classic status as an excellent business introduction to systems thinking. The original version of the book was published in 1990 and, in it, Senge introduces the concept of the learning organization.

We find that this book and the Fifth Discipline variants that have come since, such as the *Fifth Discipline Fieldbook,* provide an excellent introduction to the kind of thinking that makes Net projects effective.

There's a special set of benefits encased in Appendix B, which outlines system archetypes in a few pages. We find that, for us and for our clients, this is a great tool for insight and a handy reference.

Co-Opetition by Adam Brandenburger and Barry Nalebuff does two things that will help you use Net technology more effectively.

First, the book does an excellent job of setting your business in a competitive and cooperative context. We've picked up the term "complimentor," which we've used several times during this book from *Co-Opetition*. You'll also see that our basic model of where a value chain fits and how to analyze good places to use the Net is very similar to the material covered here.

Connections: New Ways of Working in the Networked Organization by Lee Sproull and Sarah Kiesler is an excellent, research-based book that will give you insights into how computer communication, virtual teams, and other tools that we've discussed in this book actually work. This is an especially good resource if you're interested in how virtual teams differ from face-to-face teams.

Being Digital by Nicholas Negroponte is what we call a "mind stretcher." Negroponte, who is professor of media technology at MIT, is one of the great visionaries of the digital age. This book is excellent for helping you see possibilities. Some of the predictions may reach a bit further than practical reality ultimately will, but you'll come away from the book with lots of ideas about the kinds of things that could be possible in your business and your life.

Another mind stretcher book is *The Web of Life* by Fritjof Capra. During the last 20 years, there has been a developing body of knowledge and theory about how complex dynamical systems work. Businesses and industries are complex dynamic systems, so this has some value to you. What Capra, author of the best sellers *The Tao of Physics,* and *The Turning Point,* has done in *The Web of Life* is to provide an excellent summary of this thinking as it applies to all kinds of systems. You'll have to make a bit of a leap to connect some of this with business situations, but the effort will be repaid. You'll also find that you can scan several of the chapters and skip the ones with more science than you might like and still get a lot of value from this.

Where Wizards Stay Up Late: The Origins of the Internet by Katie Hafner and Matthew Lyon is about how the Internet came to be and how it has developed. If you'd like a concise and well-written discussion of the development of the Internet and its underlying technology, this is the book for you. You'll find some good profiles of the people who developed the initial technology as well as some excellent descriptions of how that technology works. There's not much here on business on the Internet, but that's OK.

We like to speculate about the future. We love Net/Web technology. Alas, most of the predictions out there are, we think, nonsense. As an antidote to wild speculation masquerading as reasoned prediction, we recommend the book *Megamistakes: Forecasting and the Myth of Rapid Technological Change* by Steven Schnaars. Schnaars takes a good and entertaining look at why technological forecasts go wrong. It will help you keep your feet firmly planted on terra firma.

We will recommend one book about the future of technology and how to use technology for competitive advantage. That's *TechnoTrends* by Dan Burrus. It's a good survey of an array of technologies, including the Net and Web, viewed with an eye toward business strategy.

WEB SITES OF INTEREST

As you have probably noticed, this book was researched and developed entirely from resources available from the World Wide Web. When we looked at the thousands of books we have in our libraries on various business and related topics and the several hundred on the Internet, we were amazed that none of these were used directly to write this book. Lots of them provided background, and we've listed a few of those above.

We thought it only appropriate that we share some of the Web sites we found particularly valuable.

NETSCAPE COLUMNS

We found that each of these columns offered cutting-edge information on the state of the Net.

1. The Main Thing. Jim Barksdale talks about Netscape's business and offers advice on how companies can succeed in a networked world.

2. TechVision. Marc Andreessen shares his thoughts about the future of Netscape and Internet technologies and looks ahead to where we're going.

3. Intranet Executive. Guest chief information officers and other leading technology executives discuss the implementation of open standards systems in their companies.

4. Web Site Stories. Members of the Netscape Web site team, recognized designers, and technical experts focus on the processes, technologies, tricks, and successes of designing, building, and maintaining Web sites. This series is scheduled to begin in the spring.

These four columns can be found on the Web at:
http://home.netscape.com/comprod/columns/index.html

5. Build a More Productive Team with Intranet Solutions. Filled with links to all kinds of intranet/extranet resources, this site can be found at
http://home.netscape.com/comprod/at_work/index.html

IDC ROI REPORT

International Data Corporation (IDC) has conducted in-depth return on investment (ROI) case studies on Netscape intranet customers. You can read IDC's findings on each company, including company background; business challenge; "before Netscape" and "after Netscape"; subjective benefits; and details of the financial impact (including ROI, payback period, and total costs and savings). This report can be found on the Web at:
http://home.netscape.com/comprod/announce/roi.html

THE INTRANET JOURNAL

BES, Inc.'s Intranet Journal. Features include the latest intranet/extranet news with excerpts from leading publications, a Web-based moderated newsgroup devoted to intranets; an experts' corner, where guest experts provide insights into intranet/extranet building and the latest technology; resource design tools; and much more for the informed business executive using the Net technology. This site can be found on the Web at:
http://www.intranetjournal.com/

Appendix B

PRECURSOR TECHNOLOGIES

Net and Web technologies are not the only ones out there helping businesses do things more effectively. Two other technologies have been around for a while and offer solutions to some of the same problems. The two best-known are Electronic Data Interchange (EDI) and groupware. We call them the "precursor technologies" for two reasons.

One reason is that they came first. By and large, businesses were using EDI and groupware before they started using the Internet and World Wide Web and before they began looking at intranets and extranets.

The other reason is that they showed the way. Both EDI and groupware are ways to do things that many businesses are now discovering with Net/Web technology. Using them as models can help you use Net/Web technology more effectively.

Electronic Data Interchange or groupware may even be the right choice for meeting your business goals or perhaps for use as a launching pad from which you rocket into the world of open systems and Net/Web technology to achieve your business goals.

ELECTRONIC DATA INTERCHANGE (EDI)

Electronic Data Interchange (EDI) had its birth in the Berlin Airlift and the paper-strewn business practices of that time. Return for a moment in your mind to a time when businesses all used different systems and they were all based on paper.

Because we each had different forms and because there was no easy way to transfer information, what happened was that the people at my company wound up transcribing the information that people at your company had already set down. And when we were done, we transcribed it again onto different forms and sent it to other companies, that would transcribe it again. The amount of labor and the potential for error was phenomenal.

Electronic Data Interchange was developed to deal with that situation. Essentially, EDI is an attempt to automate the handling of common information through two means: standards and networks. The government, EDI associations, and other trade associations all work together to develop standards. That way, two businesses didn't have to start from scratch when they wanted to share information. Instead, they could adapt a common format and standard way of transferring information.

Electronic Data Interchange was also about developing networks. With the rise of computerization and data processing through the 1960s and 1970s, it became possible to transfer information easily and quickly from one place to another. Even if that information wasn't sent over a network, it could be put into disk form and mailed or expressed to the company you were doing business with. The simplest and most effective way for EDI, though, was a private network. Those private networks are often called value-added networks (VANs).

As you might expect, the people who made the big push to start Electronic Data Interchange were the people with the most to gain, the big players. For that reason, the government, large chemical companies such as Dupont, and large manufacturers such as those in the automotive industry were the first to get onboard and then to demand that their suppliers use EDI as a condition of doing business. This was all well and good, and it worked well with the trend toward business alliances and partnerships and just-in-time inventory. It worked well with trends toward lean manufacturing and efficient distribution.

For the large players, EDI has been quite a success. It's provided a robust, structured, and secure system for automating a lot of routine business functions. In many value chains, information is entered only once and then passed from electronic hand to electronic hand along the chain.

The use of a value-added network sitting between the partners allows different kinds of computer systems to be used. And those systems provide a level of security because of their proprietary nature. Issues like company identification, data security, and data authentication are handled routinely through the value-added networks that carry most EDI traffic.

Even in this environment, several large players have not automated things all the way through. There are several places out there where you can find stand-alone terminals accepting EDI transmissions which are then entered into the computer system of the company receiving the information. The reasons for this are various, stretching from the rational to the purely political.

Electronic Data Interchange, in its traditional form, is excellent for members of a small, stable community. And, in fact, it's most commonly seen in such a stable community where one large, dominant partner can force its will on the other players.

That leads us to the current situation. While EDI has been a success for those small, stable communities with dominant partners, it really hasn't taken hold across the board. The Department of Labor and the IRS have recently completed a study that determined that there were about 40,000 users of EDI out of the 20 million U.S. businesses. That's approximately 0.2%.

Even in those places where you'd expect lots of participation, the rates are fairly low. IBM did a survey in 1996 of 500,000 wholesale distribution companies. These are the businesses that sit between the large manufacturers and retail outlets or contractors. They'd be highly likely, you would think, to participate in EDI, but such is not the case. According to the IBM survey, less than 8% of these businesses currently use EDI.

Why? Some don't like the mandatory structures that EDI imposes. Some find it too costly and, for many businesses, the costs are quite high. Most of those costs are dictated by the necessity for a private value-added network and for pricing structures based on small, stable communities rather than broad-based business use. Some companies don't want to be locked in. Once you've set up an EDI agreement with an entity in your value chain, you're committed to it fairly strongly. You've just added switching costs that wouldn't exist without your EDI partnership.

Many small and midsized businesses find EDI too expensive, or they may simply feel that the entire process of finding and recruiting EDI partners is not a good use of their time and energy.

Even so, the use of EDI is soaring. *Traffic World* pointed out a major surge in EDI usage in 1996. Dianne Silver, vice president of information strategy for APL, Ltd. says, "Customers are requiring standard EDI as a prerequisite for accepting a bid."

Part of that is due to major industry efforts. The big three automakers announced, in June 1996, that they were banding together to prompt all their more than 10,000 first-, second-, and third-tier suppliers to adopt EDI. Silver, at APL, expects electronic commerce via EDI and other channels to grow 100% to 200% in 1997. And she sees the portion of her customer base running EDI as having doubled in 1996.

Enter the Internet. As we're pointing out throughout this book, the Internet brings two things to the party that are crucial to you when you are analyzing whether your company is going to use EDI. First, it brings a broad array of people who are connected. That dramatically improves the number of people you can do business with at various levels. The other thing that the Internet and Web technology bring to the party is a standard interface. People get used to looking at, and dealing with, a simple graphic way of handling the information on their desktop, whether they are dealing with a transaction that is going around the world or merely typing a letter into their word processor.

There are a couple of ways that the Net, Net technology, and EDI are coming together. EDI X.12 standard structured documents are treated as a special MIME attachment to e-mail. That sets up the possibility of a business buying translation software from a company like Sterling or DNS Worldwide or Premenos to convert that attachment to a standard format.

We're also seeing a number of efforts by major players, such as Harbinger and St. Paul Software (again, among others), to find ways for people to use the Internet to connect to EDI networks or simply to send EDI materials across the Net.

What we're finding is that e-mail is starting to do some of the work, online catalogs are starting to do some of the work, and special translation software and Web sites are starting to do some of the work. And the line that once clearly separated EDI from other commerce is beginning to blur.

At bottom, we see EDI as a precursor technology. It's going to remain excellent for those who need it—those small, stable communities, especially those with high security needs and dominant partners. But the lure of wider networking possibilities and a standard interface, we think, will bring lots of companies into the market to find ways to integrate the two.

We think there will certainly be an EDI-like function in the electronic commerce of the future. There is a need for standard formats and secure networks, along with a common way of doing business that automates transactions throughout a value chain. The trick is that we may not call it EDI, even though it will do the same things.

Our suggestion to you as an executive is to look for ways to do the EDI type of function. Look for ways to automate your processes all the way through the value chain. Adopt the motto Key It Only Once. Look for solutions to that automation process that are inexpensive or less expensive than traditional EDI. And consider the variety of turnkey possibilities that are already beginning to pop up. One good example of these is the Federal Express Service Business Link. Business Link, which is designed for smaller and midsized companies, links the data transfer function to fulfillment centers and to shipping, providing a one-stop shop for certain distribution and logistics functions. That may not be the answer for you, but that kind of service will be an answer for many in the years ahead.

GROUPWARE

The other major precursor technology to today's open-systems intranet/extranet/Internet is a class of software that's known commonly as groupware. As we note in the Glossary, groupware is a network-based software application that lets users collaborate.

Another way to look at that is by function. Essentially, groupware lets groups, mostly businesses, do three things. Groupware lets a group of people have a common body of information that they can easily share. Groupware generally provides a method for tracking work flow. And groupware provides a way for members of a group to work together—it fosters collaboration.

There are actually a lot of different kinds of software that do these types of things. There is software devoted to scheduling and project management. There are various calendar programs. And, of course, there are database and document programs. In fact, when many of these are set up on a standard local-area network (LAN) or other network, they might, at first glance, seem to do several of the things that groupware does.

That would be deceptive, though. The special strength of group-ware as an application is that it brings the pieces together. And the key word here is *integration*. If you can imagine a spectrum running from left to right, place individual stand-alone applications on the left. A project management package running on a single computer would go there on the spectrum. As you move to the right across the spectrum, imagine that these become more networked and more integrated.

An easy way to think of that is to think of what happens with a common office suite such as Microsoft Office. If you've got the pro-grams that are designed to work together to a certain extent, then the documents from Microsoft Word can be used in Microsoft Pro-ject. The output from Microsoft Project can be used in Microsoft Word. Clearly, this isn't limited to Microsoft. Any suite of applica-tions, such as that from Lotus or WordPerfect, would do the same kind of thing with the same kinds of programs.

Move a little bit farther to the right, and imagine that you're now integrating programs from outside the suite but still in a single-user application. This is where a calendar program such as Ecco Pro might be added to the package to provide some sophisticated cal-endar functions. Programs like this are designed to work with stan-dard word-processing packages like Microsoft Word. And so you can imagine inputs and outputs and getting things from one pro-gram to another by taking them through another and translating and so forth.

We're still on a single desktop, however. We've got the programs to work together, but we're not networked yet. That comes next.

Move a bit farther along the continuum to the right, and imagine that these same programs are now shared across the network. Several people with an Ecco Pro calendar system and using the networked version can share a common group calendar. The same is true for people sharing individual word-processing documents in Word or project files in Project. The network adds collaboration. Now, move farther to the right.

Now we're beginning to talk about what groupware really does. It brings the stuff together in a specialized, collaborative, networked application. And a groupware package would also add the ability to develop a specific application of this type. Let's take a look at the components that go into a normal groupware package.

We've already mentioned application development, so let's start there. This component allows developers to build applications to integrate and automate almost any set of office functions that you can imagine. Those functions can range from a simple e-mail application to highly complex and mission-critical tasks. This is not just your everyday sit down at the computer and crank out some stuff developer, though. People who are qualified developers for groupware programs, such as Lotus Notes, get very good at what they do. They are, in effect, specialized programmers.

Most groupware packages include a component for electronic messaging or e-mail. What this does is to allow sharing files and the electronic transmission of messages that help achieve the objectives we've already talked about.

Groupware packages include a component that allows for storage and retrieval. Memos can be put in electronic folders. Those folders can be gotten to through directories. This is generally easier and usually less restrictive than hooking things onto electronic mail. One particular advantage is that a formatted document can be sent without translations and without attachments.

Groupware usually includes a routing capability. This allows for automatic routing of documents to people with predetermined or preassigned access rights. If a group of people in a business are working on a project together, groupware allows for setting up ways in which certain kinds of messages will be routed. Some will go to all the people on the project, others to members of specific working groups, and still others to members of some groups, with notification to everyone.

Groupware usually includes a calendar or scheduling component. Everybody gets to see everybody else's calendar. Calendars can be coordinated. Calendars can be searched for available meeting times.

Groupware includes document management as well. Lots of people can work on the same documents, access can be restricted, and documents can be retrieved.

This is very powerful technology. People have been cobbling together systems to try to do this almost since we got the first computers. You could even say that the Internet itself is a kind of vast groupware application. But that would miss the point that the class of software that we're calling groupware is a highly specialized application that provides incredible benefits in the right place.

In fact, Ian Campbell, of International Data Corporation, believes that groupware is *the* unique application among computer programs. He points out that other programs are essentially variants of things we already have. Spreadsheets are variants of ledgers. A word-processing program turns a computer into a typewriter. A scheduling program is a fancy way to build charts that were already done by hand. Groupware, says Campbell, is different.

The power of groupware is that it lets people work together in ways that are different from anything we've known in history. And the payoff can be dramatic. Companies that have used groupware on projects commonly see reduction times from nongroupware methods of 50% to 70% and more. They see reduced costs.

Groupware, as we knew it, essentially grew out of a single application, Lotus Notes. That was really the first program that did all the things we mentioned earlier and integrated their operation.

Now, if you've stayed with us this long, you may be thinking, "This sounds a little bit like that Internet stuff that's in the rest of the book." And it is. But it isn't.

Groupware turns out to be a specialty application and, in that sense, it's very much like EDI. For the situations for which it is ideal, it has incredible payoff and power. But, for many situations, it's far too expensive and difficult.

Compared to open systems like the Internet and World Wide Web, groupware has several drawbacks. Groupware is not as intuitive to use in most packages as the open-systems software. Groupware is often hard or expensive to use with other applications that have not already been integrated into the proprietary software. And, compared to Web applications, groupware tends to be very expensive.

So, where are we? Basic groupware is a powerful and productive application for those limited situations in which the human and financial resources are there and the payoff is big enough to warrant the application of those resources.

Now, that doesn't mean that people aren't interested in getting the benefits that groupware provides in an easier-to-use format or one that's less expensive. We're seeing a move toward software that allows collaboration, sharing common bodies of knowledge, and tracking work flows but using an open-systems format such as an intranet. Those efforts are coming from three distinct places.

Groupware vendors such as Lotus are developing systems that work with HTML. Lotus's new Domino product is designed to do just that. A basic application here would be to translate data from a Lotus Notes database into a Web page.

The second major direction toward this open-systems "groupware" is coming from the people who develop browsers. In today's world, that's Microsoft, with its Explorer, and Netscape, with Navigator. In Microsoft's case, it's integrating its Exchange groupware product to work with its browser, and vice versa. In the case of Netscape, it's the development of a new product that incorporates the latest version of the browser. The Netscape product is called Communicator.

The third direction from which development of open-systems "groupware" is coming is individual entrepreneurial developers. There are, quite simply, lots of people out there who see this as a major opportunity to make the fortune they've always dreamed of. They're developing products as add-ons to browsers and products that stand alone. They're extending their calendar programs to work over the Internet and to add project management capabilities.

The result for you is what we term "good news." What you can pretty much expect over the next months and years is that the power of groupware is going to come to open platforms. Exactly how that's going to happen for you and who is going to make the most money at it are still open questions, but we can be pretty sure of the outcome.

Expect the pricing for groupware type of applications to drop considerably. There are simply too many players and too much competition in the market for that not to happen. In fact, it's already started to happen.

Expect standard groupware applications to get easier to use and to work more easily with open systems. That's already starting to happen as well.

And expect the big browser players to continue to add features that look, walk, talk, and quack like groupware.

SUMMARY

For all practical purposes, the situations with both EDI and groupware are the same. Both of them are incredibly powerful technologies that have big payoffs for the situations in which they can be used effectively. Both, until fairly recently, would make that payoff only for larger companies or companies with very specific sets of circumstances. That's because the dollar and time involvement required to use EDI or groupware effectively was more than many businesses were willing to put out for the specific benefits they would get.

In both cases, your organization is likely to benefit from two key avenues of development. Avenue number one is that major players in the EDI and groupware part of the business software business are going to find ways to make their products less expensive and more accessible to people operating on open systems such as the Internet. The other avenue is that lots of people out there are racing to develop open-systems software that does what EDI and groupware do in specialized applications but to make it available to anybody with a browser. Those avenues are going to meet soon, and you can be the beneficiary.

Appendix C

SALES

Throughout this book, we've looked at the "hidden profits" to be had using Net and Web technology. You'll recall that, in the introduction, we refer to these profits as hidden because they aren't the visible part, the thing that everyone has been writing about. No, most of the magazine articles and books out there seem to be about what's variously called "electronic commerce" or "Web business" or something like that. The reason that we're not writing about that is that most of it isn't profitable yet. Sure, a lot of individual efforts are profitable, but we decided to leave those to the books that were aimed primarily at people starting Web businesses.

There are already several books on this, including one of the best, Dan Janal's *101 Businesses You Can Start on the Internet*. If that's your interest, that's a great book to look at. Lots of small businesses are making money on the Net, and lots of larger businesses are doing a small portion of their business on the Net.

The fact remains, though, that most of the profits from direct sales on the Web lie out there in the future someplace. There are several projections about that.

Most studies are based on two core trends. First, the number of households with computers has been increasing dramatically for years and, in recent years, most of those are Net/Web-capable. The second is that the number of servers connecting to the Internet has been doubling every year since 1988. Put those together and you say, "Wow, a pretty good percentage of the population will be online soon—and they'll want to buy things."

The actual numbers run all over the map, but they're always big. In one recent *Wall Street Journal* story, an executive estimated that $900 million in business was done on the Net in 1996 and predicted that $3 to $4 billion will be done in 1997 and $1 trillion in 2000. A Cowles/Simba Information study, called "The Electronic Marketplace 1997," pegs 1996 Internet sales at $733.1 million, growing to $4.27 billion in 2000.

That's a pretty big discrepancy in predictions, but it's still got companies lining up to offer online sales to consumers. A recent study by Forrester Research Inc. of Cambridge, Massachusetts, found that 22 of 30 big corporations surveyed plan to offer online transactions by the end of 1997.

What we'd like to do here is to lay out what we see as the current state of the "selling on the Web" art, along with some ideas about how it's going to change in the years ahead.

Let's start by addressing why this seems to be moving fairly slowly even though the World Wide Web would seem to offer explosive potential for direct marketing.

The basic reason that things are moving fairly slowly is that new things take time to be adopted. That's been true for major consumer technological innovations like television and for business innovations like direct ordering and for banking innovations like ATMs. People don't start using a new technology until they feel that it gives them a benefit and that it's safe.

Online sales haven't been helped by the media coverage that has focused on "hackers," those evil computer whizzes who break into computers and steal information, credit-card numbers, and other things. These fears are like those that slowed the spread of earlier technological innovations. The news stories, when ATMs were first introduced, focused on the bad points, telling about how people lost money in the machines, were injured using them, were robbed using them, had their cards stolen, and lost tons of money, and other things. Sound familiar?

This is a case in which the reality of the threat is very different from the perception of it. The reality is that it is probably more dangerous for you to use your credit card in a restaurant than it is to send it over the Net using e-mail. You're probably even safer if you use a secure server and an encrypted system.

The popular media tend to portray computer criminals as brilliant hackers. Many of them are, but many of them are not. I've always liked the response of Don Delaney, an investigator for the New York State Police. After arresting one hacker group, Delaney was asked by an interviewer, "Sir, would you classify these young people as geniuses?" Delaney's response was brief and to the point, "No Sir, I'd categorize them as defendants."

That's not to minimize the real threat that's out there. If your company is going to sell things over the Net, you need to take precautions so that you and your customers are protected. You need to utilize the security expertise that's available to make your system secure. What you'll probably find, though, is that your greatest threats don't come from brilliant hackers but, instead, from sloppiness, laziness, and people who violate procedure and share their password with others. Your greatest threats are probably not as likely to come from outside your firewall as from inside.

Still, there is the reality of perception to be dealt with. Our best guess, looking at how other technological innovations and payment methods have been adopted, is that we're about halfway through a 7- to 10-year cycle. That would mean that the big money from online sales is likely to be several years in the future.

All growth has a somewhat spiraling effect. The growth in the number of people willing to try buying online leads people to develop applications and software and systems that help them do that. As the application software and systems become more effective and secure, more people are willing to try buying online, and the cycle continues.

In the next couple of years, we should see some agreement on basic standards for handling payments and settlements in secure transactions. We should also see continuing development of *middleware,* which is the software necessary to connect the order when it comes in the electronic front door with the order-processing, fulfillment, and payment systems in the back office.

Now, with all that said, what kinds of things might sell well on the Net and the Web? And note here that we're talking about the kinds of things individual consumers buy. Most business-to-business commerce is going to be handled through the standard purchase order/invoice format or the newly developing purchasing cards, both of which are based on prior relationship and regular contact.

One thing that seems to have good sales potential on the World Wide Web is anything that is a "commodity." We put the word commodity in quotes there because this is not the classic economic definition of commodity that we're talking about. Here, *commodity* means a product that is the same no matter where you buy it. By that definition, CDs are a commodity, as are books and videotapes and movies.

In these situations, a consumer knows what he or she is getting in advance, and the Web lends certain economies to the way business can be done. One basic economy comes from the ability to offer a huge selection without investing money in inventory. Amazon.com can be the largest bookstore in the world, not because it has the largest physical inventory but because it can get a book that meets a customer's specifications to that customer for a reasonable price. From the customer's standpoint, it doesn't matter where the book begins its journey to his or her front door. It only matters that it reaches the front door quickly and at reasonable cost.

We'd say that any transaction in which the customer knows what product to expect would make a good potential Web sale. We can extend the concept of commodity in two fairly distinct ways.

Some companies have positioned themselves in the customer's mind as providing a certain level of quality and service. Some of these are primarily retailers, such as Nordstrom and Nieman Marcus. Others are cataloguers such as L.L. Bean and Lands' End. And some fall somewhere between the two, like the Sharper Image and Eddie Bauer. What they all have in common is that, as a result of efforts over the years, their customers know what to expect from them. In this case, it's the merchant that provides the certainty about what the customer is getting.

Another extension of the "commodity" idea is items that are being reordered. Pretty much every retail business has some of these. Music stores sell strings, frets, and reeds. Office supply stores sell

reams of paper and sets of markers. These are all bought by customers again and again and again. These seem to have a good life
being sold over the Web.

Another item that ought to sell well on the Web is one that is
highly specialized. To some extent, this is the branded retailer phenomenon, but it can extend to certain specialties. Virtual Vineyards
offers a huge selection of wine, but one of the reasons that it can sell
a lot on the Web is the expert advice that's available on the site
about how to buy and use the wine that it sells.

Another way to look at this is the extension of a highly specialized retail operation to a much larger geographical component. The
best example we know of this is the Hot Hot Hot store based in
Pasadena, California.

The store was opened in November 1993 and put up a Web site in
1994. It sells hot sauce. By the end of 1996, Web sales accounted for
between 20% and 30% of revenues, with catalog sales taking 10%
and the balance coming through the retail location. The Web sales
are more than doubling annually. In addition, the marketing cost for
Web sales is only about 5% of revenue, compared to 20% for catalog
sales.

We see highly specialized stores as having good things to sell.
This is especially true if there's a major information component
connected with the specialty.

The last thing we see as presenting great possibilities on the Net
and the Web are information products—essentially anything that
can be digitized. Wally's publishing company, for example, is developing a line of specialized digital books. Because the books are digital, the cost of producing individual, specialized copies is primarily
the cost of the development of the material, not the production of
individual copies. That allows the publishing company to produce
a product for retailers, for example, but then to produce several
specialized versions of that for retailers in different industries. Al-
ternatively, a product on executive information strategies can be
created for executives at different organizational levels or in different industries and distributed effectively.

The ability to customize digital products makes them a potential
profit maker in electronic commerce. We're already seeing the be-
ginnings of that with specialized online information services such

as the Personal Journal Service of the *Interactive Wall Street Journal.*

Another advantage of the digital information product is that it appeals to the quest for instant gratification. As electronic commerce systems smooth out and the verification, authentication, and payment systems become automatic, the following scenario is possible. At 2:00 A.M., a consumer visits an information Web site and decides that he or she would like to purchase a digital book or a piece of software or several articles from a database. The order is placed using a credit card or a cybercash system. It's authenticated and the payment method is verified automatically. And, within seconds, the digital product is on its way across the Net.

The total time to complete that transaction would be seconds or minutes. The product that the consumer wanted would be in his or her hands (actually in his or her computer) and ready for use. The payment would have been processed.

We do have one other set of thoughts on electronic commerce and online sales that we think is important: Just as with other new technologies, we're still learning how to use this one. In the beginning of a new technology, we don't really have names for what we do. We call products by a version of an old name. Jeff, in his speeches, points out that when cars were first invented, we didn't call them *cars.* Instead, we called them *horseless carriages.* That's because we knew what a carriage was but we weren't quite sure what a car was.

In the next few years, we'll define what electronic commerce really is. And it's our suspicion that the people who will blaze the trails here, especially in information products, will not be the big companies with millions to spend. We think, instead, that, as with innovations, smaller, more flexible, and often more resource-strapped companies will blaze the trail.

Whoever blazes the trails, you can expect that, within very few years, direct online sales will be added to the other profit-building methods that we talk about here.

GLOSSARY

ASCII

American Standard Code for Information Interchange ... in the context of a file, an ASCII file is one that contains only printable text characters—numbers, letters, and standard punctuation—that is universally accepted by every software program; sometimes referred to a "simple text."

Asynchronous

The transmission of information without reference to timing factors on the receiving end (i.e., someone can type in a message and send it off, but the recipient doesn't have to be around to receive it—recipients can then read and respond when they want).

Autoresponder

A text file that is sent automatically back to someone who has sent an e-mail message requesting it. People can then download the file to their computers if they

269

choose. This file can contain such items as articles, information about you and your products/services, or whatever you want to make available for people to retrieve automatically via e-mail.

Bandwidth

The size of the data transmission pipeline. The higher the bandwidth, the faster the information can flow per unit of time.

Browser

A client program that enables users to search, often somewhat randomly, through the information that is provided by a specific type of server. This terminology is generally used in reference to the World Wide Web.

CGI

Common gateway interface; a standard that allows Web servers to run external applications such as search engines.

CGI Script

On the Web, a list of instructions used by a Web server to process data that was received via a form.

Chat

A service that allows two or more people to have an electronic conversation, a real-time, online dialogue over the Internet. Many commercial service providers, like AOL, CIS and Prodigy, also offer this service. *See* IRC.

Client

A software application that works on your behalf to extract a service from your server located somewhere on the network. A good analogy would be to think of the telephone company as the server and your phone as the client.

Collaboration software

A network-based application that lets participants share information.

Groupware	A network-based software application that lets users collaborate.
Data mining	The process of sifting through large databases of information from multiple sources (often including transactions and customer records) to extract additional information that can be used in business.
Data warehouse	A comprehensive collection of company data, organized for easy access.
Dial-up user	A person who accesses the Internet through a modem over a phone line.
Document database	An organized collection of related documents.
Domain Name System (DNS)	The system that locates the IP address corresponding to named computers and domains. A DNS consists of a sequence of information separated by dots. Thus nbn.com stands for "North Bay Network," which is located in a commercial top-level domain. Anyone can register for a domain name—an example of a domain name for a business on the Net called The Expertise Center is expertcenter.com. NOTE: DNS is often used to refer to Domain Name Service, which is a service offered by an Internet service provider that registers your domain name with the Domain Name System.
EDI	Short for Electronic Data Interchange, which is almost always abbreviated in business articles. Electronic Data Interchange (EDI) is the electronic exchange of business transactions, such as purchase orders, inventory, confirmations, and invoices, among organizations using a standard format.

Extranet   Short for extended (expanded) intranets; communications with users "internal" to the organization and with a preselected set of "external" users, usually customers and/or vendors.

FAQ   A list of frequently asked questions and their answers. Many USENET news-groups, mailing lists, and software tools for the Internet, such as Archie, Gopher, WAIS, and so on, maintain these for their participants and users so that other participants won't have to spend so much time answering the same set of questions. Although FAQs can be very helpful if you are a newcomer to the Internet, it is always advisable for the seasoned pro to check them too, so as not to violate the social guidelines when participating in a newsgroup or mailing list.

Firewall   A machine or machines that sit between a site's internal network and the Internet to restrict certain types of traffic from passing between them.

Forum   A special-interest group devoted to a single topic, which exists on many general-purpose gateways such as AOL or CompuServe.

FTP   File transfer protocol, a tool (software application) that enables you to transfer text or software files between remote computers or from a remote computer onto your computer. Its most popular Internet use is "anonymous FTP," where you log in to a remote system using the log-in name "Anonymous" and type your full e-mail address as the password. With "anonymous FTP," you don't need an account on the remote computer in order to access certain software applications or text files. You can perform FTP through Gopher, the World Wide Web, or directly with FTP application software.

Homepage

This term is actually used in three different ways. It may refer to the first page a visitor comes to on a Web site. Or it may refer to the most important page on a Web site. On corporate sites, both of these are often the page with basic corporate information. The term home page is also used to refer to the first page your browser goes to when you start it up.

HTML

Hypertext markup language, the markup language of World Wide Web (WWW) documents that tells WWW clients how to display a document's text, hyperlinks, graphics, and attached media; commonly referred to as hypertext.

HTTP

Hypertext transfer protocol, a protocol or language used by WWW servers and clients to transfer HTML documents.

Hypertext

Provides the ability to move from document to document whenever a word or concept is introduced—links documents and graphics through selected words and images; simply point your computer's mouse to a word or phrase that is underlined and/or colored, click the mouse button, and another document pops up, that gives more details about the specified subject.

Intranet

A network based on standard IP protocols that is contained within an enterprise. It may consist of many interlinked local-area networks and also use leased lines in the wide-area network. It may or may not include connections through one or more gateways to the outside Internet. The main purpose of an intranet is usually to share company information and computing resources among employees.

IP

Internet Protocol; one of the TCP/IP protocols, the basic Internet protocol used to move packets of raw data from one computer to another.

Java

An object-oriented language, developed by Sun Microsystems, for writing distributed Web applications.

LAN

Local-area network; a computer network, usually confined to a single office or building, that allows for the sharing of files and other resources among several users and makes interoperability among various systems possible.

LISTSERV

A program that automatically manages mailing lists. It responds automatically to e-mail requests sent to a mailing list and distributes them automatically to the members of that mailing list. This term is actually the name for one of the software programs that performs this function. You may also see references to Listproc or Majordomo, which are the other two popular programs, but only LISTSERV is used as the generic name for the type of program.

Mailing list

An automated message service whose subscribers receive e-mail postings from other subscribers on a given topic.

MIME	Multipurpose internet mail extensions; a protocol that allows e-mail to contain simple text plus color pictures, video, sound, and binary database; both sender and receiver need a MIME-aware mail program to read it.
Modem	A device that allows your computer to talk to another computer or the Internet via the phone lines.
Net	A short way of referring to the Internet.
Newsgroup	An automated message area, usually operated by USENET, in which subscribers post messages to the entire group on specific topics.
NNTP	Network news transfer protocol; a protocol for posting and retrieving news articles on USENET newsgroups.
Online Communities	Communications among members of an affinity group or "community."
Password	The secret string of characters assigned to your individual log-in name on a particular system; it prevents others from easily accessing your computer accounts.
Post	To place a message on a bulletin board, in a forum, or in a USENET newsgroup for public reading.
Protocol	The codes and procedures that make it possible for one computer to talk to another computer and exchange data.
Router	A computer system that makes decisions about which path Internet traffic will take to reach its destination.
Server	A computer configured to communicate with clients and provide access to the

files stored on the server computer; a file server makes files available, a WAIS server makes full-text information available through WAIS protocol, and a WWW server makes stored hypertext files available to the browser client.

Signature file (.sig file) A file, typically between four and eight lines long, that users append to the end of their electronic mail and USENET newsgroup or mailing list message postings. It's a good way to get a promotional message out about your business or yourself without offending Internet users with blatant advertisement; sometimes referred to as an "electronic business card."

SLIP Serial line Internet protocol; a protocol, like PPP, that lets a Macintosh computer pretend it is a full Internet machine using only a modem and a phone line.

Spamming The act of sending hundreds of inappropriate postings to USENET newsgroups and mailing lists. Old-time Internet users consider this to be a very serious breach of Netiquette.

SQL Structured query language, a standard language for requesting information from a relational database.

SSL Secure Sockets Layer, a transport-level technology for the authentification and data encryption between a Web server and a Web browser.

Sysop A person who monitors online conversations to be sure that they stay on tack and above board.

TCP/IP

Transmission control protocol/Internet protocol; a special computer language to guarantee the safe arrival of data at its intended destination, this is the base protocol on which the Internet is founded.

Telnet

A software tool that enables you to log in to a remote computer from the computer you are sitting at; it allows you to access and direct the remote computers to do such things as search the remote computers database.

Text file

A file that contains only characters from the ASCII character set, with no graphics or special symbols.

Thread

A series of messages or conversations that follow a single thought or topic.

UNIX

An operating system specializing in customizability and multiuser capabilities that is in wide use on the computer of the Internet; it uses a rather cryptic language that can be very difficult for the average Internet user; hence the rise and popularity of "point and click" software, which is much more user-friendly.

Upload

To send a test or software application file from your computer to a remote computer on the Internet, a commercial online service, or a bulletin board.

URL

Universal resource locator; a standard addressing system used in the World Wide Web that can reference any type of Internet file, enabling a WWW client to access that file. It contains information about the method of access or protocol, the server computer to be accessed, and the path name of the file to be accessed.

USENET A bulletin board network system linked to the Internet that houses the popular special-interest newsgroups.

VAN Value Added Network; a limited access network that provides one or more features that add value for users. Many EDI networks are VANs that provide security; other VANs are set up to facilitate purchasing by prequalifying vendors.

WAN Wide-area network; a long-distance computer network using dedicated phone lines and/or satellites to interconnect local-area networks across large geographical distances up to thousands of miles apart.

Whiteboard A collaboration software feature that allows people on the Net at different locations to type and draw in the same file in real time.

INDEX

80/20 rule, 173

A

administration, 61
  challenges online tools can solve, 62, 63
  cost reduction, administration
    basic administration, 64, 65
    benefit of Internet technology, 63, 64
    employee benefit costs, cutting using he
      Web, 67-69
    intranet/extranet systems, proprietary,
      75
    intranets, role in, 66, 67
    investor relations, employing Net technology in, 70, 71
    practical examples of, 65-67
    purchasing costs, cutting online, 72-77
  purchasing costs, cutting online, 72, 84, 85
    General Electric, 73-77
    MRO items, 72
    process simplification, 72, 73
  recent developments in, 61, 62
  role in organization, 61
  support, role of, 63
  TACTICS planning action system and, 77
    automate, 79, 80
    core functions/big payoffs, 81
    customize, 53-55
    inside/out, 80, 81
    start now, 81
    think links, 77-79
    transform, 80
    tips for employing Net technology in, 81-85
    Webmaster role, 82, 83
agility, in manufacturing, 45-48
  IT supporting manufacturing, 46, 47
  virtual process control, 47, 48
APQC (American Productivity and Quality
    Center), 41
Apria Health Care, supply-chain partners, 165,
    166

ASCII, described, 269
asynchronous, described, 269
autoresponder, described, 269, 270

B

bandwidth, described, 270
best practices, sharing, 42-44
Boeing, 3
  intranet, 25
    impact of, 25, 26
    primary goals, 25
books, Web/Net resources, 249-251
Booz-Allen, and Hamilton, 4
  service delivery, enhancing, 145
    business activities, application support,
      146
    content knowledge, 145
    coordinating growth, 145
    cultural issues and, 147, 148
    experts, access to, 146
    integrating people into practice, 145
    knowledge program implementation,
      145, 146
    return on investment, 147
Braxton Associates, 3
browser, described, 270
budget issues, 243, 244
Business Edge
  strategic objectives, 7
business strategy
  business environment, 6
  driving forces in, 2
    attitude to organization, 3-5
    leanness and efficiency, 2
    organizational changes, 2, 3
  recent changes in, 1, 2
  strategic objectives, determining, 7
  strategy analysis, 7
    business processes, 8-10
    customers, 10, 11
    key supplier, 10

partners, 11
strategy determination, 7, 8
TACTICS planning action system, 12
  automate, 12, 13
  core functions/big payoffs, 15, 16
  customize, 13, 14
  inside/out, 15
  start now, 16
  think links, 12
  transform 14

C

CAD (computer aided design) products, Web
    migration, 23
call center costs, reducing, 177, 178
Caterpillar, customer responsiveness, 39, 40
CATIA (computer-aided, three dimensional,
    interactive applications), 25, 26
CGI (common gateway interface), described,
    270
  script, 270
chat, described, 270
Chrysler
  customization and Net sales, 39
  intranet use in product development, 24
CKO (chief knowledge officer), 145
client, described, 270
collaboration
  product development, 22, 23
  software, described, 270
Columbia/HCA Healthcare
  recruitment online, 88
    companywide information, 90
    education, 90
    physicians, 90, 91
    scope of Web site, 89
    strategic objectives, 7
    training development, 98-100
    training via the Net, 94
      administration functions, 96, 97
      cutting travel costs, 94, 95
      executive training, 96
commodity, Web sales, 266, 267
communication, Net seminars for, 214
competitive strategy via training, 102, 103
concurrent engineering, 19
conformance quality, 41
core business strategy, profit margins, 210-212
core process, 8

cost reduction. *See also* administration
  basic administration, 64, 65
    key components in, 65
  benefit of Internet technology, 63, 64
  employee benefit costs, cutting using the
      Web, 67
    caveats in, 68
    making information available on
        intranet, 67, 68
    outsourcing of benefit management, 68,
        69
  intranet/extranet systems, proprietary, 75
  intranets, role in, 66, 67
  investor relations, employing Net technolo-
      gy in, 70, 71
  practical examples of, 65-67
  purchasing costs, cutting online, 72
    General Electric, 73-77
    MRO items, 72
    process simplification, 72, 73
Countrywide Home Loans
  Internet technology cost benefit analysis,
      63, 64
  service delivery, enhancing, 139, 140
    customized applications, delivering, 141
    fax delivery costs, reducing, 140, 141
    security, meeting concerns, 142
culture concerns, plan implementation, 240, 241
customer service, 175
  call center costs, reducing, 177, 178
  challenges of providing high quality, 176
  customization, 197
  dealer network, improving responsiveness
      using, 181, 182
  delivering using the Net, 185
    automation and customization, 186, 187
    FAQ files, 185
    infobot, setting up, 185
    links, providing in infobot message, 186
    productivity, improving, 187, 188
  information flow, importance of, 196
  impact of good, 176
  mailbots, 182
  responsiveness, improving, 178
  small companies and, 188, 189
    mailbots, 192
    online professional support, 189-191
    tracking software for, 189
  TACTICS planning action system, 193
    automate, 193, 194
    core functions/big payoffs, 195

customize, 194
  inside/out, 194, 195
  start now, 195
  think links, 193
  transform 194
value, adding to product/service, 176, 177
Web-based, 184
  savings potential, 184
  tracking package calls, cutting, 184
customization
  customer service, 197
  digital products, sales on the Web, 268, 269
  increasing importance of, 39
customized applications, delivering, 141
cycle time, 19

D

Darwin, product development system, 24, 25
data mining, described, 271
data warehouse, described, 271
database technology
  administration, 83
    cost reduction, 65
delivery of service. *See* service delivery
design issues, plan implementation, 239, 240
dial-up user, described, 271
Digital, sales support via the Web site, 126
directed content, 212, 213
distribution. *See* fulfillment and distribution
distributor relationships, improving, 160, 161
DNS (domain name system), described, 271
document database, 271

E

EDI (Electronic Data Interchange), 73, 253, 273
  bringing to Web, 160
  cost drawbacks of, 256
  implementation of, 255
  limitations of, 172
  need for in the future, 257
  purchase cycle prices, cutting, 159
  purpose of, 254
  success of, 255
  summary, 262
education, Net seminars for, 214
electronic commerce, intranet/extranet use and,
  162, 163

Eli Lilly & Company, information sharing, 128,
  129
e-mail
  as team communication tool, 206, 207
  discussion groups, product development,
    29, 30, 32
Ernst & Young, virtual world consulting, 149
  benefits of, 150
ERP (enterprise resource planning), 46
extranet, 272
  developing partnerships via, 213
  drawbacks of using, 24
  use in product development, 24, 33
Extron Electronics, competitive strategy in
  training, 102, 103

F

FAQ (Frequently Asked Questions) files, 272
  customer service, 185
  product development, 33
fax delivery costs, reducing, 140, 141
Federal Express
  automatic fulfillment, 169
  tracking package calls, cutting, 184
Financial Services Corporation, sales force
  effectiveness, 113
  cost analysis, 115
  extranet site map, 117-120
  intranet, setting up, 114, 115
  motivating affiliates to use extranet, 116, 117
  WWW adoption, 113, 114
financial Web site, full-service, 143, 144
firewall, 272
  collaboration and, 24
  fulfillment and distribution, 172
food-chain, 156
Footlocker, supply-chain partners, 164, 165
Ford
  manufacturing, 37, 38
  product development, 17
forum, described, 272
FTP (File Transfer Protocol), 206
  described, 272, 273
fulfillment and distribution, 152
  80/20 rule, 173
  challenges, of, 155
    cost reduction, 156, 157
    demand-driven requests, meeting, 156
    relationships, enhancing, 156

using as competitive advantage, 155, 156
cross-platform applicability, 172, 173
EDI limitations of, 172
firewall considerations, 172
Pareto's law and, 173
solutions to challenges, 157, 158
  customers, knowledge of, 166, 167
  distributor relationships, improving, 160, 161
  EDI, bringing to Web, 160
  integrated solutions, 167, 168
  intranet/extranet use, electronic commerce and, 162, 163
  network development with key partners, 161, 162
  outsourcing services, 163, 164
  purchase cycle prices, cutting, 159
  supply-chain management, 158
  supply-chain partners, 164-166
  TPN, improving efficiencies, 159, 160
supply-chain, 156
  defined, 157
TACTICS planning action system and, 168
  automate, 169
  core functions/big payoffs, 170, 171
  customize, 169, 170
  inside/out, 170
  start now, 172, 172
  think links, 168, 169
  transform, 170
tips for handling, 172, 173
training, employee, 173

G

General Electric
  cutting purchasing costs online, 72, 73
  business-to-business software, developing, 74
  outsourcing multiple bids, 73, 74
  supply-chain management, 76, 77
  TPN goals, 74
  purchase cycle prices, cutting, 159
General Motors, intranet use in product development, 24
Goodyear, setting up retail sales via the Web, 126-129
groupware, 253, 271
  application suitability, 260, 261
  components, of, 259, 260
  described, 257, 258
  functions of, 258
  future expectations of, 262
  integrating from outside, 258, 259
  open systems direction, 261
  summary, 262

H

HBO, Internet tools administration cost reduction, 66
Heineken, integrated solutions to fulfillment and distribution, 167, 168
Hewlett Packard, intranet use, 49, 50
home banking, Internet, 143
homepage, described, 273
Horner, Townsend & Kent, extranet customer service, 188
Hot Hot Hot store, 2367
HTML (hypertext transfer markup language), described, 273
HTTP (hypertext transfer protocol), described, 273
hyperlinked Web pages, use in product development, 33
hypertext, described, 273

I

IBM
  account information, developing, 120-122
  administration cost reduction, 66
  core processes, 9, 10
  customer service, Web-based, 184
IDC ROI report, Web/Net resources, 252
improved speed to market, 19
Industry.Net, 75, 76
infobot, setting up in customer service, 185
information products, sales on the Web, 267
information sharing, using online tools for, 62, 63
InfoTest, customer responsiveness, 41, 42
internet as strategic planning tool, 216-219
internal Web, use in product development, 25, 26. See also intranet
intranet, 273, 274
  Boeing Internal Web, 25
  impact of, 25, 26
  primary goals, 25

/extranet use, electronic commerce and, 162, 163
human resources and, 81, 82
product development and, 24
intranet/extranet systems, proprietary, 75
Intuitive Technologies, virtual process control, 47, 48
investor relations, employing Net technology in, 70, 71, 84
IP (Internet Protocols), 274
ISO9000 (International Standards Organization), quality and, 44, 45
IT (Information Technology) support for manufacturing operations, 46
ERP (enterprise resource planning), 46
MES (manufacturing execution systems), 46
process control, 46, 47

J

Java, described, 274
Johnson Controls
distributor relationships, improving, 160, 161
network development with key partners, 161, 162

K

knowledge exchange networks, setting up, 123-125
knowledge, leveraging using Net, 145-149
Knowledge On-Line. See KOL
KOL (Knowledge On-Line), 4, 146, 147
2.0, described, 148, 149

L

LAN (local-area network), described, 274
leadership
challenges of, 200, 201
communication, Net seminars for, 214
directed content, 212, 213
education, Net seminars for, 214
e-mail as team communication tool, 206, 207
extranets, developing partnerships via, 213
information sharing, 205
internet as strategic planning tool, 216-219
intranet scope, 203

issues, handling, 244-246
Netscape SuiteSpot, applications offered via, 203, 204
open-door policies and, 208, 209
profit margins, boosting as core business strategy, 210-212
purpose of, 199, 200
TACTICS planning action system and, 219
automate, 221
core functions/big payoffs, 222
customize, 221
inside/out, 222
start now, 223
think links, 219-221
transform, 221, 222
team development, 206
training, Net seminars for, 214
virtual teaming, 206-208
Web set development of mini, 205
lean manufacturing, 19
Liberty Mutual Insurance Company, purchasing costs, cutting online, 72, 73
LISTSERV
described, 274
product development use, 32
Lockheed Martin
e-mail as team communication tool, 206, 207
information sharing, 205
intranet scope, 203
Netscape SuiteSpot, applications offered via, 203, 204
payoff on technology implementations, 204
recruiting Web site, 91, 92
team development, 206
virtual teaming, 206-208
Web set development of mini, 205
logistics, 156
Lotus Notes, information gathering, 41

M

mailbots, customer service, 192
mailing list
described, 274
use in product development, 21
manufacturing, 37
agility, in manufacturing, 45-48
IT supporting manufacturing, 46, 47
virtual process control, 47, 48
challenges to, 38-48
agility, 45-48

customer responsiveness, 39-41
quality, 41-45
IT support for manufacturing operations, 46
ERP (enterprise resource planning), 46
MES (manufacturing execution systems), 46
process control, 46, 47
quality, in manufacturing, 41-45
best practices, sharing, 42-44
conformance quality, 41
ISO9000, 44, 45
quality control, 41
shipping control, 41
TACTICS planning action system and, 52
automate, 53
core functions/big payoffs, 56
customize, 53-55
inside/out, 56
start now, 56, 57
think links, 53
transform, 55
technological limitations, traditional, 37
Marshall Industries
competitive strategy in training, 103
core processes, 8
electronic commerce and intranet/extranet
use, 162, 163
profit margins, boosting as core business
strategy, 210-212
McDonnell Douglas
outsourcing bids electronically, 75
security, Web concerns for, 57, 58
virtual factory, 50-52
MES (manufacturing execution systems), 46
middleware, sales on the Web, 265
MIME (multipurpose internet mail extensions),
described, 275
modem, described, 275
MRO (maintenance, repair, and operations) supplies, 72

N

NASA Ames Research Center
cost reduction using Internet tools, 64, 65
product development system, 24, 25
National Semiconductor
information availability, 28
intranet, 28, 29
National Sporting Goods Association, supply-
chain partners, 165

newsgroups, product development 29, 30, 33

O

outsourcing, 3
fulfillment and distribution services, 163-164

P

Pareto's law, fulfillment and distribution, 173
password, described, 275
post, described, 275
precursor technologies, 253
EDI, 253
cost drawbacks of, 256
implementation of, 255
need for in the future, 257
purpose of, 254
success of, 255
summary, 262
groupware, 253
application suitability, 260, 261
components, of, 259, 260
described, 257, 258
functions of, 258
future expectations of, 262
integrating from outside, 258, 259
open systems direction, 261
summary, 262
process control, 46, 47
benefits of, 48
product development, 17, 18
developing ideas, 20
internal sources, 20, 21
internal Web, 25, 26
mailing list use, 21
product design, speed of, 22-25
surveying via the Net, 21, 22
primary challenges solvable with Internet
technology, 18
build speed, 18, 19
exceeding customers needs, 18
productive project team, 19
reduce costs/maintain quality, 19
TACTICS planning action system and, 30
automate, 31
core functions/big payoffs, 32
customize, 31
inside/out, 32
start now, 32, 33

think links, 31
transform 31
Web assisting in
e-mail discussion groups, 29, 30
information availability 28
information gathering, 28
newsgroups, 29, 30
professional support online, customer service,
189-191
project start up, 227
steps in, 230, 231
changes, dealing with, 244-247
plan development, 237, 238
plan implementation, 239-244
starting point assessment, 231-233
strategy and tactics analysis, 235-237
teams, setting up, 233-235
types of, 227
changing technology, 227, 228
champion, 228
from the top, 228, 229
spontaneous, 229, 230
voice of God, 228
Web site, 230
protocol, described, 275
Prudential Securities, customer service, 179,
180
accessibility, improving, 183
e-mail standardization, 183
full-service brokerage ion the Web, providing, 181, 182
intranet development, 182, 183
Technology Advisory Team, setting up, 180
Publishers Marketing Association, 21
purchase cycle prices, cutting, 159
purchasing costs, cutting online, 72. *See also*
administration
General Electric, 73-77
MRO items, 72
process simplification, 72, 73

Q

Quaker Oats, open-door policy, 208, 209
quality
control, 41
maintaining, 138
manufacturing, 41. *See also* manufacturing
best practices, sharing, 42-44
conformance quality, 41
ISO9000, 44, 45

quality control, 41
shipping control, 41

R

rapid prototyping, 19
recruitment and training, 87
challenges of, 87, 88
Columbia/HCA Healthcare
recruitment online, 88-91
scope of Web site, 89
training development, 98-100
training via the Net, 94-97
competitive strategy via training, 102, 103
computer-based courses online, 97
continuing-education courses, 97, 98
make or buy decision, 98
fulfillment and distribution training, 173
Lockheed Martin, recruiting Web site, 91, 92
online recruitment
applicants viewpoint, 93, 94
ongoing trends in, 92, 93
TACTICS planning action system and, 103
automate, 104, 105
core functions/big payoffs, 107
customize, 105
inside/out, 106, 107
start now, 107, 108
think links, 104
transform, 106
tips for using Web technologies in, 108, 109
training via the Net, 94
administration functions, 96, 97
considerations for developing own, 99,
100
cutting travel costs, 94, 95
executive training, 96
training partnerships, 100
reduced cycle time, 19
reengineering, 2
Resource Financial Group, 2, 3
employees benefits outsourcing, 68-70
resources
books, 249-251
Web start up, 263
IDC ROI report, 252
The Intranet Journal, 252
Netscape columns, 251, 252
Web sites, 251
responsiveness, improving
customer service, 178

service delivery, 137, 138
router, described, 275
routine tasks, using online tools to combat, 62, 63
RSA encryption, 57, 58

S

sales effectiveness, enhancing, 111
  challenges for enhancing sales force effectiveness, 111
    cost reduction, 113
    distance management, 112
    information availability, 112
    sales force development, 113
    selling challenges, 112
  Financial Services corporation, 113
    cost analysis, 115
    extranet site map, 117-120
    intranet, setting up, 114, 115
    motivating affiliates to use extranet, 116, 117
    WWW adoption, 113, 114
  IBM, 120
    account information, developing, 120-122
  knowledge exchange networks, setting up, 123-125
  learning curve for representative, shortening, 123
  opportunity development, 129
  sales support via the Web site, 126
    company promotion, 126, 127
    internal information dissemination, 128, 129
    ordering online, 127
    try before you buy online, 127, 128
  TACTICS planning action system and, 130
    automate, 130
    core functions/big payoffs, 132, 133
    customize, 130, 131
    inside/out, 132
    start now, 133, 135
    think links, 130
    transform, 131, 132
  tips for using Net technologies in, 134-136
  trade show planning using the Net, 125
sales on the Web, 264
  customization of digital products, 268, 269
  discrepancies in figures, 264

information products, 267
  item suitability for, 266, 267
  middleware, 265
  security perceptions, 265
  slow growth of, 265
sales support via the Web site, 126
  company promotion, 126, 127
  internal information dissemination, 128, 129
  ordering online, 127
  try before you buy online, 127, 128
San Jose Mercury News, online recruitment, 93, 94
Schlumberger, investor relations on the Net 70, 71
SCOR (supply-chain operations reference), 158
security
  actual issues, 242
  meeting concerns, 142
  perceived issues, 242
  perceptions, sales on the Web, 265
  Web concerns for, 57, 58
server, described, 275, 276
service. *See* customer service; service delivery
service delivery, enhancing, 137
  challenges in, 137
    competing effectively, 138, 139
    delivery format, 137, 138
    quality, maintaining, 138
    responsiveness, improving, 137, 138
  consumer benefit, determining, 153
  control of projects, maintaining, 153
  extranet, setting up, 154
  flexibility, importance of, 152
  solutions to challenges, 139
    customized applications, delivering, 141
    fax delivery costs, reducing, 140, 141
    full-service financial Web site, 143, 144
    home banking, Internet, 143
    knowledge, leveraging using Net, 145-149
    security, meeting concerns, 142
    virtual world consulting, 149
  TACTICS planning action system and, 150
    automate, 150, 151
    core functions/big payoffs, 152
    customize, 151
    inside/out, 151, 152
    start now, 152
    think links, 150
    transform, 151
  tips for, 152-154

usable systems, developing, 153, 154
user needs, identifying, 153
shipping control, 41
signature file, described, 276
SLIP (serial line Internet protocol), described,
    276
Southern California Gas, intranet use, 79
spamming, described, 276
SQL (structure query language), described, 276
SSL (Secure Sockets Layer), 58
    described, 276
Stanford Federal Credit Union, 142
    service delivery, enhancing, 142, 143
        full-service financial Web site, 143, 144
        home banking, Internet, 143
strategic
    alliances, 2
    objectives, determining, 7
    planning tool, internet as, 216-219
strategy analysis, 7. *See also* business strategy
    business processes, 8-10
    customers, 10, 11
    key supplier, 10
    partners, 11
    strategy determination, 7, 8
supply-chain, 156
    defined, 157
    management, 76, 77, 158
    partners, 164-166
supporting sales via the Web site, 126
    company promotion, 126, 127
    internal information dissemination, 128, 129
    ordering online, 127
    try before you buy online, 127, 128
surveying via the Net, product development, 21,
    22
sysop, described, 276

T

TACTICS planning action system, 12, 235, 236,
    249
    automate, 12, 13
        administration, 79, 80
        customer service, 193, 194
        fulfillment and planning, 169
        leadership, 221
        manufacturing, 53
        product development, 31
        recruitment and training, 104, 105
        sales effectiveness, enhancing, 130

    service delivery, 150, 150
    core functions/big payoffs, 15, 16
        administration, 81
        customer service, 185
        fulfillment and planning, 170, 171
        leadership, 222
        manufacturing, 56
        product development, 32
        recruitment and training, 107
        sales effectiveness, enhancing, 132, 133
        service delivery, 152
    customize, 13, 14
        administration, 79, 80
        customer service, 194
        fulfillment and planning, 169, 170
        leadership, 221
        manufacturing, 53-55
        product development, 31
        recruitment and training, 105
        sales effectiveness, enhancing, 131, 132
        service delivery, 151
    inside/out, 15
        administration, 80, 81
        customer service, 194, 195
        fulfillment and planning, 170
        inside/out, 222
        manufacturing, 56
        product development, 32
        recruitment and training, 106, 107
        sales effectiveness, enhancing, 132
        service delivery, 151, 152
    start now, 16
        administration, 79, 80
        customer service, 195
        fulfillment and planning, 171, 172
        inside/out, 222
        manufacturing, 56, 57
        product development, 32, 33
        recruitment and training, 107, 108
        sales effectiveness, enhancing, 133, 134
        service delivery, 152
    think links, 12
        administration, 77-79
        customer service, 193
        fulfillment and planning, 168, 169
        leadership, 219-221
        manufacturing, 53
        product development, 31
        recruitment and training, 104
        sales effectiveness, enhancing, 130
        service delivery, 150

transform 14
  administration, 80
  customer service, 194
  fulfillment and planning, 170
  leadership, 221
  manufacturing, 55
  product development, 31
  recruitment and training, 106
  sales effectiveness, enhancing, 131, 132
  service delivery, 152
TCP/IP (transmission control protocol/internet
    protocol), 277
technology. *See also* business strategy
  changes, handling, 246, 247
  project start up, 227
    steps in, 230-247
    types of, 227-230
Telnet, described, 277
Texas Instruments
  core processes, 8, 9
  quality practices, 42
text file, described, 277
TPN (Trading Process Network), 74
  fulfillment and distribution efficiencies, 159,
    160
  supply chain, 157
trade show, planning using the Net, 125
training. *See also* recruitment and training
  Net seminars for, 214
  via the Net, 94
    administration functions, 96, 97
    considerations for developing own, 99,
      100
    cutting travel costs, 94, 95
    executive training, 96
    training partnerships, 100

U

UNIX, described, 277
upload, described, 277
URL, described, 277, 278
USENET, described, 278

V

value chain, 6, 156
VAN (Value Added Network), described, 278
virtual
  organizations, 2
  teaming, 206-208
  world consulting, 149
virtual factory, McDonnell Douglas, 50
  benefits of, 52
  possibility of achieving, 51

W

Wang, knowledge exchange networks, setting
    up, 123-125
Web, product development
  e-mail discussion groups, 29, 30
  information availability 28
  information gathering, 28
  newsgroups, 29, 30
Web sites, Web/Net resources, 251
Web Week, Net surveys, 21, 22
Webmaster, role in administration function, 82,
    83
whiteboard, described, 278
  online, 23

X

XtX Internet Communications Suite, white-
    boards online, 23

Author Contact Information

Wally and Jeff are available to help your organization use the Net to cut costs, boost profits, and improve operations. For more information or to have either Jeff or Wally speak to a group, contact

Jeff Senné
(800) 786-4421
jeff@sennegroup.com

Wally Bock
(800) 648-2677
wbock@wallybock.com

AND

Check out the Net Income Web site for more information at
http://www.netincometactics.com